NATIONAL UNIVERSITY LIBRARY
ORANGE CO.

Humanistic Psychology and the Research Tradition:
Their Several Virtues

Humanistic Psychology and the Research Tradition: Their Several Virtues

Irvin L. Child

John Wiley & Sons, Inc.,
New York · London · Sydney · Toronto

To Alice, Dick, and Pam

Library of Congress Cataloging in Publication Data:

Child, Irvin Long, 1915–
Humanistic psychology and the research tradition.

Includes bibliographical references.
1. Humanistic psychology. 2. Psychology, Experimental. I. Title. [DNLM: 1. Humanities. 2. Psychology. 3. Research. BF 121 C536H 1972]
BF204.C48 150 72-6595
ISBN 0-471-15570-5

Printed in the United States of America

10 9 8 7 6 5 4 3 2 1

Preface

The aim of this book is to establish a new image of psychology by showing that each of two traditional images is incomplete, and that through a fusion of their virtues a more viable psychology is gradually taking form.

Psychology traditionally presents two images to the world. One is the concerned effort to understand persons. Here, like the humanities, psychology is centered on the individual and, like other humane endeavors, is aimed at promoting personal welfare and growth. The second image is the quest for abstract knowledge about human behavior. As in the other sciences, the object of study is looked at only as object, and is considered not for its own sake but for the generalizations that can be based on it. Psychology, in this second image, may forget the person in order to study only the processes occurring within him.

The first image is represented in an extreme form by the recent movement known as humanistic psychology, but it emerges from a long tradition of centering psychology on humanity. I am extending to this long tradition the same term: humanistic psychology. The second image is represented in an extreme form by the experimental study of behavior, with its restrictive emphasis on method and evidence.

When people first learn about psychology, which image do they encounter? If they are reading books on their own, they are most likely to encounter the friendly humanistic image of psychology. If they are taking an introductory course in psychology, they may encounter principally the rigors of the research tradition. My argument is that both are incomplete. The first is of the flesh alone, the second is all bones. The two images need to be brought together.

Psychology, as it is pursued today at the frontiers of research and practice, is a full-bodied enterprise that has been developed through the fusion of these two traditions. But images outlive the events that have created them. Introductory textbooks of psychology, even those that incorporate considerable humanistic influence, still bear a heavy mark of the narrow objectivism of earlier decades. Humanistic books on psychology, on the other hand, do not yet draw as they could on the changing research tradition and rely too exclusively on the unsystematic clinical observation and the reflective thought that have been their great source of strength.

For a course on humanistic psychology, this book shows the impressive influence that the humanistic viewpoint has already had on psychological research, and suggests that humanistic theory has much to gain from a careful consideration of research. For a course stressing the research tradition, this book points the way toward loosening the conservative bonds in which the research tradition is so often held, so that all psychology can share the positive values of that tradition.

This book is useful, then, for introductory courses in psychology, for courses on humanistic psychology, and for courses in advanced general psychology. But my objective has been to write a book that might interest anyone, in or out of a course or college, who is curious about psychology as a path toward understanding people.

My definition of psychology is very broad. In professional practice there is, of course, despite great overlap, some real distinction between psychology and psychiatry; fields of knowledge need separation, too, for administrative purposes, and I think universities would be worse run if departments were altogether abolished. But good science respects none of these boundaries, and psychology is the most appropriate single word for the range of inquiry that I discuss.

Irvin L. Child

Acknowledgments

A book of this kind has personal origins too numerous to trace and acknowledge in detail. But I am especially grateful to the following colleagues and friends: Rosaline S. Schwartz, who read everything at least twice and is responsible for great improvements throughout in substance and style; Charles Walters, who in commenting on the entire manuscript gave me the advantage of his keen intelligence united with the freshness of having recently come to psychology; Steven H. Lewis, who introduced me to the humanistic research on schizophrenia; Jane Olejarczyk, who eased the work by her secretarial skills, understanding, and good judgment; Stephen Fleck, Gertrude Schmeidler, and Elliot Turiel, who generously shared with me their special knowledge and wisdom in a review of particular chapters; and my philosopher brother, Arthur Child, who without having seen the manuscript has yet exerted his usual influence toward humanism.

I. L. C.

Contents

. . . for several virtues
Have I liked several women; never any
With so full soul, but some defect in her
Did quarrel with the noblest grace she owned
And put it to the foil.

—SHAKESPEARE, *The Tempest*

1 Introduction

The feeling many people have for their profession is akin to love, and similar conflicts arise. Psychologists in particular often are in conflict between the attractions of two kinds of psychology, sometimes referred to concisely as hard and soft psychologies.

As a psychologist I am interested above all in studying personality and esthetics, and when a distinction is made between hard and soft psychology, these topics are usually placed in the latter category. The hard psychology of rigorous experimentation also has great attraction for me. Yet both fall short of my ideal of what psychology should and could be at the present time.

It sometimes surprises me that we psychologists ever make or accept so superficial a distinction as hard and soft in carving up the subject matter of our discipline.

But a light touch can make tolerable the tedium that frequently accompanies intellectual discipline. I view hard and soft as the humorous distortion of a valid distinction, slick terms useful in calling one's attention to contrasts that are genuine but far more complex than those terms suggest.

The hard psychologies are founded on the rock of experimental method. Their great strength lies in the firm establishment of knowledge about small circumscribed aspects of behavior and experience. Examples of their achievements would be a precisely defined curve relating the apparent brightness of a very dim light to the number of minutes the eyes have been in darkness, or a graph showing how the number of errors made in learning a list of nonsense syllables is related to the length of the list or to the time between successive rehearsals.

The soft psychologies are warm and sensate, faithful to and aware of the immediately felt reality of human experience and human personality. They take as their starting point the multi-faceted reality of conscious experience, the dynamic diversity of the integrated person as he knows himself and is known to others. From this starting point it is not easy to move on to scientific investigation, to framing limited questions testable by systematic observation. The soft psychologist may not see this as a great inadequacy. He wants first of all to be faithful to human reality as he knows it. He hopes a psychology that takes the conscious experience of the organized person as its subject matter will eventually lead to understanding man better than can a psychology that denies these obvious realities and clings to precise methods even at the possible expense of irrelevance.

Psychology has at all times been somewhat polarized between soft and hard, between experiential reality and scientific precision. In recent times the two poles are well represented by humanistic psychology and by the sterner aspects of the psychological research tradition. The research tradition has long dominated American psychology. Even today, when the tradition is expressed in many diversified and fruitful ways, there remains within it a tight traditional core of orthodoxy that influences even psychologists working at the varied boundaries of the research tradition. Humanistic psychology is new as a major psychological movement in the United States, though it has never been completely dormant. The extremes of the two contrast sharply, and are often exaggerated by partisans of either side. But I think if the contrast is heightened in argument, it is in preparation for eventual synthesis. I, too, shall at first exaggerate the contrast, not to provoke controversy, but to show that each extreme is by itself defective and that a fusion of virtues is needed.

If this were played upon a stage now, I could condemn it as an improbable fiction.

—SHAKESPEARE, *Twelfth Night*

2
The Research Tradition

The research tradition in psychology is devoted to advancing the general knowledge of man by systematic factual inquiry. Concepts and theory are valued for their help in guiding the researcher to interesting topics, and for their help in organizing and interpreting the facts he arrives at. But where conflict arises between the pursuit of ideas and the pursuit of fact, the latter tends to be favored. The important idea is what the psychological research tradition values most highly, of course, in common with other scientific traditions; but the measure of importance is bound to the clarity with which an observational test of the idea can be envisioned. Adding one more trivial fact to the body of well-established knowledge often gains readier support than inventing or presenting ideas that might possibly in the future, but not certainly or immediately, guide effective research. Ideas are respected most when they are closely linked to the prospect of being tested against evidence.

The research tradition in American psychology, as in other disciplines, has been very strong. We might expect a major effect to be an abundance of triviality, a proliferation of knowledge about an infinity of specific topics that have little relevance to general ideas. That expectation would be mistaken. The outsider can pick up a psychology journal and be greatly amused by the highly specific titles of some of the articles. The insider generally finds, under the specificity of title, immediate relevance to general issues in psychology. The research tradition in psychology has not been especially characterized by triviality, and my purpose here is not to expose the instances of triviality that could be found. I am concerned with how the valuable research of psychologists could be still more valuable if it were more influenced by ideas that derive from humanistic psychology.

The research tradition appears in its ideal form in experimentation in the psychological laboratory. A general topic which has received much of the attention of experimental psychologists through many decades is learning, conceived as modifications of behavior brought about by past interaction between organism and environment. The research tends to develop around particular techniques of experimentation. One body of research is concerned with college students' memorization of nonsense syllables, another is concerned with the rate at which pigeons will peck at a gadget that sometimes responds to their attack by yielding a bit of food, and another is concerned with rats' learning to thread a maze swiftly and efficiently toward the food box that lies at the end. In each body of research, a standard technique is generally used to measure some variable of behavior—for instance, percentage recalled of a set of syllables previously memorized. Other variables may then be studied as causal influences. Different groups of subjects, for example, can be assigned various tasks to do between memorizing the syllables and later recalling them, and the average percentage of recall is determined for each group. The outcome—the dependence of recall on interpolated activity—can then be compared with what is known about other influences on recall, as one step in moving from narrow statements of experimental fact to broad theories integrating a variety of those statements.

Virtues

A basic virtue of the psychological research tradition is its emphasis on objectivity in definition and measurement of concepts. Suppose that, like some students of learning, I use a concept of response probability and do experiments on a particular response observable in laboratory rats, seeking to relate its occurrence to various factors that may influence it. I may put the rat in a laboratory box provided with a lever, a food delivery chute, and a device to produce a clicking sound, arranging the controls so that whenever a click occurs, and only then, the rat can obtain a pellet of food by pressing the lever. I can then define response probability, for purposes of my experiment, as the proportion of times that a click is followed by the rat's pressing the lever. If I have described adequately the box, the food, the timing of the click, the system of recording the rat's pushes on the lever, and the like, then anyone reading about my research could put his own rats into a similar situation and can apply my definition of response probability to similar data that he could gather for himself. If the animals are treated in the same way, and are observed in the same way, the concept of response probability should have the same meaning in his experiment and mine. Here a very useful form of objectivity is attained: concepts can be given the same meaning, in relation to what is observed, by different researchers working at different places and times. The concept has a repeatable public meaning, and scientists distant from one another can share in developing knowledge about it.

The objectivity here can be, in part, illusory. That the measurement of response probability, or any other concept in a particular experiment, is thoroughly objective does not mean that everything the experimenter does with the concept is objective. He may generalize his conclusions in a manner just as subjective as that of a poet who extends the meaning of words in metaphorical expression of his personal feelings.

Still, the original objectivity remains a virtue. If a general concept such as response probability is measured in different objective ways in different research, the conclusions reached may appear contradictory. But objectivity of method permits the combination of the various measures in a new and broader program of research that may indicate how the different measures relate to each other, and to what general concepts each may be pertinent. Thus objectivity of method permits the solution of controversy, the reconciliation of apparent contradictions. Objectivity of concepts is not enough to give thoroughly dependable knowledge; but without it we have difficulty in acquiring dependable and communicable knowledge.

The research tradition also can achieve another virtue, that of precision. This is a by-product of objectivity, in those instances where the method used yields measurement rather than gross classification of events into categories. We can, of course, have important and useful knowledge that is not quantitatively precise. Often we do not need or care about precision even where it could be had. For most scientific purposes, as for practical purposes in daily life, we would not want to measure things or events nearly as accurately as we could. Precision, moreover, is itself at times illusory. Measuring the length of a line with a ruler scaled to the sixty-fourth of an inch, we may forget to place the ruler's end carefully enough to warrant such precise reading. Even those who especially value precision can forget that some of it may be pseudo-precision, and many examples are to be found in psychological research. But where precision is genuine and useful, a method that provides it is obviously desirable.

Another virtue, essentially a consequence and justification of those already named, is that the research tradition contains and sustains a tradition of obtaining verifiable knowledge. If conjectures about human behavior or experience can somehow be made amenable to the methods of the research tradition, then we can test whether those conjectures are true or false. In prescientific tradition, "Absence makes the heart grow fonder" and "Out of sight, out of mind" could peacefully coexist as contradictory generalizations. If a traveling husband yearned for home, he could be explained by the former saying. If another exploited the erotic opportunities of travel, he could be explained by the latter. Those who participate in the research tradition are inclined to be impatient with such pseudo-explanations, unverified statements which can be applied confidently only to facts already known. Wherever the research tradition is successfully applied, such statements give way to verified generalizations, capable of being stated in advance of an event, as a help in predicting or even controlling it. Prediction and control may remain very imperfect, but even so they may be far preferable to complete ignorance.

Defects

The defects of the research tradition in psychology are not uniform, since the activities carried out within it are extremely diverse. Indeed, one half of my main thesis is that the research tradition itself contains much of great value to humanistic psychology, neglected by most humanistic psychologists because it is intertwined with elements alien or inimical to their concerns. The defects I describe are especially characteristic of the orthodox core of the experimentalist tradition. Much recent research in psychology, intrinsically free from these defects, has been often presented and interpreted in a context provided by this orthodox core. It is thus associated with an ideological tradition not altogether consistent with the actual practice of the researchers. If I seem, in describing here what I consider defects, to be attacking without justification the entire tradition of psychological research, I want to point out that my argument is directed only at certain strands of thought; those strands are very conspicuous in the research tradition, but I hope they will become less so. I am pointing them out because I think that exposing them for inspection will lead to their more general discard, so that the psychological research tradition may move on with greater relevance to human interests.

The basic defect is a restriction of topics of inquiry to those that can be most directly studied by the most precise and objective methods available. The subject of inquiry is determined partly by historical accident; the availability of methods determines the subject matter studied. Because the first experimental psychologists had studied how sensory experience is related to physical dimensions of stimuli, and had developed excellent methods, experimental psychology was for a long time almost entirely confined to that study, rather than turning to the development of equally objective and precise methods for learning how responses are related to pertinent motives and stimuli. Then at a later time, when the recitation of nonsense syllables had been elaborated as a method for studying responses, an inordinate amount of effort went into studying those problems of learning that could be successfully studied with nonsense syllables. Because so much was known about this method, and it was so precise and objective, psychologists lost sight for a while of aspects of the learning process that were not readily investigated by having subjects recite nonsense syllables. The virtues of verifiability, objectivity, and precision, then, carry with them the danger that psychologists in the main stream of the research tradition, by holding those virtues to be the absolutely essential ones, will restrict their discipline by discouraging its extension to problems whose study can only be pursued by methods somewhat lacking in these virtues. Self-esteem, for instance, is a concept difficult to objectify or to measure with precision, and many notions you or I might develop about it from our own experience would be difficult to verify as broad generalizations. So self-esteem, central though it seems to many people's sense of what topics psychology should illuminate, tends to be left out of psychology. When self-esteem is considered, moreover, the dominant research tradition usually leads to its being immediately given a narrow objective meaning—self-esteem as measured by a particular questionnaire—though this may be but a blurred shadow of the original concept.

Another defect of the research tradition is related to the special power of the experimental method. Where it is possible to vary experimentally some condition that may influence behavior or experience, the changes that follow may confidently be considered to be a consequence of the experimental variation that was introduced. Where causal factors cannot be deliberately manipulated to observe their effects, the experimental tradition may discourage making any observations at all. Thus self-esteem may not be studied even by the objective methods available, because the experimental manipulation of factors influencing it is either impossible or unethical. The defect of the research tradition here lies in the neglect of problems to which an experimental approach cannot be immediately applied.

Beyond the restriction of topics of inquiry, however, is a much more subtle influence, an influence on the very nature of the psychologist's thought. Exclusive devotion to experimental methods permits a psychologist to think of science as being concerned exclusively with relations between cause and effect (although he may prefer more cumbersome terms, such as independent and dependent, or antecedent and consequent variables, hoping to avoid controversies about the nature of causation). If he considers the purpose of scientific inquiry to be restricted entirely to determining such relations, he will miss much of the potential subject matter of a science, and may even hamper its development in such a way as to prevent the future attainment of a good understanding of the very relations that he is studying. An example is the theory of biological evolution. Although not a simple assertion of a relation between an antecedent and consequent, a theory of evolution contains within it a number of such statements. And it is hard to see how they could have been arrived at except as a result of long efforts by many people to learn about the variety of plants and animals. To confine early biology to experimental study would have prevented the descriptive research from which the theory of evolution emerged, and which thus helped provide the conceptual framework out of which developed much of the later experimental research on mechanisms of heredity.

Most serious among the defects that characterize much of the psychological research tradition is the attempt to exclude experience or awareness from the subject matter of psychology, to define psychology exclusively as the scientific study of behavior. I call this an *attempt* because it is not generally carried out very consistently. In the current psychology textbook I know best, the first chapter defines psychology as the science of behavior. This, the authors say, is preferable to the older definition as science of mind, consciousness, or experience, "chiefly because behavior is objective in a way that mind, consciousness, and experience are not," and the initial chapter is presented as "an elaboration of this basic point." But later in the book, a chapter on perception is written primarily in terms of conscious experience, with only an occasional bow to behavior. One of the chapters on learning argues that awareness is probably required for any learning to occur. A chapter on anxiety and coping behavior frequently uses the word *unconscious* and occasionally *conscious,* and is rather more experiential than behavioral. Despite what is said in the first chapter, in fact, consciousness and experience often recur, either explicitly or implicitly, although at the end of the book they are again almost completely excluded from the glossary and index. Recently I have read two new introductory textbooks. Unlike the other, these books do not give a general impression of trying to maintain a consistently behavioral definition of psychology; they both give a great deal of attention to studies of experience. Yet these, too, present at the outset a definition of psychology as the scientific study of behavior, and in neither is there any substantial effort to resolve the apparent contradiction.

B. F. Skinner, a leader of modern behaviorism, manages to be only a little more consistent, and at the expense of cutting out much of the subject matter of psychology—either directly or by making it so cumbersome to discuss by circumlocution that it is easier to leave it alone. In a published interview that probed him on these concepts, he admits awareness only as "something imposed upon us—we become aware of what we are doing and why we are doing it because society insists that we talk about these things." Having been asked about awareness, he has answered by discussing self-awareness, either dodging the original question altogether or not recognizing that awareness and self-awareness are distinct concepts. When later in the interview he discusses perception, he avoids the terms awareness or consciousness, yet seems to refer to part of the same concept with a substitute term, "perceptual phenomena." He will not admit that perceptual phenomena are a proper part of the subject matter of psychology, saying "it is always a response that is being studied, not what you see."*

* This is the only footnote in the book and is to let you know that most of the articles and books I refer to are cited in notes beginning on page 185. (I thought it prudent not to identify the introductory textbooks mentioned above, and some other references are probably omitted for no reason at all.) Each note begins with the number of the page to which it is relevant; if you want to know where I found the statement by Skinner, look up the note for page 8. Some of the notes cite articles or books I do not mention in the text but thought someone would like to know about in pursuing an issue further.

Skinner and others like him are here converting method into madness. We have no way of studying another person's experience except by observing his behavior or products of his behavior. That is a sound point, whose true and significant implications for method are by no means so obvious as might be thought. Concluding that the subject matter of psychology must be behavior alone seems to me, however, a foolish aberration.

Consider the parallel in paleontology. Through the centuries men had collected fossils—stones that seemed to embody remains of once living organisms. There was a temptation to think they could profitably be used as a way of learning about those organisms. Some people who were fearful for their souls felt that the temptation was too risky; the fossils may have been placed in the earth's surface by God to test the constancy of man's faith in the biblical account of biological history. This timidity of inference could, like Skinner's, have been based on scientific caution alone; extinct life can never be observed, so it cannot be the subject matter of any science. Had such caution won the biological battle of the nineteenth century, fossils might now be arranged in museums only to please the eye rather than to exhibit sequences of evolutionary development.

Or consider astronomy. A few years ago it might have been defined as the science of telescopic photographs. The systematization of knowledge of the photographs would have been difficult without an underlying assumption that they were related to radiation from stars. Yet the purist might have wished to dispense with the concept of star, since at most only the radiant energy reaching the earth could be known—and for most stars only the marks produced on a photographic plate through lengthy exposure to very weak energy. This extremely objective definition of astronomy as the study of photographs might well have discouraged the development of techniques for recording radiant energy at frequencies to which photographic plates are not sensitive. If stars are not what are being studied, why look for other ways of studying them?

Absurd examples? Of course. But in some ways the behavioristic exclusion of experience is more absurd. The psychologist, like any man, sees other people acting like himself, and his inferring in them an awareness like his own is much more immediate than other scientists' inferring from photographs or fossils the existence of remote nebulae or extinct animals. Anyone, too, has some personal knowledge of the inaccuracies and uncertainties of inference to others' awareness. But it is reasonable to expect that scientific study of a subject matter will involve improvement of inference rather than the elimination of the subject matter.

How has the maintenance of such an absurdity been possible? Surely it can be only because of some real differences between psychology and either paleontology or astronomy, differences that render incomplete the

A few notes, too, are comments I wanted to include but felt would interrupt the flow of thought unless put in a separate place.

analogies I have drawn. I think the important differences are three in number:

1. Some sense can be made of behavior alone without inferences to experience, much more than of fossils alone without inference to organisms. I do not want to press this point, because it has been greatly exaggerated by innumerable psychologists. But it has some reality.

2. Behavior has greater intrinsic interest for people than do fossils or telescopic photographs. Neither scientist nor ordinary citizen would be much concerned about the latter two except as sources of knowledge about events distant in time or space. Behavior is of intrinsic practical interest to everyone. We can accept the food a waiter puts before us with no thought about his state of mind; we count on oncoming drivers to stay beyond the center line, without guessing what separate feelings each may be experiencing. A pure psychology of behavior, if that were the only psychology possible, would still be worthwhile. Although a person's behavior is often of special interest for the information it gives about his experience, his state of mind, it is also a psychological datum in its own right. Experience alone cannot be the total subject matter of an adequate psychology; behavior must be included too.

3. A more important difference, I believe, is that unwitting intrusion of the forbidden subject matter is easier in psychology, and perhaps inevitable, so that the behavioristic psychologist is not really giving up as much as he thinks he is. Since the tabooed subject matter is not really banished, the absurdity of the effort can go unnoticed. Talk about fossils could, perhaps, be conducted with no thought about the extinct organisms that may be inferred from them. Talk about aggressive responses, however, almost inevitably blurs with forbidden thoughts about feelings of aggression. Even more, the concept of stimulus, or of a specific stimulus, is likely to involve a latent reference to the psychologist's experience and a latent assumption that the person he is studying will have a similar experience. For instance, a researcher who believes that he is thoroughly objective may use as stimuli spoken words or sentences; yet spoken words or sentences exist as stimuli only in the awareness of a person hearing them who understands the language of which they are a part. Thus awareness is built into the fundamental operations of psychological research without being noticed.

Most psychologists, if they had to choose between behavior and experience as the subject matter of psychology would choose behavior, and the choice would be wise. Behavior is the more inclusive concept. We know another person's experience through evidence provided by his behavior, and not the reverse. We ordinarily infer another's experience, of course, from knowing our own experience in a comparable situation; but to verify such an inference we depend on his describing his experience or giving other behavioral evidence of it. For any experience, then, there must theoretically be some way of stating what behavioral evidence, when put together with knowledge of the circumstances, would justify a belief in its occurrence. So a behavioral definition of psychology can be twisted, contorted, extended to embrace experience as well. Yet to be constantly restating conscious experience in behavioral terms is very cumbersome. Moreover, it is distracting and confusing. We really do want to understand people's experience as well as their behavior, and will not tolerate verbiage that conceals our understanding. That, I am sure, is why behavioristic textbooks do not generally try to make their treatment of perception consistent with the behavioral definition of psychology.

Most important of all, when psychology tries to be persistently behavioral it becomes seriously inadequate through omitting much of its subject matter and much of the relevant context for what is left. To be always stating experience in terms of behavioral evidence for it is a practice too complicated and confusing to keep up. Hence, we begin to omit experience and try to persuade ourselves to views that seem to justify, even to ennoble, this mutilation of psychology.

The research tradition in psychology does not have to remain marred by these defects. Much of what is called cognitive psychology has come from adapting the methods of the research tradition to studying more complex phenomena of the human mind—accepting the useful standards of objectivity developed in the research tradition, and rejecting the assumption that only simple relationships can be studied by a discipline holding to those standards. Much of cognitive psychology is not itself humanistic, and seeks models that will remain mechanical even if complex. But by taking as model the computer or its programming rather than the simple reflex arc, cognitive psychology promises to develop a mechanistic psychology complex enough to have a relevant place in a more general humanistic psychology. Even more immediately pertinent is much recent research in developmental psychology, as I will show in a chapter on the psychology of moral development. These and other movements within the psychological research tradition represent a real break with the orthodox restrictions of that tradition. But this fact is often not manifest; and its relevance to the humanistic movement, originating in the clinical tradition, often goes unnoticed. My purpose is to make that relevance clear.

Among our students, I trust, there will be many adventurers. Shall we not teach them that in the pastures of science it is not only the sacred cows that can yield good scientific milk?

—GORDON W. ALLPORT

3
Humanistic Psychology

The research tradition is defined by method, a firm insistence on good evidence as a basis for making new entries in the record of scientific knowledge. Humanistic psychology is defined by its model of man, by its insistence that the body of scientific knowledge about man will develop most usefully if it is guided by a conception of man as he knows himself rather than by some nonhuman analogy. While they cover different domains, these two definitions are not incompatible, and their domains may include a large common ground. Investigations carried on within the psychological research tradition may perfectly well be guided by, or lead to, a humanistic orientation. Psychologists with a humanistic orientation may perfectly well seek to verify their ideas by observations that are gathered in accordance with the traditions of systematic psychological research.

Why then do I bother to demonstrate this compatibility, if it follows from the very definitions of humanistic psychology and of the research tradition? It is because there has been something of a psychological incompatibility, even though there is no logical one.

Many humanistic psychologists become so absorbed in arguing for a human model of man that they neglect the systematic observational side of science. While discussing their model in the light of their everyday experience or clinical practice, they may not notice that a great body of systematic scientific evidence is also pertinent to their argument. Many psychological researchers, on the other hand, become so absorbed in perfecting their methods of inquiry that their thinking comes to be dominated by the method rather than by the topic of inquiry. When method is generalized into a way of thinking, experimentalists are prone to adopt a mechanistic or manipulative way of thinking. The experimental method is based on manipulating what is done to people or animals serving as subjects, and observing the effect on their behavior. Psychologists who use exclusively the experimental method, or who hold it always in mind as their ideal, are encouraged to believe that psychological processes are analogous to the simple physical relationships they have studied in the physics laboratory. With gas confined in a tight chamber, changing its temperature leads to precisely predictable changes in its pressure. Psychological research, they assume, should likewise confine itself to measuring the dependence of one quantitative variable, such as response probability, on other quantitative variables such as delay of reward. Were the same psychologists more concentrated on understanding their subjects, they might notice that the outcome of the human experiment is generally much less precise than that of the physics experiment. Variations in the behavior being observed are often so great that a model of mechanical control of one quantitative variable by another is far from adequate, and may be so unrealistic that it lessens rather than increases understanding. So followers of the research tradition, through devotion to what they consider the best methods, are often led to adopt models of man that the humanistic psychologist feels to be hopelessly wrong. Humanistic psychologists, on the other hand, engaged in finding and defending the most appropriate models for understanding man, often forget that this understanding cannot go far until it is adequately related to the test of observation.

In American psychology, the humanistic tradition was present from its earliest days, well represented by the most notable of early American psychologists, William James. James' forthright espousal of a humanistic model of man was not entirely shared by the "functionalist" and "structuralist" psychologists who succeeded him, and it was altogether rejected by the behavioristic movement which came to dominate American psychology through the middle decades of the twentieth century. Apart from practicing clinical psychologists, who could hardly fail to be somewhat humanistic, only a few voices—notably those of Gordon Allport, Gardner Murphy, and Henry Murray—continued to cry out against the narrow and mechanical view of man that was associated with the research tradition. Humanistic models of man remained more prominent in Europe, and European writers were the most influential in keeping an awareness of such models alive among American psychologists. Especially important were the psychiatrists and clinical psychologists—Jung, Adler, Rank, and eventually a host of others—who reacted against the mechanistic elements in Freud's early theory, and while developing their own humanistic views may also have pushed Freud and Freudians toward the more humanistic orientation that characterizes psychoanalysis today. Europe was the locus, also, of the development of existentialist psychology and psychiatry. Taking, as the central problem any person faces, his sense of his own existence—the meaning of his life and of his relation to others—the existentialists obviously hold to a humanistic view of man.

15 *Humanistic Psychology*

In recent years "humanistic" and "existentialist" have been widely used as labels for theoretical movements or emphases, for therapeutic techniques, and for types of training in American psychology and psychiatry. The term "humanistic" has been espoused above all by those who argue for self-fulfillment as a main theme in human life, and stress in clinical practice the removal of barriers to personal growth. Abraham Maslow and James Bugental are among the best-known writers who have applied the term "humanistic" to this particular emphasis. Recently established "growth centers" such as the Esalen Institute are devoted to devising and applying a variety of techniques to foster personal growth, and the development and the communication of these techniques have been a central concern of many members of the Association for Humanistic Psychology. This use of the term is appropriate and well established, but so, too, is the broader use I wish to make of it. These recent developments in psychological technique are one manifestation of a long tradition in psychology. They are especially important for that tradition in occasioning its resurgence, in restoring it to the position of major importance it had earlier in American psychology and has retained in some other countries. The term, *humanistic psychology,* which has been generally applied to these new developments is a useful term for the whole mode of thought that they exemplify and promote.

Humanistic psychology, then, consists of all those currents of psychological thought in which man is viewed somewhat as he normally sees himself—as a person rather than only as an animal or a machine. Man is a conscious agent; that is the starting point. He experiences, he decides, he acts. If there are conditions under which man can usefully be looked at entirely from the outside, as responding to external stimulation with the regular predictability of a machine, a mechanical model may be useful for those conditions. But humanistic psychology starts with the presumption that such conditions are special cases, that to build the whole of psychology on them would mean an impoverishment of psychology, a restriction that would prevent its general application to the understanding of man.

A humanistic point of view also implies attention to the person as a whole and to his understanding of the context of his action. Behaviorists in the research tradition, in their effort to push objectivism as far as possible, have tried to define stimulus and response in physical terms—a flash of light, for instance, or pressure of the index finger on a switch. This sort of definition may work very well in the experimental laboratory, where a person's clues to oncoming shock can be restricted to the flash of light alone, and where his contract with the experimenter may guarantee his including finger pressure as a part of his total response. In the more varied situation of real life, both stimulus and response may more usefully be defined psychologically—danger signal and avoidance of pain, for example—because a person may use any of an infinity of clues in inferring the danger of future pain, and may choose among many devices for the avoiding of it.

What the person perceives or understands about the situation and its potentialities must be taken into account, and they depend on highly organized processes in the person.

Humanistic psychologists generally share a sense of the person as an integrated whole. The issue of the relation between body and mind can be used to clarify this point. Some philosophers of earlier centuries discussed psychological processes almost as though they occurred in a bodyless mind —a mode of approach that makes scientific study difficult, to say the least. The research tradition, fearful of encountering difficulties in applying a scientific approach, has often tried to confine its view of man to what can be classed as "body"—that is, to those psychological functions for which some sort of anatomical or physiological account can at the time be given or reasonably imagined. In general, humanistic psychologists reject the timidity of this approach and view it as perpetuating an unnecessary distinction between body and mind. They tend to trust the naive impression that a person is a total functioning organism, and to conclude we should not disregard any part of its functioning just because we have at present no adequate guesses about the anatomical or physiological aspect of that part.

Body and mind—or words more or less synonymous with them—remain useful terms. They represent polar extremes useful to recognize in studying man. Anatomy deals only with the body; theology perhaps only with the mind. Branches of psychology are not likely to be so focused on one extreme or other, and yet they vary in emphasis. Humanistic psychologists, like their colleagues, vary individually in whether their individual interests approach one pole or the other. In the recent proliferation of techniques for promoting personal growth, some especially attend to the body pole of functioning—Ida Rolfe's technique of structural integration, for instance, or Alexander Lowen's bioenergetic analysis. Others, such as techniques of meditation, attend especially to the mental pole. But it is not surprising to find training in meditation associated with training in breathing and bodily movement. For what tends to characterize humanistic psychology in the United States is a presumption that a person is a single integrated organism, with no part of him to be disregarded because we do not yet understand how it is related to the rest.

Virtues

One virtue of humanistic psychology, although it may be a passing one, is its fit to present values. It is a virtue not to be disregarded even if it be ephemeral, for science like other activities is after all to a considerable extent a creature of its time. The special elements I have in mind are respect for individual initiative and freedom, and the desire to expand them. In the United States, these values are especially conspicuous in the quest of modern youth for better ways of life. The vigorous complaints against mechanization are due not just to the specific frustrations it occasions but to a sense that extreme mechanization is incompatible with each individual's importance and dignity as a unique center of awareness and freedom. Guilt among white Americans about the positions traditionally accorded to black Americans also stresses this value; recognizing and resenting the denial to some of your fellows of individual opportunities open to the rest makes for a livelier appreciation of those opportunities. But increased respect for the individual, and extension of this value to more individuals, is not exclusively an American phenomenon. Parallel developments in other countries and the rapid absorption of national and cultural differences into a homogenized world culture threaten everywhere the normal assumption of, or aspiration to, individual integrity and dignity. Under threat, the salience of these values increases.

Humanistic psychology also has the virtue of fitting what seems to be an enduring and universal value of human life—a regard for individual responsibility. Perhaps the expansion of individuality, too, should always be highly valued, but it seems not always to be. There are and there have been societies in which the individual is accorded much less freedom and opportunity, is subordinated much more thoroughly to the mass or to superiors, than in the dominant cultural tradition of the United States and Europe. Yet it is hard to imagine a society in which the individual is not expected to be responsible for whatever limited aspects of his life remain within his choice. Humanistic psychology, in taking as its basic model the responsible human being freely making choices among the possibilities open to him, presents a view of man compatible with this enduring value of human society.

But what of all this? Surely the scientific approach is one of understanding fact rather than of elucidating value. A conception that things below the earth's surface must be of lower value than man—and at the ultimate depths be hell itself—and that things above the earth's surface must be of higher value the farther they are, was surely a barrier to the development of a sound astronomy and geology. But here man was imposing his own values on alien objects that are irrelevant to them. When man is studying man he is studying objects that, like himself, are characterized by orientation toward values. A psychological model that makes values irrelevant to man's behavior may, of course, have bad moral consequences. But the point I intend is that it is likely also to make a bad fit with factual observation.

Another virtue often claimed for humanistic psychology is that it readily leads into the discussion of personal ideals, of fulfillment, of self-actualization. The research tradition sometimes challenges people's sense of personal worth—as when it makes people feel that they are automatons with no control over their own actions. More often it is irrelevant, and this disappoints an expectation people bring to their reading of psychology. If humanistic psychology can be relevant to these human interests without losing the advantages of the research tradition, psychology and mankind will be the richer for it.

The openness of humanistic psychology is another of its virtues. Where the organized person is taken as the general pattern for understanding human experience and behavior, it is natural to expect novelty. Every one of us discovers in childhood that he has a private world of experience not directly accessible to others; his naive conception of being a person is bound to include a sense of uniqueness. Emphasis on *the person* is therefore likely, in my opinion, to predispose anyone to grant uniqueness to others as well, to expect that in exploring other people we will learn things we did not already know. Humanistic psychology, for this reason, has a certain readiness to be surprised, an openness to possible facts which a more rigid and uniform theory would lead one to dismiss as impossible. It encourages the advance of psychology into new fields, the serious investigation of topics lacking in current scientific respectability.

Perhaps the most persuasive virtue of humanistic psychology is the intuitive rightness of the model. The sciences studying man are unique in having this criterion to appeal to. In claiming "intuitive rightness" I do not mean that a human model of man is certainly correct because it is intuitively known to be so. Nor, indeed, do I think absolute correctness is a property of a scientific model; usefulness, or scientific value, is all I would argue for. In claiming intuitive rightness for a human model of man, I mean to assert that this model agrees with most people's intuitive impression of what it is like to be a human being, and that this agreement is one important item of positive evidence for the scientific value of the model. I may seem to be making a very modest claim, in arguing only that this item should be considered, and that it offers some support for the value of a human model. But many psychologists would reject even this modest claim. Seeking to understand their point of view, I can only suppose that their admiration of the more rigorous and precise sciences leads them to reject any criterion not relevant there. I would argue that there is an important and pertinent difference between psychology and the other sciences. Even where the subject matter of another science would theoretically lend itself to "intuitive rightness" as a criterion, we have no access to the information. Consider the zoologist trying to characterize the innate behavior patterns of the wolf, the tiger, and the sea gull. We may imagine some kind of consciousness in the members of each of these species. If we could communicate with them at an adequate intellectual level the choice among competing accounts of the species differences might then in theory be based partly on the intuitive rightness of those descriptions to the animals described—just as an anthropologist often profits from presenting to an informant something of the understanding he has thus far reached of the culture the informant represents. But this option is not open to the zoologist, and for the physical sciences, of course, the objects of study—earth, stars, light, electricity—seem to be just objects or events, so that few people would even playfully think of applying a subjective criterion to the validity of statements about them.

When it comes to man, our subject matter is really quite different. Here we know that each person who studies our theory will himself be one of the subjects to which the theory is applied. Is his judgment of how applicable it is to himself not one of the criteria to take into account in considering the theory?

I would certainly not want to suggest carrying this criterion very far. When psychoanalytic theory proposes that many of a person's motives are not available to his conscious awareness, because of emotional factors that will prevent him even from realizing their absence from his awareness, intuitive reaction to the model cannot be taken as very good evidence against it. But humanistic psychology can claim in its favor a sense of intuitive rightness about some basic characteristics of its model of man with which no one's conscious experience is likely to yield a sense of real discrepancy, whereas some of the competing models do, indeed, pose a radical discrepancy. If humanistic psychology were to claim that all human action is completely free, in the sense of being determined only by the person himself, the claim would be so gross a violation of everyone's experience as to be rejected out of hand. (To be sure, a great variety of other evidence could be adduced against this extreme position, but I believe everyone's experience from his own life would be adequate to reject it with complete confidence.) The opposite extreme, of viewing every detail of a man's behavior as being completely determined by separate, isolable stimuli and motivational states, is equally incompatible with the testimony of personal experience. Yet that extreme is adopted as a model by some forms of behavioristic psychology. Such a model, however implausible it is as a perfectly general view of man, may of course have great value for predicting behavior under some limited conditions. But as a general basis for approaching the understanding of man, the humanistic model seems to have great advantage. In assuming that experience and behavior, although partly determined in simple external ways, are also in part brought about through the initiative or decisions of the person himself, the humanistic model has the great virtue of probable long-range value to be inferred from its fit with the general evidence of everyone's personal experience.

Defects

One difficulty with the writings of humanistic psychologists is a frequent vagueness. The concepts used are often far enough from relation to specific fact that they have a real ambiguity. It is difficult to tell what precisely is meant, and easy to suppose that nothing very definite is meant. *Authentic-*

ity, a favorite concept of recent humanistic psychologists, provides an example. How are we to recognize an authentic person, or an authentic act? Can we expect that the person himself and an outside observer of his acts will usually agree about its authenticity? Can we even expect that two outside observers will agree? The concept may be capable of clarification. But it certainly invites differences of interpretation, differences that could become so great as to deprive the concept of all usefulness. Humanistic psychology does not stand alone in having somewhat vague concepts; in varying degrees, the characteristic is shared by all forms of psychology that are based on clinical practice or the observation of cases rather than on systematic research, nor is it absent from the sternest of experimental psychologies. However, vagueness certainly seems to be an especially severe problem in humanistic psychology.

Related to vagueness of concept but also partly independent is a marked tendency toward lack of verifiability. This difficulty, too, is quite in the tradition of clinical psychology and psychiatry. Where the verification of a statement resides entirely in the judgment of the clinician interpreting what he sees in individual cases, the process lacks the objectivity aimed for in the scientific tradition. Even the highly qualified observer, if left to evaluate essentially private evidence in a private manner, may not be easily convinced that the theory to which he is devoted is in error. This may be seen, for example, in the career of Sigmund Freud. A man unusually persistent in his adherence to scientific canons of evidence, and set to regard his theories as tentative and open to modification, even Freud seemed to require years of experience to become convinced that any particular aspect needed change. Some of the theories to which he was brought by the evidence of his clinical experience, moreover, have not been widely accepted by other psychoanalysts exposed to the same kinds of evidence. A notable instance is Freud's division of basic motives into a life instinct and a death instinct; the observations on which Freud based this idea were, presumably, unrepresentative or mistaken, yet once persuaded of its validity he was not easily dissuaded.

Humanistic psychologists seem especially prone, then, to make statements that are not easily verifiable. Since all psychologists of theoretical bent must necessarily look far beyond present fact, this is not in itself very troublesome. More disturbing is the apparent lack of interest in possible future verification. An instance of this is provided by the work of Abraham Maslow, one of the pioneers of humanistic psychology. With a background in experimental psychology, he clearly had the competence to carry out well-planned research that might lead to a testing of his ideas. In his work as a humanistic psychologist, he devised at least two novel techniques of observation and applied them in research on points of great interest to humanistic psychology generally. One was a device for measuring the individual's sensitivity to artistic styles. He and some of his colleagues wrote suggestively of research using this tool, but seem never to have presented the research in full. The other and more significant case appears in Maslow's extremely valuable investigations of peak experiences (uniquely absorbing experiences exemplified in extreme form by religious ecstasy) and the study of self-actualizing persons from which he developed his interest in peak experiences. Although he evidently spent a great deal of time in interviewing people, and in gathering data with well-planned interviews and questionnaires, his report of the outcome was always extremely informal. He seemed to suggest, for example that self-actualizing persons are especially prone to report many peak experiences. Had he retained along with his humanistic orientation a great concern for testing ideas against fact, it should have been relatively easy for him to pursue the research that could have tested this suggestion. Though obviously master of the necessary skills, he seemed not greatly interested in applying them. Perhaps he was simply making a wise decision about what activity of his could contribute most effectively at the time to the movement of which he was so important a part. If his example were to set the general pattern for humanistic psychologists, however, the theoretical work he and others have done would remain sterile; pertinent factual study is equally essential to the breeding of new generations of scientific knowledge.

The defect of nonverifiability is especially severe when it is set beside another defect that I sense in the writings of some of the humanistic psychologists. I feel that those who term themselves humanistic psychologists tend to be smug about their understanding of people. Perhaps we all are smug—those in the research tradition about their methods, and those in humanistic psychology about their intuitive understanding. Both forms of smugness are a threat to the development of significant psychological knowledge that can be shared and improved.

Even if we could feel confident that the best of the humanistic psychologists have a thorough intuitive understanding of mankind, there would still be a need for objectively verified knowledge as one way of increasing the number of such highly qualified people in the future. It may be claimed that a high order of intuitive understanding cannot be developed by way of abstract scientific knowledge but, instead, requires training in intuitive skills, or is not trainable at all. The very claim itself, however, is doubtful until it is tested by adequate inquiry into how various kinds of pertinent training affect intuitive understanding.

A fourth and somewhat related defect of humanistic psychology is a trend toward sentimentality. Descriptions of man by humanistic psychologists—and they are presumably intended as descriptions of man generally, not just of the person writing—are sometimes reminiscent of the concept of man that is associated with simple religious optimism, emphasizing the power of positive thinking, the infinite capacity of the human will to achieve good. Humanistic thought is a valuable counterweight to the behavioristic emphasis on the purely mechanical functioning of man and to Freud's early emphasis on the power of innate biological urges. It is a valuable antidote to the tendency, arising in these and other currents of thought, to picture man as basically evil or as totally driven by forces beyond his control. But where humanistic psychological writers encourage anyone to hold a one-sided view of man as totally under his own control or totally beneficent toward others, they depart from common observation into a realm of sentimental fantasy. For such a psychology to retain any usefulness, there must be much more to it than this obvious sentimentality. And, of course, there is a great deal more, as I hope to show.

Bogachevsky often urged me not to adopt any conventions, either those of my immediate circle or those of any other people.

He said: "From the conventions with which one is stuffed subjective morality is formed, but for real life objective morality is needed, which comes only from conscience.

"Conscience is everywhere the same. As it is here, so it is in St. Petersburg, America, Kamchatka, and in the Solomon Islands. Today you happen to be here, but tomorrow you may be in America; and if you have a real conscience and live according to it, it will always be well with you wherever you may be.

"You are still quite young; you have not yet begun life. Everybody here may now call you badly brought up; you may not know how to bow correctly, or to say the right thing in the proper manner, but this does not matter if only when you grow up and begin to live you have in yourself a real conscience, that is, the foundation of objective morality.

"Subjective morality is a relative conception, and if you are filled with relative conceptions, then when you are grown up you will always and everywhere act and judge other people according to the conventional views and notions you have acquired. You must learn not what people round you consider good or bad, but to act in life as your conscience bids you."

—G. I. GURDJIEFF

4

Psychology and Moral Development

What are the sources of a person's sense of right and wrong? If a person does something he considers wrong, why does he afterward—at times—feel guilty? Why do people so often choose a course of action they judge to be morally good and stick to that choice despite the prospect of pleasures, profit, and comfort to be gained by other choices?

Two extremes are found among attempts to answer these questions. One extreme is the simplest supernatural view. God has decided that certain human acts are right and others are wrong and has made these decisions known to man; guilt is the consequence of a departure from divine command. Another extreme seems more common today. Based on rebellion against this simple supernatural view, it holds that right and wrong are pure convention; each particular social tradition has arrived arbitrarily at a definition of right and wrong, teaches this definition to its participants, and by the threat of social retribution develops guilt in those who fail to conform to the standards set.

The supernatural view is frequently accompanied by a sort of absolutism —right and wrong are considered to be uniformly defined for all time and all circumstances by divine ordinance. Contraception, for example, may be viewed as absolutely wrong under all conditions, regardless of how much suffering and how many other wrongs result from failure to practice it. The social convention view, in its extreme form, is altogether relativistic. Any standards whatever may become the accepted ones in a particular social tradition, and once accepted they are completely valid; no considerations about human life in general can reasonably be used to criticize the moral conventions of any one human tradition.

One of these two views is associated with a particular form of psychology. Behavioristic psychology, with its external view of the individual as responsive only to rewards and punishments from outside, can readily encourage acceptance of the relativistic view of morality as pure convention. Behaviorism *need* not lead to such a view—but for many people behavioristic psychology forms a part of the background and justification of an extreme moral relativism.

The absolutistic extreme seems to have no close connection with any school of modern psychology. A possible psychological version of this extreme is to hold that God-given standards of right and wrong are built directly into the inherited nature of man, but our present understanding of genetics would make this an unlikely position. There must be psychologists who, as a part of their religion, believe in divinely ordained moral absolutes, but I do not know of any who as psychologists hold that knowledge of moral absolutes is uniformly built into inherited human nature.

Certainly neither of these views is likely to be an outgrowth of a humanistic psychology. If we take the manifest characteristics of the individual human being as a model for psychological understanding, we are led to view morality as something that the individual arrives at, through his attempts to understand and cope with the world in which he is immersed. What he arrives at seems certain to be influenced by the moral judgments he encounters, especially those conventional in his society, whether or not associated with supernatural beliefs. What he arrives at seems certain to be influenced, too, by the uniformities of man's biological inheritance and, perhaps, by his individual genetic makeup. But a humanistic view would suggest that a person's moral judgments and actions will neither be a direct product of biological inheritance nor a simple, passive absorption of the morality he encounters in his environment—that they will rather be something he arrives at through a creative interaction with these and other facts about himself and his world.

Just such a psychological theory of moral development has been proposed in recent years by the psychologist Lawrence Kohlberg. Kohlberg's theory deals most directly with moral judgment; yet many aspects of the accompanying research demonstrate its relevance to moral actions and moral feelings as well. It did not grow out of the intellectual movement commonly known as humanistic psychology; nor has it, so far as I know, received special notice from writers on humanistic psychology. But it deserves such notice; the research associated with Kohlberg's theory provides some of the most substantial and pertinent evidence for the value of a humanistic approach to the psychological study of personality and social interaction.

Background in Piaget's Work

The account of moral development formulated by Kohlberg has two principal sources.

One source is found in theory. As a baby gradually becomes a child, and the child becomes an adolescent and then an adult, he obviously improves his capacity for knowing, and this general improvement seems to be accompanied by changes in style or mode of knowing. Playful rehearsal of a situation somewhat as if actually in it, for example, seems to be a technique much more used by young children than by adults in seeking to master challenging situations; adults, on the other hand, make more use of abstract thought. As methods of science came to be used in the study of man, this gradual growth and change in cognitive capacity and modes formed one of the topics studied. Among its students, the Swiss psychologist Jean Piaget has been outstandingly successful in arriving at general principles. Piaget's developmental theory of cognitive growth is one source of Kohlberg's work, and Kohlberg's ability to add ingeniously to the theory of his predecessors is one reason for the notable success of his work.

The other source is in observation. Drawing on techniques of research again especially associated with Piaget, who had himself applied them to begin investigating the development of morality, Kohlberg devised an excellent method for observing moral judgment, and for analyzing his observations to obtain systematic data useful in testing and modifying his theory.

I think an initial glance at both these sources—Piaget's theory and method—will help prepare the way for a clear account of the research initiated by Kohlberg.

Piaget's theory, as I have said, is about how a person's ways of knowing change as he matures. It is not about *what* a person knows at different ages, except where this follows from answering the main question Piaget confronts: *how* does a person know at different ages? In seeking to answer this question, Piaget has explored highly varied aspects of human knowledge. He has studied perception; confronted, for instance, by a pattern of lines which for an adult makes one of two equal lines appear much longer than the other, does a child, too, see the lines as unequal? Piaget has studied the child's understanding of space and of time, the child's conception of number, and of cause and effect. He has explored the process of reasoning that the child goes through when faced with various kinds of problem or question. With all this diverse subject matter Piaget has been concerned to show how the knowledge processes of the child differ from those of adults. In everyday life, when we notice the evidence of these differences, we readily impute adult thought to children and facilely judge children to be inadequate copies of adults. The numerous studies of how children perceive and think, conducted or inspired by Piaget, have thus produced a corrected picture of what children are like and how they know.

The correction is badly needed; childhood, Piaget shows, is more distinctive than most of us had thought. In a great variety of ways, for instance, Piaget shows that the young child's understanding is more egocentric than that of the adult. The young child's conception of reality is limited by the point of view created by his size, his position in space and time, and his maturity and previous experience. An understanding of how things look to another particular person, or an objective formulation of the agreement among different persons' views, is not easily come by. A young child may even be an animist, naively attributing to a physical object a point of view like his own; that is, he may assume that every object shares his own characteristics, including that of being a living center of awareness.

Concerned primarily with the process of change, however, Piaget has never been content only with demonstrating that children are vastly different from adults. For practical interests, perhaps, it may be enough to know that thought processes are often very different in children; this awareness may in itself prepare us to avoid misunderstandings in our interactions with children. To understand change in thought processes, however, we must be prepared to study change wherever it occurs. Cognitive change, all students of human development find, does not occur just during a transition from childhood to adulthood; it characterizes all of childhood, and it does not cease when biological growth is completed.

Piaget's research over several decades has been directed at portraying and understanding this change. It began with a series of intensive studies of various aspects of children's knowing; a comparison of these various studies led Piaget toward an ever more adequate and general theory of cognitive development. For various specific aspects of the knowledge process, Piaget has sought to define successive stages of development (each *stage* is an organization or structure, the pattern of thought characteristic of a particular age or point in development). He has succeeded, too, in identifying some broad similarities between the way different aspects of thought develop, and thus in delineating very general stages of cognitive development. One of these broad stages, characteristic of infancy, is called sensori-motor. Here, thinking takes place by overt response to a stimulus actually present, or through maintaining the response during the temporary absence of the stimulus; the infant has no internal devices for symbolizing something not represented, whether it be milk, a toy, or a parental smile. Another of these broad stages, that of formal operations, begins to appear in adolescence; here, thinking is facilitated by the capacity not only to symbolize but to symbolize very abstractly, and to manipulate abstract symbols. This kind of thinking is well represented by formal mathematical reasoning, but Piaget shows that the same basic modes of thought are often involved in everyday reasoning about physical events and about social interactions. A person moves from the sensori-motor thought of infancy toward the stage of formal operations, Piaget finds, through a fairly regular sequence of intermediate stages.

In addition to portraying the sequence of stages through which the structure of thought develops, Piaget has also undertaken a more difficult task, that of analyzing the progress made within each stage and, especially, the transition from each stage to the next. A *stage* is a concept that describes or summarizes the pattern of thought almost visible in the careful observation of a child working at a problem or stating his reasoning. The *transition* from one stage to another is a concept referring to long sequences of events occurring over months or even years, and only indirectly evidenced through direct observation. As might be expected from this distinction, Piaget's account of stages is clearer, better elaborated, more closely related to observation, and more persuasive than his account of transition. Yet his account of transition is, perhaps, more essential to our purposes here. The concept of stage is likely to be sufficiently clear from the material I present on moral judgment. The concept of transition may need more preparation, for in moral development as in cognitive development generally, it is more remote from observable fact, more inferential, than the concept of stage.

Piaget's general conception is that the structure of thought at a particular stage is an attainment by the person. It is a pattern of functioning that the person has arrived at in solving problems posed by his interaction with his physical and social environment. This particular pattern of thought is likely to be successful or effective in some ways, and yet to pose certain problems, to encourage certain questions, whose nature follows from the particular pattern of thought. Those problems or questions, if the person does encounter them and is aroused to deal with them, have a particular solution most likely to be developed by a person thinking in this way. There is a strong tendency, hence, for a particular pattern of thought to be succeeded by another particular pattern (even though the discovery of the next pattern depends on the person's own curiosity and inventiveness and he may not attain it). There may, indeed, be only one particular pattern that is at all likely to be a satisfactory resolution of the problems posed by a particular structure of thought. This new pattern is, moreover, a structure likely to be created only in this way. Thus the development of entirely different individuals, though completely independent, may most often follow a very similar or even identical sequence of stages.

For an example, consider how the child arrives at a conception that a physical object normally retains a certain constancy of substance. In investigating this aspect of thought about physical reality, Piaget uses the following situation: the child is shown a rounded pellet of modeling clay, and is asked to form another exactly like it. When the two pellets have definitely the same size and shape, the examiner picks up one and by rolling it between his fingers converts it to a sausage shape, while the child watches. The examiner then puts the sausage down beside the remaining pellet and asks a variety of questions to learn just how the child understands what has changed and what has remained the same. For example, he may ask, "Is there the same amount of clay in both pieces now?" At the age of 7 and 8, Piaget reports that the child's pattern of thought is to concentrate on just one of the features involved—in this case usually the length of the lump as the most conspicuous feature—and to reason that the longer piece has more clay. With experience in this pattern of thought, in his many interactions with the physical world, a child becomes more likely to notice other related features, less conspicuous at first, and to base equally simple reasoning on them; in this instance, he may notice the thinness of the sausage-shaped piece and reason that since it is thinner than the round pellet it must have less clay. In this stage, he may oscillate, on different occasions, between two such lines of reasoning. This may give rise to noticing on a single occasion both of the features, and the dissonance of the reasoning separately based on them. The puzzle then posed by this discordance finds its most probable solution in a new pattern of thinking, which Piaget describes as follows:

> "If there is oscillation, the probability of the subject's noticing some correlation between the two variations (when the sausage becomes longer it becomes thinner) *becomes* greater (third stage). But as soon as this feeling of the solidarity existing between variables appears, his reasoning has acquired a new property: it does not rest solely on *configurations* any more but begins to be concerned with *transformations:* the sausage is not simply 'long,' it can 'lengthen,' etc."

This redirecting of thought from configurations to transformations readily leads to the consideration of how one transformation relates to other transformations, and out of this consideration the child arrives at a notion of conservation of substance:

> "As soon as the subject's thought takes transformations into account, the next stage *becomes* more probable in which he understands (alternately or simultaneously) that a transformation can be reversed, or that the two simultaneous transformations of length and width compensate, because of the solidarity he has glimpsed. . . ."

The kind of transformation portrayed here in the child's developing understanding of simple aspects of the physical world, Piaget considers also to characterize the child's developing understanding of the human world. On that use of Piaget's theory Kohlberg bases his theory of the development of moral judgment.

Its origin in Piaget's theory leads us to expect that Kohlberg's account of moral development will be humanistic. Of the few people whose highly innovative ideas have had a profound influence on the course of psychology, Piaget is the one whose approach has been most consistently humanistic. Like Pavlov and Freud he came to psychological problems with a biological bias, but the three men differed widely in what aspect of biological thought they drew on. The differences are pertinent to differences in the degree to which their work is humanistic; Pavlov is the least humanistic and Piaget is the most.

Pavlov, studying in dogs the learned modification of what seemed to be simple reflex connections between stimulus and response, initiated the custom of studying man's learning by methods applicable also to lower animals, and—more importantly—of understanding man so far as possible with the relatively simple principles of learning that could be extracted from the study of lower animals. In its rigorous form, this line of thought obviously involves looking at man externally and mechanically. Freud derived from his biological background a theory of innate drive pressing for reduction, and sought to extend it to all of human behavior and thought. This effort was most influential in the clinic but has also greatly influenced the course of laboratory research on human motivation. While Freud's approach, too, views man as somewhat mechanically impelled by forces alien to his conscious self, it holds the relevant forces to arise inside the organism rather than outside; it thus presents and encourages an inner view, a psychology that embraces a person's own experience as well as his actions seen from outside. To that extent the Freudian model was from its beginning humanistic. The biological sources of both the Pavlovian and the Freudian movements, though, provide a mechanism of explanation, a model of automatic or mechanical determination of human thought or action. It took a number of years for Freud and his followers to modify their model in the direction of greater humanism; it took longer for the students of learning, and some of them have never made the change.

Where Pavlov and Freud borrowed from biology a segmental concept about the functioning of some part of the organism, Piaget borrowed from biology the concept of the whole intact organism constructing and maintaining itself through interaction with the environment. The organism takes in materials and energy from the environment—such as food, water, air, and the sun's radiation. It uses them to maintain and strengthen its existing structure or to transform it; the latter use is especially conspicuous in growth and in the healing of wounds. From its beginning as a single cell, the organism is a continuous flow of structural transformations. The structure at any moment is an outcome of the active processes of growth and repair carried on by the organism itself, using the materials it obtains from the environment. These processes take account of the input from outside, accommodating the organic structure to environmental characteristics, as in summer tanning of light skin; but they also represent a constant assimilation of materials from outside into the existing structure of the body.

This is the biological model that Piaget extends to psychology. The human being exists and develops psychologically as well as anatomically by active processes of interchange with the environment. Piaget's theory of cognitive growth, which I have sketched above, is based on viewing psychological development as akin to anatomical development. The embryological analogy has obvious dangers. The processes involved in nutritional interchange with the environment are very different from those in informational exchange. The great strength of Piaget, among the founders of developmental psychology, seems to me to lie in his success in using the embryological analogy only as a general framework, obtaining the details of his theory directly from the systematic study of psychological development itself. He sees the organism as constructing its knowledge of the world by a progressive development of appropriate psychological structures, which are, on the whole, capable of assimilating ongoing experience because they have been devised in accommodation to problems that were encountered in attempting to assimilate earlier experience. Experience is not, though, a passive reception of mechanical input; it is an active interchange. The child does not just stare at a strange object. He moves to another position for a different view, he picks it up, perhaps tries to bite or bend it, or uses it to prod or smash other objects. His experience with the object is an interaction, in which the object may be changed more than he; how much he will be changed may depend on whether this interactive experience permits him to fit the object neatly into categories that he has already developed through earlier experience, or poses problems that require a new solution. The conditions and the processes involved in psychological development, when compared with those in anatomical development, seem likely to lead to much greater variation from one person to another. Any belief in uniformity must emerge from research; it is not predicted in advance by the general theoretical model. Piaget's theory, thus, is also humanistic in setting the observer to expect individuality and to seek to understand each person on his own terms.

Kohlberg's method, as well as his theory, derives from the general approach of Piaget. Given an aspect of thought to which he wishes to extend his research, Piaget seeks to devise a situation in which it will occur and to which a child may reasonably be subjected. The problem of the altered pellet of clay is typical of many that Piaget invented to study the child's understanding of the physical world. Piaget has given less attention to studying how the child understands the social world, but moral judgment is one aspect of social thinking that Piaget has studied. His research on moral judgment was done in the early years of his research and could not have the benefit of his own later-developed theory to guide its planning. Starting so much later, Kohlberg had a broader theoretical foundation on which to base his research; the general method he used, however, follows the path first broken by Piaget.

In setting out to study moral reasoning, Piaget was aware that he could not use so direct a method as he could use in studying the child's thought about physical reality. Unable to have the child resolve actual moral dilemmas, he could still tell the child stories related to moral issues, observe the child's spontaneous comments and probe his thought with suitable questioning. One of the stories Piaget told children was the following:

> "Story I. Once there were two children who were stealing apples in an orchard. Suddenly a policeman comes along and the two children run away. One of them is caught. The other one, going home by a roundabout way, crosses a river on a rotten bridge and falls into the water. Now what do you think? If he had not stolen the apples and had crossed the river on that rotten bridge all the same, would he also have fallen into the water?"

Response to this story clearly revealed young children's belief in immanent justice or moral realism. Of six-year-olds, 86 percent held that the child's fall was a consequence of his bad behavior, implying that justice is inherent in a natural sequence of events, and not dependent on the actions of parents or policemen. The proportion holding this view diminishes with age, but only around ten or eleven did Piaget find it to fall below 50 percent.

Stages in Moral Reasoning

Kohlberg wished to study more of the total span of moral reasoning than Piaget had considered. In adapting Piaget's methods, therefore, he had to devise stories that would be seriously considered by people varying widely in age—both children and adults. He began by studying boys of four different ages: 7, 10, 13, and 16. Each of the stories he prepared tells of someone facing a moral dilemma, torn between two alternatives each of which has some legitimate claim to be considered morally right. One story tells of an air raid warden on duty where there is no immediate threat, who can see that some blocks away his wife and children are in immediate danger;

by leaving his post he might be able to save their lives. The story ends with the question: "Should he stay by his post or leave it to save his family?" More important than a person's answer to that question is the reasoning behind his solution of the moral dilemma. On precisely what grounds does he view each alternative as legitimate, and how does he resolve the conflict? That reasoning and how it changes with age, form Kohlberg's special topic of inquiry.

Studying boys spread out in age from 7 to 16, Kohlberg found a development of moral reasoning that seemed to him to break up very naturally into six stages. As a first step let's look at what these stages are, and how characteristic they are of different ages. Then we can consider what sort of general sequence of change they suggest.

First in the sequence of development is what Kohlberg calls an *obedience and punishment* orientation. A person ought to obey because if he does not he will get punished. For example: "If he doesn't stay at his post, he'll be arrested and they'll put him in jail or maybe even shoot him." Or, "If he doesn't help his family, his wife will probably divorce him and take away his children." Statements of this kind are found to make up over 70 percent of the statements that seven-year-old boys make in response to questions about their moral choices. The proportion declines to just 10 percent of the statements made by 13- and 16-year-olds.

A second stage is *naively egoistic,* oriented around the immediate interests of the central actor, attending primarily to his major needs in the situation. For example: "It's according to what he wants most. If his family are most important to him, he ought to go and help them. If all the people in this neighborhood matter more to him, he ought to stay and protect them." Statements of this sort are a little under a quarter of the statements made by seven-year-olds and rise to somewhat above a quarter at the age of ten. Then this kind of reason also declines, forming about 10 percent of the statements made at the two later ages.

In a third stage, moral reasoning is still oriented around the central character, but it emphasizes his maintaining good relations with other people. Kohlberg calls this a good-boy orientation. Here for the first time appear notions of right and wrong, of good and evil, but they are expressed in thoughts about the socially defined role played by the central character. Society has definite rules or expectations for each role, and conforming to them is good. "He'd have to go help his family. It wouldn't be natural for him to do anything else. People would think he was crazy." Or, in support of the opposite choice: "People would say he was a coward if he deserted his post. His family wouldn't want him to be a coward either." Such statements are only about 5 percent of those made by seven-year-olds, but rise to 20 percent at the age of ten and to almost 25 percent at the age of thirteen. Then they, too, begin to decline, forming only about 20 percent of the statements made by the 16-year-olds.

The fourth stage seems oriented toward authority rather than toward the central character himself, and Kohlberg calls it an orientation toward *authority and social order.* A course of action is justified by its being demanded or supported by whatever individual or group is seen as the possessor of proper authority for the maintenance of social order. For instance: "The civil-defense officers have to know just where everyone is, if their job is to be done. For him to run away is just as bad as for a soldier to desert." Or, "He ought to do what the civil-defense officers would order him to do if they knew what was up; when his family's in trouble and the others aren't, they'd order him to go help his family." Statements of this form were missing in Kohlberg's 7-year-old subjects, made up about 15 percent of the reasons offered at the age of 10, and rose to 30 percent at the age of 13. At 16, such statements still seemed to be somewhat the most frequent type, forming 32 percent of all the statements made.

The fifth stage in moral reasoning is legalistic, appealing to such concepts as *social contract.* For example: "It wouldn't be right for him to leave his post to help his family. After all, the only reason his family's generally been safe is because other men were on duty there. Now they have to count on him to protect their families, even if it hasn't been possible this time to keep his family safe." Or: "I think he'd have to go help his family, even though there might be a bit of a risk in leaving his post. His wife expects this of him, and he's obliged to take care of his children; that's the kind of commitment a man makes when he gets married. The other men on duty would agree that he should take care of his own family first." This sort of reasoning, completely absent in Kohlberg's 7-year-olds, was found in only 3 percent of statements made by his 10-year-olds; but it rose to 15 percent at age 13 and to 20 percent at age 16.

The sixth and last stage is oriented toward abstract principles of conscience. Here, reasoning depends on universal principles viewed as products of human nature rather than of convention or agreement. For instance: "It's wrong to place the interests of a few people, even close relatives, above the general welfare of people at large. The warden is the person this whole neighborhood counts on for safety, and his first duty is toward them, even though he ought to help his family if he were free to do so." Or "Protecting to the best of one's ability the life and welfare of relatives must be a major aim for anyone. It has to be balanced against the responsibility this man has for protecting others as well, as we all should do to the best of our capacity. But now when these others are not really threatened, he should go help his family. Human life should be safeguarded, so he must help those whose life is threatened." Moral reasoning of this sort was not found by Kohlberg at age 7 nor at age 10, and it remained rare at the higher ages; only 4 percent of statements at age 13 and 5 percent at age 16 formulated universal principles in justifying moral choices.

At first glance this sequence may seem haphazard. It seems to work almost randomly back and forth between emphasis on the individual and on something outside him, and between emphasis on the bad consequences of the wrong choice and on the good consequences of the right choice. Yet when studied with care, the sequence of six stages may be seen to be systematic

The first two stages are grouped together by Kohlberg as premoral. In effect they both deny the existence of anything that would justify a special term such as morality. One says all that matters is the whim or chance of the punishing person or situation—what actions will happen to be punished? The other says all that matters is the whim of the actor—what particular needs does he consider most urgent?

The third and fourth stages introduce some consideration that might justify the term morality, and have in common that they justify it solely by reference to convention. In the third stage a person should choose whatever will lead him to be accepted by others as a "good boy," and this reasoning implies acceptance of the conventional values of the group—any group—as a basis for choice. The fourth stage, although referring to authority rather than to group acceptance, implies a conventional basis for definition of authority.

The fifth and sixth stages have in common a reference to some kind of abstract principle. The fifth stage justifies morality by reference to a global principle of contractual reciprocity; in accepting the benefits of group living each person has incurred the obligation to help provide the corresponding benefits to others. In the sixth stage the principles are both more abstract and more specific; they are generalizations about various morally relevant aspects of human living.

The six stages fall into three groups, then, and the significance of the sequence of stages is, perhaps, most readily introduced by looking at the order in which the three groups appear. First there is no morality. Then there is morality imbedded in convention. Finally there is morality independent of convention. As one grows older, this seems to imply, there is a movement toward fuller or richer knowledge, accompanied by greater abstraction and differentiation. Could it be that the sequence occurs because a person is gaining better understanding as he grows older? This is just what Kohlberg proposes. His interpretation of why this sequence occurs as it does is the central point of his work, and the aspect that particularly relates it to a humanistic view of man.

The sequence begins at the first stage with a simple and global view of any situation in life: action occurs and results follow. The person acts, for instance, and punishment follows. No special attention is given to the makeup of the person, nor to how he differs from another person. The punishment, too, is not analyzed; it occurs, but no special attention is given to who administers it, nor to why. The understanding represented in these statements is reminiscent of Piaget's description of the immanent justice that he encountered in the moral understanding of young children, who see punishment just as a natural part of the entire sequence of events, inherent in the situation rather than administered by authority.

In the second stage, this global understanding becomes a little more differentiated. The actor is distinguished from the rest of the total situation, and he is not an empty person; he has definite needs. It is these needs, a part of him, that press him on to justifiable action. The self is thus the first part of the global situation to become subject to a more enriched understanding.

In the third stage, the self remains the central focus, but it is now seen in relation to other people. A person's internal needs do not determine what he should do; the key is how other people will respond. Kohlberg finds, too, that other people are often viewed here as evaluating a person's behavior in the light of his intention, rather than just in the light of his overt behavior. This is consistent with a continuation and improvement of the differentiated understanding of the self which was already begun in the previous stage with the recognition of *needs* as one part of the person; here a more refined understanding brings the recognition of *intentions* as another distinct part.

In the fourth stage the outside world which had begun to be differentiated in the previous stage is now subject to further analysis. Among external realities the role of authority is singled out for special attention, and decisions that authorities make become the prime criterion for morality.

In the fifth stage, for the first time, a rule or principle is distinguished from the situation in which its application occurs and from the particular person acting or responding to action. People have an implied social contract—a contract that has an existence or validity outside the actions of the particular individual involved in the choice and its immediate consequences. Here is a still further step in differentiated understanding of the world, one in which laws or principles can be separated from the specific situations to which they are relevant. Along with this greater differentiation comes greater ability to face conflict. The person reasoning at this level more explicitly recognizes that conflicting interests are present, and that a resolution cannot altogether satisfy all interests. Here is more complex thinking; in the earlier stages the individual seeks some simple understanding to conceal the underlying ambiguity.

In the sixth stage, where principles come to be stated in the abstract, there is further differentiation. Principles are now stated outside any specific social matrix; they are seen as generally valid truths about human beings.

The six stages that Kohlberg portrays in the development of moral reasoning, then, form a sequence of steadily increasing capacity for realistic understanding of the world and for abstract reasoning about it. This is true, he argues, for many aspects of moral reasoning. In giving examples of reasoning at different stages, I have especially stressed the values held and the motives considered especially relevant. A variety of other concepts might have been stressed instead—for example, the way in which rules are conceptualized, or the purposes attributed to punishment. Kohlberg asserts that these diverse aspects of moral reasoning all show a progression through six stages of development, with each aspect consistent with the others though, perhaps, not entirely predictable from the others. Kohlberg recognizes, too, that a person's reasoning is not all at a single stage. When a child is questioned about a number of moral dilemmas, his answers will sometimes be at one stage and sometimes at another; indeed, variation may appear even among the parts of his reasoning about a single dilemma. Yet a person's position in the developmental sequence may be determined by the general trend of his reasoning, and Kohlberg asserts that almost 50 percent of a child's moral reasoning is generally found to be at a single stage. As this fact implies, of course, the stages are constructs we psychologists use in understanding a reality that is much more complex than the constructs themselves. Only an exceptional person—perhaps, indeed, no person at all—could be found to fit in every detail one of the stage constructs. Yet these constructs help in characterizing the way one person differs from another, and in understanding how each person changes through time.

The evidence for a fairly regular sequence of development is beginning to accumulate, and from diverse sources. Various psychologists have used Kohlberg's techniques in studying moral judgment in other societies, including several peasant or tribal villages. Thus far, these studies have found the same sequence that Kohlberg found in his urban American subjects; in some communities the rate of development is much slower and the proportion of the population ever reaching the highest stages is probably lower, but the stages appear in a constant order. The finding of a similar order of development in communities as diverse as those studied in Taiwan, Yucatan, and Turkey supports the Piagetian theory about how the development takes place. The cultural pressures on the child differ greatly from one of these communities to another. The common element that can be related to the sequence of moral thought is that every community contains children each one of whom is progressing in a more or less panhuman fashion toward cognitive maturity; the structure of moral thought is a specific instance of the considerable regularity in the order in which this progress occurs. Cultural variation induces great differences in the speed with which one stage is replaced by the next, or in whether it ever is replaced; but what the next stage can be seems to be limited by universally valid facts about what problems can arise from using a given mode of thought, and about what change in mode of thought can solve those problems.

A parallel finding begins to emerge from the comparison of different groups within a single society. Boys and girls, for example, often differ in characteristic experience, and sometimes in ways that have been thought likely to produce sex differences in the substance or structure of moral judgments. Only for one society, the United States, is there the beginning of adequate comparison of the sexes in moral development. In a number of social settings boys and girls have been found to progress through the same sequence of stages. Although in one social setting boys were more advanced than girls, in other social settings no such differences in timing appeared. In each sex, and in each social setting, the same sequence of stages was found.

That stages of moral reasoning appear in a fairly regular order, related to cognitive development, is also indicated by several studies of how people respond when they encounter the moral reasoning of stages other than their own. An experiment by Kohlberg's student and colleague, Elliot Turiel, found subjects most likely to modify their own reasoning in the direction of arguments at the stage just above their own; hearing arguments at a still higher stage or at a lower stage is less likely to induce change. Although little change of any kind seems to be produced by exposure to other arguments, this tendency for change to be toward the next stage above has been confirmed in later experiments. The special status of moral reasoning at the stage just above one's own characteristic level is also indicated by experiments that test subjects' understanding and evaluation of reasoning they are asked to read or listen to; moral reasoning at the stage just above is valued more highly, although moral reasoning at lower stages is understood much better.

The sequence of stages Kohlberg finds for moral development makes good sense, too, in relation to our more general knowledge of children's intellectual development. Kohlberg has also pointed out that the sequence fits well with attempts made thus far to view the growth of the self or ego in relation to intellectual development. As our knowledge of moral development advances through the research initiated by Piaget and Kohlberg, there may be many changes of detail, but Kohlberg's picture of the general sequence seems to be well established.

Transition from One Stage to Another

Why does moral reasoning change as a person develops? This question has been most often put in a more specific form: why does a person's moral reasoning change from the structure of one stage to the structure of the stage just above? This more specific question is a bit artificial, because it suggests that a person's moral reasoning is at one time all of one character, and that it may all then suddenly change. As I have already indicated, a person ordinarily exhibits at any one period the moral reasoning of various stages. Different structures of thought may dominate his reasoning about different issues, about different topics pertinent to a single issue, or perhaps in different moods or different situations. During the period a person might be classified as principally at one stage of moral reasoning, he may be undergoing change just as steadily as during a period when he is obviously between one stage and the next. A person is an ever-changing process. The concept of stage, and movement from one stage to the next are, however, useful abstractions, helpful in understanding the myriad little changes that occur through time, none of them in actual fact so clear-cut and decisive as the abstract theory might suggest.

Movement from one stage to another emerges, according to the theory of Kohlberg and his fellow developmental psychologists, from each person's interaction with the world. Changes in a person's moral reasoning are above all an achievement by the person himself, a solution he produces to the problem of understanding the social world. In his daily life a person repeatedly formulates moral judgments, perhaps with awareness and perhaps not; at times he feels these judgments, and the reasoning that forms them, to be challenged. How a challenge arises, and what follows, will perhaps be clearer from the example presented later than from an abstract statement of general theory. However, the abstract statement may at least serve as a useful introduction, and here it is: the structure of the thought process at any one stage defines to a considerable extent what will constitute a challenge to it, and it also defines what kinds of change in thinking would provide a satisfactory answer. A person may not feel the challenge. If he does, he may not choose to cope with it. But if he does cope with the challenge, there may be only one general kind of change to be discovered (though with ample room for variation in detail) that will meet precisely this challenge. That change is what defines movement to the next stage.

The sequence of stages, according to this theory, thus depends on a certain requiredness in the interaction between person and world. The mode of thought at a given stage defines what kind of interaction with the world is required for that mode of thought to be challenged. The mode of thought and its challenge define what new mode of thought is required to eliminate the challenge and, hence, what the next stage must be. A particular person may or may not be challenged, and he may or may not rise to the challenge; but if he does, and meets it successfully, we can, according to Kohlberg's theory, predict what general kind of solution the person will arrive at. One kind of solution is required, or at least rendered most highly probable, by the nature of the person's interaction with the world.

A parallel, with an instructive difference, is provided by historical developments in technology. The production of high temperatures, in order to process food and other products, is an example. For early man, able to keep fire going once he had obtained it from a forest fire, the challenge was to find how to start a fire at will. Once he was able to set wood afire whenever he wished, a new challenge might be to raise its temperature; blowing might provide a first technique, and bellows and controlled drafts would provide a further improvement. Only with the mastery of ceramic and metal techniques thus available, could the further challenge of still higher temperatures and greater concentration be met, and then only in the way permitted by the tools and materials at hand. There is in technological development, thus, an element of requiredness about the succession of techniques. But an individual does not need to go through the same stages as has mankind as a whole. A child who has never nursed tinder into flame, who has perhaps never struck a match, can readily turn on the electric stove. The stages of technological development, in their implications for the typical individual, represent changes in external conditions, not necessarily changing the basic nature of what he must do. Turning a switch, like striking a match, is a simple act a person can learn at almost any time.

Stages of development in moral reasoning, on the contrary, involve basic changes in what the person himself does. The processes characteristic of a stage are not in a matchhead nor an electric circuit; they are in the functioning organism. They are not, moreover, simple acts that can be readily taught. They are complex patterns or structures of thought, not obviously or easily teachable. The structure characteristic of one stage, perhaps, is something that can come into being only as a modification of the structure found at the previous stage—much as a ceramic bowl is brought into being only by taking a clay bowl and subjecting it to high temperature. Despite our remarkable control over many physical processes, we cannot make a ceramic bowl by a more analytic procedure, taking each of the chemical elements in the right amount and somehow making them each take its proper place. The structure of the ceramic bowl can only be formed by modifying, through heat, the structure of a clay bowl. We can hardly be surprised that—at least, in the primitive condition of psychology, and perhaps forever—a complex psychological structure can be brought about only as a modification of a certain previous psychological structure.

We can hardly be surprised, either, that very limited knowledge has thus far been obtained, in the few years of research, about how changes in the structure of a person's moral reasoning are achieved.

Kohlberg in his initial study observed moral reasoning in different groups of boys spaced out in age at three-year intervals from seven to sixteen. Subsequently, a student of Kohlberg's, Richard Kramer, was able to reinterview many of Kohlberg's subjects when they reached the ages of twenty and twenty-five. Changes and consistencies in the same persons' reasoning could thus be traced over a period of years, although of course without any information about day-to-day or month-to-month change. Another student of Kohlberg's, Elliot Turiel, initiated the experimental study of developmental change over short periods of time, as I have already mentioned, and this sort of research has been continued both by him and by others, partly with the practical aim of improving educational procedures. I have indicated, too, the striking similarities and variations obtained by applying Kohlberg's technique in different communities. All this research provides a rich background for theoretical speculation about the process of transition from one stage to another, and most of the research has been planned to test particular aspects of the theory. Turiel has recently written several excellent articles about this theory and research, and I have drawn on his articles to give the following brief account, stressing the general themes which emerge, while leaving aside the uncertainties that necessarily characterize the early years of any new field of knowledge.

A specific transition in moral reasoning may be the best place to start, and Turiel has given careful consideration to one that has been most studied. It is movement from the fourth stage, oriented toward authority and social order, to the fifth stage, involving social contract reasoning. Some curious observations pertinent to this transition had been made in two quite separate studies, and Turiel has put them together in an illuminating way.

The observations suggest that transition from authority to social contract type of moral reasoning often involves a regression to the much more primitive naive egoism of Stage 2. The clearest suggestion of this comes from Kramer's follow-up of Kohlberg's original subjects. A joint article by Kohlberg and Kramer describes the evidence in this way:

> "Between late high school and the second or third year of college, 20% of our middle class sample dropped or retrogressed in moral maturity scores. Retrogression was defined as a drop in maturity scores greater than any found in a two-month-test-retest sample. This drop had a definite pattern. In high school the 20% who dropped were among the most advanced in high school, all having a mixture of conventional (Stage 4) and principled (Stage 5) thought. In their college sophomore phase, they kicked both their conventional and their Stage 5 morality and replaced it with good old Stage 2 hedonistic relativism, jazzed up with some philosophic and sociopolitical jargon. . . . Every single one of our retrogressors had returned to a mixed Stage 4 and 5 morality by age 25, with a little more 5 or social contract principle, a little less 4 or convention, than at high school. All too are conventionally conforming in behavior, at least as far as we can observe them. In sum, this 20% was among the highest group at high school, was the lowest in college and again among the highest at 25. The correlation of moral maturity from age 16 to age 25 is .89, the correlations from high school to college and from college to 25 are only .41."

The other pertinent observations come from the study of students at the University of California at Berkeley, shortly after the Free Speech Movement activities there in 1964. This was the first of the major student protests in this period of United States history. It grew out of circumstances that led a majority of students to consider the protest movement important and morally justified, and led a substantial minority to support the sit-in and other tactics eventually used in the protest. In these conditions, who were the student activists who pursued their moral convictions at the risk of arrest and various other punitive consequences? Among the research techniques used in attempts to answer this question was Kohlberg's inquiry into moral reasoning.

One outcome was very strong evidence that a large proportion of the activists were at very high stages of moral reasoning as assessed by Kohlberg's technique. Of the students who had been arrested for sitting-in, 23 percent were assessed as being at Stage 6 (abstract principles of conscience) and 36 percent at Stage 5 (social contract reasoning), while in a control group representing a random sample of Berkeley students the corresponding figures were only 3 percent and 11 percent. Moral reasoning appealing to convention rather than to principles (Stages 3 and 4) was, on the other hand, much more frequent in the control group than among sit-in participants. People whose moral judgments were supported by more mature structures of thought were much more likely, then, in this particular crisis, to act in accordance with their moral judgments.

A second outcome was that the premoral egoistic reasoning of Stage 2 was also more frequent among the activists than in the control group (13 percent as against 5 percent). The Berkeley researchers took this to indicate that the protest movement, although it grew out of the moral concerns of the most mature members of the student community and continued to be dominated by those concerns, also offered gratifications of a different kind to some of the least mature. The researchers thus took at face value the level of moral reasoning indicated by the Kohlberg technique, assuming that this small group of activists were, indeed, at the naive egoistic level. Kohlberg and Kramer, in their later discussion of these results, suggest that this may be too simple a view. There is, indeed, a marked similarity of general structure between the reasoning of the college egoists and of children and delinquents whose statements are placed in the same category. But along with this similarity are differences that must be considered. The researchers offer the following samples:

"*Table III.* Examples of sophisticated and unsophisticated Stage 2 responses to one story

"Story III American.

"In Europe, a woman was near death from a very bad disease, a special kind of cancer. There was one drug that the doctors thought might save her. It was a form of radium that a druggist in the same town had recently discovered. The drug was expensive to make, but the druggist was charging ten times what the drug cost him to make. He paid $200 for the radium and charged $2,000 for a small dose of the drug. The sick woman's husband, Heinz, went to everyone he knew to borrow the money, but he could only get together about $1,000 which is half of what it cost. He told the druggist that his wife was dying, and asked him to sell it cheaper or let him pay later. But the druggist said, 'No, I discovered the drug and I'm going to make money from it.' So Heinz got desperate and broke into the man's store to steal the drug for his wife.

"Should the husband have done that? Why?

"Guide for scoring Story III at Stage 2—as oriented to instrumental necessity of stealing:

1. *Value.* "The ends justify the means.' Says has to, is best to, or is right to steal, to prevent wife from dying. (Without implication that saving the wife is a good deed.)
2. *Choice.* Little conflict in *decision to steal.* Implies decision is based on instrumental reasoning or impulse.
3. *Sanction.* Little concern about punishment, or punishment may be avoided by repayment, etc.
4. *Rule.* Little concern about stealing in this situation. May see stealing in this situation as not hurting the druggist.
5. *Husband role.* Orientation to a family member or a relative whom one needs and is identified with. May be an act of exchange, but not of sacrifice or duty.
6. *Injustice.* Druggist's 'cheating' makes it natural to steal. However, not actually indignant at the druggist, who may be seen as within his rights to charge whatever he wants.

"*Roger* (age 20, a Berkeley Free Speech Movement student).

"He was a victim of circumstances and can only be judged by other men whose varying value and interest frameworks produce subjective decisions which are neither permanent nor absolute. The same is true of the druggist. I'd do it. As far as duty, a husband's duty is up to the husband to decide, and anybody can judge him, and he can judge anybody's judgment. If he values her life over the consequences of theft, he should do it.'

"(Did the druggist have a right?) 'One can talk about rights until doomsday and never say anything. Does the lion have a right to the zebra's life when he starves? When he wants sport? Or when he will take it at will? Does he consider rights? Is man so different?'

"(Should he be punished by the judge?) 'All this could be avoided if the people would organize a planned economy. I think the judge should let him go, but if he does, it will provide less incentive for the poorer people to organize.'

"*John* (age 17, reform school inmate).

"Should the husband steal the drug for his wife? would eliminate that into whether he wanted to or not. If he wants to marry someone else, someone young and good-looking, he may not want to keep her alive.'

"(How about the law, he is asked): He replies, 'The laws are made by the rich, by cowards to protect themselves. Here we have a law against killing people but we think it's all right to kill animals. In India you can't. Why should it be right to kill people but not animals? You can make anything right or wrong. To me what is right is to follow your own natural instincts.'

"*Hamza* (Turkish village, age 12).

"Yes, because nobody would give him the drug and he had no money, because his wife was dying it was right.'

"(Is it a husband's duty to steal the drug?) 'Yes—when his wife is dying and he cannot do anything he is obliged to steal. If he doesn't steal his wife will die.'

"(Does the druggist have the right to charge that much for the drug?)

'Yes, because he is the only store in the village it is right to sell.'

"(Should he steal the drug if he doesn't love his wife?) 'If he doesn't love his wife he should not steal because he doesn't care for her, doesn't care for what she says.'

"(How about if it is a good friend? 'Yes—because he loves his friend and one day when he is hungry his friend will help him.'

"(Should the judge punish him?) "They should put him in jail because he stole.'

"*Jimmy* (American city, age 10).

"It depends on how much he loved his wife. He should if he does.'

"If he doesn't love her much?) 'If he wanted her to die, I don't think he should.'

"(Would it be right to steal it?) 'In a way it's right because he knew his wife would die if he didn't and it would be right to save her.'

"(Does the druggist have the right to charge that much if no law? 'Yes, it's his drug, look at all he's got invested in it.'

"(Should the judge punish?) 'He should put him in jail for stealing and he should put the druggist in because he charged so much and the drug didn't work.' "

Kohlberg and Kramer call attention to the fact that college egoists such as the one quoted above understand reasoning of much higher stages, as we might well guess from the complexities and abstractions of phrasing in the quotation. They also note that the college egoists make occasional use of reasoning at the higher stages, where the children and delinquents do not. Of obvious importance, too, is Kramer's finding that the college egoists later return to the higher stages of moral reasoning, and thus differ from the many persons at stage 2 who are likely never to reach Stages 4, 5, or 6.

Turiel puts these and other facts together to argue that the apparent naive egoism demonstrated by some college students on the Kohlberg questionnaire is genuinely different from the similar reasoning found in children. We have here in fact, he argues, an instance of the slow struggle many people go through in achieving a transition from one structure of reasoning to the one that can eventually supplant it. The transition is a gradual transformation that may, at times, lead to behavior or statements seemingly quite inconsistent with the structure of the stage at the beginning and of the stage at the end of the transition. The particular behavior or statement may then be an inadequate index of the structure that produces it. A larger context is needed for its correct interpretation.

To be specific, then, about the transition involved here: the authority-oriented morality of Stage 4 takes social conventions as absolutes, distinguishing little between moral and other conventions. The principled reasoning of Stages 5 and 6 must distinguish between the arbitrary aspect of all conventions and the basic principles of moral import (such as equality and justice) underlying or embodied in those conventions. The principles have universal validity, even though the conventions based on them are relative to the particular social matrix in which they arise. As Turiel puts it, "The change to principled thinking must, therefore, include a greater recognition of the arbitrariness of conventional values—that is, more relativism. At the same time, it must include a greater recognition of the universality of moral principles—that is, less relativism." This transition is a very difficult one to make, and few people ever make it; in some communities studied where verbal skills are not highly developed, very little principled reasoning is found. In a person who has already developed special skills in abstract reasoning, perhaps, recognition of the relativism of convention may be readily accompanied by the realization of the universality of underlying principles, and by the integration of relativism and universality required in Stages 5 and 6. But more characteristically, Turiel seems to suggest, high skill in reasoning with general principles—at least on moral issues—has not been attained in advance; recognition of the relativism of convention can then for a long time be accompanied only by an intuitive understanding of principles, whose lack of clear formulation prevents a satisfactory integration into a coherent structure of thought. The characteristics of transition from Stage 4 to Stage 5, exhibited by the college students who seem to regress temporarily to the naive egoism of Stage 2—are stated by Turiel in the following way.

> "Thus, in the initial attempts to apply principles of equality and justice, there occurs a reorganization of thought about conventions so that they are seen as relative and arbitrary. In consequence, we find more relativity: in the sense that there is greater awareness of actual differences between individuals and between societies, and in the sense that many of society's non-moral values are no longer experienced as categorical imperatives. Along with this criticalness of Stage 4 thinking comes the moral attitude that differences among people and societies should be respected. Clearly, this increased relativism represents a developmental advance over Stage 4, within the context of the theoretical structure of the moral development sequence. This type of relativism also represents an obvious advance over the relativism of Stage 2 thinking.
>
> "The concomitant attempt to understand universal principles is not entirely successful because, during the period of transition, virtuosity in

> principled functioning has not been attained. Consequently, there is some confused application of moral principles—principles are at times confused with conventions and treated relativistically. It is inevitable that in any transitional phase (which involves disequilibrium) there will be some inherent cognitive confusion. However, the form of confusion we are considering still represents an advance over Stage 2 or Stage 4 thinking because the relativistic view of principles serves a different function from that employed at Stage 2. Furthermore, principles are often *not* treated relativistically within this transitional phase. . . . We may conclude, then, that during transition from Stage 4 to Stage 5, conventions are subordinated to principles, although principles are still neither clearly articulated nor fully integrated with the conventional system."

The passage I have just quoted from Turiel suggests that complex theory may be needed to deal adequately with the complexities of human moral development. A preliminary sketch of an adequate theory, perhaps, is what we have today. The research it is inspiring may lead to modifying it almost beyond recognition, or may leave it almost intact, modifying it only by filling in details. For my part, I feel strongly the promise of adequacy here, and I find it partly in the humanistic character of the theory. It portrays moral development as brought about by the striving of each active human being for understanding and control of his world and his relations with it. The regularities in it come from universalities of human nature and of the human situation, from the implications of a structured mind interacting with a structured world.

As I indicated earlier in the chapter, this new and humanistic understanding of moral development has not occurred in isolation from the rest of developmental psychology. It has been possible because of the example and guidance provided by theory and method in developmental psychology generally, and especially by Piaget's study of the development of cognition, of the substance and skills of a person's knowing. In his developmental psychology of cognition, Piaget offers a humanistic view of the human being as forming the structure of his thinking by progression through a succession of stages. The structure of a child's thought at a particular stage defines, in interaction with the facts of the physical and social world, what points of difficulty or conflict are most likely to arise, and what modification of thought structure will most adequately resolve those difficulties or conflicts. If the child achieves the requisite transformation of thought-structure, he is then prepared to encounter the difficulties it, in turn, occasions in interaction with the world, and to have the possibility of moving on to a structure that will resolve those difficulties.

This is a very different, and a vastly more complicated, view of human development than those that have dominated American psychology until recently. One view was purely external and descriptive: the development of intelligence, for instance, was portrayed as a curve representing average performance on an intelligence test at successive ages. Another view was biological in a rather naive way; drawing an analogy between intellectual growth and a rather too simply understood physical growth, it represented development as an unfolding, in genetically determined order, of a preestablished sequence of forms. Another view was environmental in an equally naive way; viewing exclusively as cultural convention the selection of tasks to be imposed on children at each school grade, it extended this exaggeration to other aspects of adult regulation of children's behavior, neglecting all active functioning of the child himself. When we try to use any of these simpler theories alone to account for the facts about the development of moral reasoning, or about the development of cognition generally, serious difficulties arise. The Piagetian approach, loyal to intuitive impressions of what it is like to be a human being, promises to be far more productive than any of the simpler theories alone. On the other hand, even this developmental approach needs to be supplemented by using, along with it, other theories and the research findings to which they have given rise. The developmentalists have taught us the importance of the person's own attainments in building the structure of thought with which he understands and tries to master his life. A humanistic point of view, however, must recognize the limitations as well as the power of the individual, and in the processes studied by simpler theories will identify many factors that constrain the development of the individual.

Say even that this complete simplicity
Stripped one of all one's torments, concealed
The evilly compounded, vital I
And made it fresh in a world of white,
A world of clear water, brilliant-edged,
Still one would want more, one would need more,
More than a world of white and snowy scents.

There would still remain the never-resting mind,
So that one would want to escape, come back
To what had been so long composed.
The imperfect is our paradise.
Note that, in this bitterness, delight,
Since the imperfect is so hot in us,
Lies in flawed words and stubborn sounds.

—WALLACE STEVENS

5

Psychology of Art

The human traditions we call art and science each offer to the other challenges and opportunities. Art has responded to science in several ways. It employs techniques derived from scientific progress; the art of the film depends on them for its very existence. Scientific activity and scientific knowledge are alluded to in many stories, plays, and poems, sometimes providing the main theme. Most importantly, perhaps, all the arts respond to the issues science raises concerning man's sense of his own origins, existence, and future.

Of all the sciences, it is psychology that could most confidently be expected to be concerned with art. Psychology seeks to understand as much of human activity as it can; and art is a human activity that impresses many people as especially difficult to bring even partially within a framework of scientific understanding. Hardly had psychology begun its independent history as a science, in the latter part of the nineteenth century, than this challenge was felt, and psychology began to be applied in advancing the understanding of art.

One effort was made by experimental psychologists in academic laboratories. Their effort, called experimental esthetics, consisted of applying the methods of experimental science to problems suggested by the arts. Claims had been made, for instance, that architectural features are more pleasing when made in particular shapes—that building facades, windows, and other segments of buildings are especially pleasing if they have the so-called "golden proportion." The issue was controversial, and a simplified version of it was testable in the laboratory: rectangles of various shapes could be presented to experimental subjects who would be asked to say how well they liked each. This was one of many issues tested in simplified form by experimental estheticians; though this tradition has not yet seemed to fulfill its early promise for understanding art, it has made valuable contributions to psychology. A recent book by Daniel Berlyne, *Aesthetics and psychobiology*, suggests the great contribution of this tradition in moving experimental psychology toward the recognition of human complexity, toward the study of cognition, and toward finding in cognition distinctive sources of motivation and of pleasure.

The other effort to relate art and psychology grew out of the clinical tradition, and especially out of psychoanalysis. Readers of Freud know that the founder of psychoanalysis was greatly interested in the arts. Perhaps at first entirely personal, this interest became important for Freud's scientific work. The major evidence for Freud's theories, the private revelations of his patients and intensive analysis of his own dreams and memories, failed to provide the objective, repeatable test by which Freud, trained in medical science, would have liked to establish the truth or falsity of his ideas. Works of art, Freud found, could to some extent make up this deficiency. If a sceptic doubted that thoughts of incest are common, as Freud was forced by his clinical observations to believe, Freud could not offer the sceptic direct access to his interviews with patients. But Freud could refer the sceptic to Dostoevsky's novels, to the classical Greek tragedies, or to mythology for clear evidence of preoccupation with incest.

Freud argued that underlying thoughts about sexuality (not incest alone, of course) are important and influential even in a person who is quite unaware of them. Unconscious sexual thoughts, therefore, need to be taken into account to understand a patient. Turning to art, Freud argued for a parallel need; anyone who wishes to analyze thoroughly the meaning of a work of art must consider unconscious sexual thoughts in the author and in the audience. Freud used this approach, for instance, in reinterpreting Shakespeare's *Hamlet*. He argued that the full meaning of the play for author and for viewer includes their unconscious attribution to young Hamlet of residues of his childhood Oedipal fantasies, and that any interpretation omitting this point fails to grasp adequately the way many details fit into the integral meaning of the play. Freud's argument here pertains to what he considered art does for man. He holds that art offers a sublimation of sexual interests. Art permits us to have sexual fantasies in a socially acceptable form; often a work of art is so ingeniously arranged that it even permits us to have sexual fantasies without realizing what we are doing. Freud's initial point, that art provides evidence for psychoanalytic ideas, seems to me generally valid. The theory of art to which this led him, that the basic function of art is to permit sublimated expression of repressed impulses, seems much more questionable.

Both the early approaches I have mentioned have a strongly mechanistic element—the experimental approach, in considering a person's enjoyment of art as an automatic consequence of some simple feature of the stimulus; the psychoanalytic approach, in considering it an automatic consequence of his partially satisfying some hidden impulse. Objections to Freud's theory of art, made by other psychologists or psychiatrists with clinical experience and artistic interest, led to the development of a humanistic psychology of art. Beginnings of a more humanistic approach may be seen in some of the allusions to art in the writings of Carl Jung. More especially devoted to studying art, however, and from an earlier time, was Otto Rank, a disciple and co-worker of Freud's from about 1905 until the early 1920's and an independent theorist from then until his death in 1939. Rank's attempts to apply early psychoanalytic theory to understanding art were one of the important influences leading him to differ from that theory in a humanistic direction.

The general trend of the theory Rank eventually developed was to turn away from biological drives as the principal source of man's discontent and striving, to emphasize instead man's existential status, his sense of himself and of his relation to the world. The details of his theory combine striking anticipations of later thought with some elements no longer viable. Relevant to my purposes here is that his possession of a humanistic theory gave him the courage to attempt an understanding of artistic creativity. Where Freud, for the most part, had limited himself to asking why certain themes are incorporated in art, Rank pressed on to raise more insistently the question Freud usually feared to ask: why do some people create art and others not?

Rank's answer is offered as a solution to the problem of creativity in general, although he developed it especially through considering artistic creativity. The part of the answer I want to present here is one that recent research has brought closer to test than any of it was when Rank wrote. Then we can look at the research, noting how valuable it is through giving empirical meaning to the theory and yet how valuable the theory is when it can give a broader meaning to the facts of the research. In presenting this point, I am following the argument of one of the main researchers to whose work I am referring—Donald MacKinnon, who has particularly stressed the good fit between his findings and Rank's theory.

The aspect of Rank's theory to which MacKinnon especially directs attention is its account of three types of mental state, or types of person. One, the normal or adjusted type, accepts himself and the world as they are, adapting without complaint, even though this means making less of life, less of each moment perhaps, than might be possible. As Rank puts it, "The so-called adaptability of the average man consists in a capacity for an extensive partial experience such as is demanded by our everyday life, with its many and varied problems." To be thoroughly "adjusted" a person must renounce his independent will and accept the external, partial, abstract definition of himself established by the social system of which he is part. To do this successfully, he must enter into all experience in socially defined ways, renouncing the possibility of the fuller and more varied experience perhaps achievable through the autonomous strivings of his will.

People who do not choose the easy but shallow course of "adjustment" —that is, entire acceptance of external demands and definitions—are termed by Rank the nonconforming. Their experience, he says, is more intense; they tend to concentrate their "whole personality . . . . whole self, on each detail of experience, however trivial or insignificant." The nonconforming include both the second and the third of Rank's three types. One of these he often refers to as the neurotic type; but this term is an inconsistency, for elsewhere he argues against the concept of neurosis, anticipating more recent humanistic attacks on other concepts of sickness, which I mention in a later chapter on schizophrenia. Better terms are the synonyms he offers—conflicted type or thwarted type. Here the nonconformer goes no further than the negative step of rejecting the inadequacies of adjusted life. He loses thereby the comforts or securities provided by the partial satisfactions of a thoroughly routine life, without gaining the distinctive rewards accessible to the third type.

The third type—referred to variously as the productive type, the creative type, or the artist—goes beyond this rejection;

> ". . . he avoids the complete loss of himself in life, not by remaining in the negative attitude, but by living himself out entirely in creative work. This fact is so obvious that, when we intuitively admire some great work of art, we say the whole artist is in it and expresses himself in it."

Another way Rank expresses the difference among the three types is this: the creative type and the thwarted neurotic are both

> ". . . distinguished fundamentally from the average type, who accepts himself as he is, by their tendency to exercise their volition in reshaping themselves. There is, however, this difference: the neurotic, in this voluntary remaking of his ego, does not get beyond the destructive preliminary work."

The creative person, on the other hand, goes beyond this negative step of rejecting complete external control. He goes on to positive constructive assertion of his will. He objectifies something of his own self by creating, or helping to create, in the outside world something uniquely expressing himself and enduring beyond himself. In this picture of the creative type of person Rank was anticipating the recent emphasis, by Abraham Maslow and other humanistic psychologists, on personal growth and self-actualization as major life objectives. Like Maslow, Rank supposed that heightened realization of one's individual potentialities could give a special zest to life, that many people do not follow a course which leads in that direction, and that those who do are not likely to renounce their chosen course.

The Berkeley Research on Creativity

Much of the recent writing on creativity is, like Rank's, theoretical. But there has been a great deal of research, too, that attempts to establish on a firmer factual basis our knowledge of creativity. Of special importance have been the long, varied, and coordinated series of studies done at the Institute of Personality Assessment and Research, a unit within the University of California at Berkeley.

The Institute has had a humanistic orientation from the outset. Its founder and director, Donald MacKinnon, brought with him attitudes that he had formed or strengthened during his years of association with Henry Murray of the Harvard Psychological Clinic. Murray is a psychologist who did much to keep alive the fruitful interplay of humanistic speculation and empirical research at a time when psychological research in the United States was almost exclusively imbedded in a mechanistic context. Among the first studies to be completed at the Institute was Frank Barron's investigation of personal soundness—notable for its orientation toward better-than-normal health, toward human potential rather than limitations.

The Berkeley studies of creativity focused on several occupations, and two of these are artistic: architecture and literature. MacKinnon directed the study of architects, and Barron directed the study of writers. Both studies bear equally on my thesis that humanistic thought and the research tradition need each other. I am concentrating first on the study of architects because of its special pertinence to Rank's theory. It is through MacKinnon's discussion of this relation, indeed, that I was led, long after first becoming familiar with the Berkeley research, to read Rank's varied works, which until then I had (except for *The Trauma of Birth,* Rank's best-known but far from most valuable book) willingly left undisturbed on the library shelves.

MacKinnon and his colleagues studied three groups of United States architects. One was a group intended to be the most creative architects available. The list of potential members of this group was carefully assembled through nominations and votes by an appropriate group of knowledgeable experts; forty out of the sixty-four invited to form this most creative group accepted and took part in the research. A second group of architects was restricted to persons who were not on the list of most creative but had been associated with someone on that list for at least two years of work experience. The third group were chosen from the general body of United States architects, with the proviso that they did not meet the criteria for eligibility in either of the first two groups. The purpose of studying these three groups was to sample the whole range of creativity found among architects; measures of creativity obtained in the research itself amply showed that the three groups, despite a great deal of overlap, differed markedly in the typical degree of creativity. The first and third groups yielded the high and low averages in creativity measures, as expected, and the second group fell between. All three groups cooperated in a number of psychological procedures—questionnaires, tests, inventories—intended to assess personality and life background, and the most creative group also took part in supplementary procedures for more intensive study.

Thinking about this grouping after the data had been gathered, MacKinnon noted that the three groups might reasonably be expected to correspond somewhat with Rank's three personality types. The most creative group clearly should be the most likely to show the characteristics of Rank's productive or artistic type. The third group might be expected on the average, doubtless with many exceptions, to have characteristics of the adapted type; having no reputation for special originality themselves, and having no history of close association with those who do, they might reasonably be suspected to include many persons of conformist bent. For the intermediate group, the expectation is less strong; their history of association with high creativity, though, suggests that many of them value creativity and seek it, without fully realizing creative originality in their own career. A possible similarity may be seen to Rank's conflicted type, unsatisfied with simple conformity yet unable to break loose sufficiently to realize the full human potential for creative action.

Here is an initial schematic correspondence between the defining characteristics of the three groups of architects and Rank's theoretical definition of three types of personality or mental state. The usefulness of Rank's theory, as a guide to understanding creativity, may then be tested by seeing whether the research findings about the three groups correspond with the expectations based on Rank's theory. MacKinnon states several theoretical expectations, and reports their confirmation by the outcome of the research.

First, a variety of personality measures indicates the greater conformity of the least creative group of architects. They score higher than the other groups on scales indicating responsibility, deference, concern for others and, in general, all traits that are indicative of conventional socialization. The most creative group scores lowest on these scales, and the intermediate group falls between. Just the opposite order is found for two scales that indicate traits contrary to conventional socialization—that is, aggression and independence. This kind of difference in personality is reflected in how members of the several groups picture their own architectural practice and their conception of the ideal architect. The most creative group, says MacKinnon

> ". . . see, as most characteristic of themselves and of the ideal architect, some inner artistic standard of excellence and a sensitive appreciation of the fittingness of architectural solutions to that standard."

The least creative group tend to stress the need for meeting a standard set by the profession, rather than the person's own standards. The intermediate group, as though suspended in conflict between personal and social standards, seem inclined to stress technical standards of aptitude and skill.

A second set of expectations is concerned with the richness or complexity of psychological development, which Rank's theory suggests should distinguish the groups in the same order as their basic degree of creativity. Here again a variety of measures pertain, and they all tend to confirm the expectation. Architects of the most creative group have the highest average, for example, on measures of perceptiveness, intuitiveness, esthetic sensitivity, preference for complexity, flexibility, and having interests characteristic of the opposite sex as well as those characteristic of their own sex. In general, the group intermediate in creativity are intermediate on these measures, too, though on most of these measures they are very close to the most creative group.

A third set of expectations has to do with the difference between the two most creative groups, expectations arising, of course, from considering them as exemplifying Rank's conflicted and productive types. On the measures thus far discussed, these two groups deviate from the least creative group of architects in the same direction, as I have reported above; they both deviate in the direction of a less socialized orientation and greater personal richness or complexity. These characteristics would be expected from Rank's picture of nonconformers. Rank's theory leads to the expectation that the intermediate group (as representatives of the conflicted type) should show signs of conflict about these nonconforming characteristics, signs of lacking constructive control or command over them. On a variety of measures of emotional stability, personal soundness, and ego strength, the intermediate group in the Berkeley study is, indeed, found to show low average scores, and on a measure of anxiety a high average score. They are by these indexes the most conflicted or disturbed of the three groups, no longer intermediate as they are in creativity.

MacKinnon argues, finally, that Rank's theory permits predictions about experiences most likely to be found in the background of the most creative group, and that these, too, are confirmed by the data of his study:

> ". . . in the life-history protocols of our subjects we have obtained supportive evidence for many of the kinds of early interpersonal experi-

> ences which Rank would have thought most strengthening of positive will and most conducive to the fullest development of the individual. They may be briefly summarized as follows: an extraordinary respect by the parent for the child, and an early granting to him of an unusual freedom in exploring his universe and in making decisions for himself; an expectation that the child would act independently but reasonably and responsibly; a lack of intense closeness between parent and child so that neither overdependence was fostered nor a feeling of rejection experienced, in other words, the sort of interpersonal relationship between parent and child which had a liberating effect upon the child; a plentiful supply in the child's extended social environment of models for identification and the promotion of ego ideals; the presence within the family of clear standards of conduct and ideas as to what was right and wrong; but at the same time an expectation, if not requirement, of active exploration and internalization of a framework of personal conduct; an emphasis upon the development of one's own ethical code; the experience of frequent moving within single communities, or from community to community, or from country to country which provided an enrichment of experience, both cultural and personal, but which at the same time contributed to experiences of aloneness, shyness, isolation, and solitariness during childhood and adolescence; the possession of skills and abilities which, though encouraged and rewarded, were nevertheless allowed to develop at their own pace; and finally the absence of pressures to establish prematurely one's professional identity."

MacKinnon regarded his study as providing marked confirmation of that part of Rank's theory to which it was relevant, and obviously regretted that an intent to test Rank's theory had not entered into the detailed planning of the research. The relevance of Rank's ideas was missed in the planning of the study, despite MacKinnon's familiarity with them years before. The reason, I think, lies in the separation of humanistic psychology and the research tradition. A humanistic theorist such as Rank does not think of the need to test his ideas, and does not try to cast his ideas into testable form. A humanistic researcher such as MacKinnon readily applies his technical knowledge and ingenuity in gathering data, but may not fully pursue the possibility of adapting them for greater pertinence to ideas that have been stated so abstractly that their potential relevance to observation is vague and uncertain. Only when humanistic psychology and the research tradition are brought together, as in MacKinnon's reconsideration of his results, does either begin to reach its full potentiality.

The Berkeley study of writers, directed by Frank Barron, included only two groups—one identified by nomination as outstandingly creative, and one representative of other successful writers—apparently most nearly comparable to the first and third of MacKinnon's groups of architects. Rank's theory comparing three groups—adjusted, thwarted, and creative types—thus cannot be tested for writers. Nor do we have parallel studies of painters or other kinds of artists. The full detail of MacKinnon's application of Rank's theory must remain for the present a suggestive line of thought, its value confirmed in its first use but not yet further tested. The differences between a highly creative group and a group more representative of the total range can, however, be tested for writers and, indeed, a variety of pertinent studies of other professional or student groups are also available for comparison.

Professions do vary somewhat in the personality characteristics associated with high creativity. Ronald Taft has proposed a useful distinction between hot and cold styles of creative process. *Hot* creativity draws strongly on emotional sources and depends on freedom of emotional expression. *Cold* creativity draws more on rational thought and depends on the integrated control of thought processes. Aspects of both styles may be present in the same person, even at the same time, but effective creativity of certain kinds may be possible with one practically absent. The hot style, Taft argues, is especially prominent in creative artists, and the cold style in creative scientists. Architecture might be expected to call for a blend of the two, combining esthetic considerations with those of science and engineering.

Despite these variations among the professions, however, there seem to be some constancies in what kinds of persons are especially likely to be highly creative; the agreement seems even greater, of course, when only the artistic professions are considered. Rank's distinction between the adjusted and the creative type provides a remarkably good advance prediction of what would be found. But the research has added other points and has provided a solidity not possible without it. The emerging picture of creative personality is nowhere given with greater skill than in the various writings of Frank Barron, who evidently chose for study a profession for which he was himself especially fitted.

When Does Creative Thinking Occur?

The Berkeley studies of creative artists portray the personal characteristics generally favorable to producing creative thought. Can we focus on this even more closely and see precisely what momentary psychological conditions especially favor creative thinking? Various people have tried to do this. An especially promising attempt, in my opinion, is the one recently made by a psychiatric researcher, Albert Rothenberg. His work is especially important for my present purpose, too, because it illustrates how the research tradition can benefit by drawing on the methods of inquiry more commonly employed in the humanities. The greater use of these methods facilitates rapprochement between humanistic psychology and the research tradition. Although these methods direct our attention first toward the detailed understanding of the individual person, they may of course lead to generalizations just as broad as those that are developed through experimental work in the laboratory. The generalizations that emerge from intensive study of the individual, however, are especially likely to be faithful to the complex realities of human life. Their absorption into the general stream of psychological research, then, influencing the research done by other methods as well, promotes a genuine blending of the separate virtues of humanistic psychology and the research tradition. Many years ago Gordon Allport made essentially this argument, in urging the greater use of personal documents in psychological science. Thus far his plea has been too little heeded by psychologists; Rothenberg's approach to studying creativity well indicates that it merits attention.

Rothenberg began with studying in detail the genesis of a specific work of art, Eugene O'Neill's play, *The iceman cometh.* He could not use experimental procedures, obviously, nor even interviews with O'Neill, who had died some years earlier. He had to depend on an analysis of documents, the traditional basis for historical research. The manuscript records of O'Neill's successive drafts and revisions of the play had been preserved in a library for the use of scholars. Rothenberg studied them in much the way a literary historian or biographer might, but watching especially for clues to the thought processes important in permitting O'Neill to achieve an artistic success in writing this play. Rothenberg supplemented his documentary approach only by interviewing O'Neill's widow; this he did later to check on definite hypotheses he had developed in the documentary research.

From this detailed inquiry into the sequence of events in O'Neill's construction and development of *The iceman cometh,* Rothenberg emerged with a definite hypothesis. It is that creative activity is especially favored by bringing into simultaneous juxtaposition two or more ideas contradictory to each other. He first called this *oppositional thinking,* and later decided that *Janusian thinking* was a better label. Using as a symbol the two-faced Roman god, who saw constantly with one face in each direction, this label aptly suggests that what is important is the simultaneous awareness of opposites. Contradictory elements must be brought together in a moment of one person's awareness, just as the views of front and back, or past and future, given by the two faces of Janus, were pictured by the ancient Romans as being brought together in a moment of divine consciousness. Rothenberg has summarized in the following way the emergence of his hypothesis from textual analysis, comparison of the successive versions of the play, and the information he could assemble about the author's life. For O'Neill, he says

> ". . . the central iceman symbol in the play *The Iceman Cometh* had at least three different connotations: (1) the iceman was death (this is stipulated in the play itself); (2) the iceman was Christ (the phrase

'the iceman cometh' refers to the biblical phrase 'the bridegroom cometh' and the play is structured as a modern parable of the Last Supper); and (3) the iceman was a sexually potent adulterer (based on an old joke known to O'Neill which goes as follows: a husband comes home from work and calls upstairs, 'Dear, has the iceman come yet?' His wife calls back down, 'No, but he's breathing hard!'). Substituting these meanings into the central creation of the play, the notion of the iceman coming, produces four or more logically opposite ideas: (1) Christ's coming or deliverance is the opposite of bleak death; (2) sexual potency is the biological and, according to Freud and others, the psychological antithesis of death; (3) a bridegroom and an adulterer are polar extremes; and (4) infidelity is opposed to the ultimate tenet of Christian faithfulness, Christ's coming. A potential fifth and probably more implicit opposition is the celebration and elevation of sexuality, particularly illict sexuality, in conjunction with Christ himself. Christ was not only the opponent of illicit sex, especially adultery, but his teaching could be considered to be generally antisexual or antihedonistic. In the unconscious, of course, many of these oppositions can be significantly equivalent and one of the sources of the awful strength and beauty of the iceman symbol is its ability to connote logical contradiction and basic truth simultaneously—in other words, the integration of opposites.

"In this same study, I also presented evidence that suggested that O'Neill arrived at a central idea in the play, an idea which led in part to his creation of the iceman symbol, by means of a *simultaneous* conceptualization of opposites. This idea pertained to the suicide of the man who was O'Neill's roommate during the year 1912, a man upon whom the 1939 play was based in large part and who was represented in the play by a character named 'Jimmy Tomorrow.' O'Neill came to realize that this roommate committed suicide because, as the man had said, he was upset about his wife's infidelity with another man, but also because of an opposite feeling—he had unwittingly wanted his wife to be unfaithful to him. All his life, O'Neill had been plagued by the memory of this man's suicide and plagued by the man's assertion shortly before he died that his wife's infidelity had brought him to his state of deep depression. It appears that only in his later life did O'Neill come to realize that the man had also wanted his wife to be unfaithful and that this was a motivating factor in the suicide. This insight was incorporated into *The Iceman Cometh* and the evidence indicates that it had a good deal of influence on the structure of the play and O'Neill's motivation to write it."

Here, then, a general psychological hypothesis comes from the study of a single literary text and the history of its composition. Literary critics have, through their own analyses of texts, often arrived at a somewhat similar point, especially emphasized in the scholarly tradition known as "The New Criticism." Their point is that the artistic value of a poem is greatly influenced by the presence, often subtle, of opposites in the very text itself or the ideas it suggests to any careful reader. The "new critics" emphasize the role of irony and paradox in the rich texture of meaning that characterizes poems most generally regarded as great works of art. The thesis of the literary critics, then, pertains to the text itself and is directed at explicating and evaluating literature; the literary critics are content to rest their argument on the evidence of their own analyses of texts. Rothenberg is, on the other hand, concerned with the text (and its successive revisions) only as one source of evidence for the psychological processes through which it came into being. And having emerged with a general hypothesis about those processes, he is not content with the evidence from which he has induced the hypothesis. Instead he seeks further, feeling that as a general statement about psychological processes, the hypothesis should if valid be testable in other ways as well.

One other source of pertinent evidence is provided by the clinical studies of creative writers. As part of a long program of research on creativity, Rothenberg has conducted a series of interviews both with established poets and novelists and with novice writers who display originality. The interviews resemble in style psychiatric interviews with patients, but they are clearly defined as having a research rather than a therapeutic intent, and they are especially focused on actual incidents of creative thought and work in progress. For comparison, Rothenberg has conducted similar interviews with other persons who, as paid research subjects, have attempted to write a poem or story; they are not themselves writers, but are matched with both the creative groups in age, sex, and socioeconomic and ethnic background.

Rothenberg finds in these clinical studies a decided confirmation of his hypothesis that Janusian thinking characterizes the creative thinking of writers. He reports that instances of Janusian thinking are frequent in the interviews with creative writers, and absent in the noncreative persons undertaking a writing task. Here are two examples:

> "In the course of discussing the circumstances surrounding the genesis of a particular poem, a poet subject told me that he got an idea for a particular poem while walking on a beach. He came upon some rocks and thought that they were heavy and were weapons but that, *at the same time,* they felt like human skin. The poetic ideas that followed this inspiration and the final poem itself were a comment on the relationship between sex and violence in the world. Indeed, the idea that sex and violence had many things in common was an early realization in this poet's mind as he wrote the poem.
>
> "In another instance, a poet was cooking cream of celery soup and began to think of arguments she had heard as a child at school that

things had no form unless they had boundaries or were in a container. She thought of the fact that cream of celery soup had no form outside the pot and simultaneously thought of the first line of a poem which went as follows: 'Cream of celery soup has a soul of its own.' In this case, using the term 'soul,' she was thinking of an entity which was both formed and formless. The total poem went on to become a vibrant statement of conflict between herself as a child and as an adult."

The methods of systematic quantitative research can also be applied to Rothenberg's hypothesis, and he has already begun to apply them. He has used a word association test, in which a person hears a number of single words and is instructed to reply to each one as quickly as possible with the first word that occurs to him. Various kinds of association are found whenever this test is given. To the word *health,* for instance, a person might reply with a rhyme (*stealth*), with a grammatical transformation (*healthy*), with a superordinate word (*condition*), with a concept associated in time or space (*body*), with a seemingly unrelated word (*fence*), and so on. Fairly frequent, and of special interest here, is the possibility of responding with a word opposite in meaning (for instance, *disease*). Perhaps a special tendency to respond with opposites in this test would be related to a general tendency toward Janusian thinking. Accordingly, Rothenberg administered the test to his creative writers, and he did, indeed, find a high frequency of opposites among their word associations. In addition, he administered the test to over a hundred college men, who also completed a questionnaire designed to provide a rough assessment of creative orientation and performance in the arts and in science. Dividing these students into more and less creative groups according to this questionnaire, he found the more creative to give the higher proportion of opposites. Both here and in the study of writers he also found that, when giving opposites on the test, the creative group tended to answer more rapidly than the noncreative. This point seems especially pertinent to the element of *simultaneity* specified in his hypothesis about the processes involved in creative thought.

The hypothesis of Janusian thinking could also be tested in experiments, though it has not as yet. Research subjects could be assigned at random to experimental and control groups. The experimental subjects could be instructed, or trained, to think of opposites, while this step would be omitted with control subjects. Then in their performance of a challenging task (perhaps writing a poem) in the laboratory, where this training or instruction might remain effective, the creativity displayed by the two groups could be compared.

If the experimental group showed greater creativity, this result would argue that the Janusian hypothesis has very broad validity. If this result were not obtained, though, would the Janusian hypothesis thereby be disproved? If the hypothesis had been tested only by experiment, of course, the only evidence available would be this negative finding, and the hypothesis might well be discarded. A great deal would have been missed by this exclusive reliance on experimental method. Rothenberg's diverse studies give us much reason to believe that a pattern of oppositional thinking, well established in a person's approach to his serious work or characteristic of his whole personality, is an important element in permitting him to work creatively. This belief would not in itself be seriously challenged by an experimental finding that oppositional thinking established only momentarily within the laboratory fails to influence creativity. Experimental procedures, while giving special certainty about exactly the issues to which they are narrowly addressed, may be quite misleading when the results are generalized to other or broader questions. It can be equally misleading to generalize too broadly and confidently from the individual case study based on historical documents or on clinical experience. Psychology needs to blend methods, as well as ideas, that are diverse in origin.

As Rothenberg points out, there is no reason to believe that Janusian thinking, or any other specific element, is the single and unique key to creativity. But Rothenberg has clearly delineated one specific part of the creative process; has shown that his picture can be tested by observation; and with several different kinds of evidence gives us reason to believe that he has portrayed a genuinely important part of the creative process. The picture he gives is consistent with the Berkeley personality studies. They did not involve measurement specifically of oppositional thinking. But some of the more general measures found correlated with creativity—a preference for complexity, for instance—are clearly more compatible with oppositional thinking than with its absence. MacKinnon's view that the Berkeley results fit well with Rank's schema is also thoroughly compatible with an emphasis on oppositional thinking; while all nonconformers share rejection of the commonplace, the ability to bring the commonplace ideas into simultaneous contrast with their opposites could be a major source of the distinction between the creative and the thwarted outcomes of nonconformity. But Rank's speculations are vague about just what psychological processes are involved; Rothenberg's greater specificity leads, I think, toward a more definite understanding.

Response to Art

Early attempts to apply psychology to art, as I have implied at the beginning of the chapter, were equally or more concerned with understanding the other side of human interaction with art—not its creation by the artist, but the viewer's experience of it, and the effects of this experience. This has been my concern in the research that I have been engaged in for more than a decade. As my own studies illustrate well the interdependence of humanistic ideas and the research tradition, and are the pertinent research I know best, I draw here principally on them. They also illustrate how change may be induced in psychology by giving appropriate attention to other disciplines, and to the humanities in particular. The research itself would not have been done without my attending seriously to the arts. Doing the research, moreover, altered my views as a psychologist, bringing me more and more into the humanistic position that previously I had only viewed with distant respect.

The only humanistic psychologists whose writings I knew well at the time that I started were Gordon Allport and Henry Murray. Both had greatly influenced my thought on other matters. Yet on this particular topic, I was not aware of any influence from their work. Looking back, I see that I must have been influenced, but only in general orientation; both of them vigorously expressed respect for the autonomous power of the individual, an attitude important for my research.

When I began my research, I was best acquainted with behavioristic and early Freudian theories. But these were not the source of the ideas that I proposed to test. The source was rather my own experience of art and my impressions about the experience of many other people who were interested in art. The pertinent aspect of experience I am referring to is a sense of esthetic value, the feeling that one work is more satisfying, beautiful, interesting, or provocative than another of its kind. Some people claim no such feelings or regard them as simply a personal preference for one style or subject matter over another—like the special fondness a yachtsman may have for sailing prints, or an adolescent for *Le Sacre du Printemps*. My own sense is that I can distinguish to some extent between this kind of purely personal attraction and a feeling that a poem or painting is an especially admirable work of its kind. Feelings of the latter sort—that a particular work is esthetically good or poor—were in earlier times taken for granted as a part of normal human experience of art. In recent decades complete scepticism has supplanted the earlier acceptance of esthetic value as a concept with substantial real meaning. Might it be worthwhile to reconsider the question?

The history of literature, music, and visual art in the European tradition offered, I felt, a good deal of support to my own feelings. There has been a remarkable tendency to esteem certain works of art and their creators very highly, and to disregard many as having much lesser value. Recent writers on the history of taste are fond of calling attention to variations in judgments from one period to another; in reading them, however, I have always been much more impressed by the evidence of agreement and continuity. Writers on the history of taste come from the tradition of the humanities, where the confidence of some persons in the objectivity and permanence of esthetic value not long ago was absolute, and even today is very much alive. A person reared in that tradition may be distressed to hear it said that Shakespeare has not always been considered the greatest of English writers, or that J. S. Bach was discovered to be a great composer only long after his death, and may give too much weight to isolated instances such as these, overlooking a general pattern of substantial agreement.

The relativistic current of recent thought, on the other hand, can lead to the expectation of complete chaos in responses to the arts. Many people today seem to hold seriously the view that praise or condemnation of any work of art whatever is equally appropriate. Two persons considering the same work should not, according to this view, show any tendency toward agreement in their response, except when one person influences the other or when they are both influenced by evaluations they know others to have made. Wherever we find agreement in esthetic evaluation not plausibly attributable to such influences, the position of complete relativism in esthetic value is challenged.

The greatest challenge of all, potentially, comes from comparing esthetic evaluations made in separate cultural traditions. In Japan and China, for example, just as in Europe, certain art has through the centuries come to be regarded as outstandingly excellent. For the most part, these were until recent times traditions almost entirely separate from the European one. Yet I have the impression that critics reared in the European tradition when encountering Oriental art usually found themselves in general agreement with the Oriental evaluations, and vice versa. I wish that we had careful comparative studies of the history of esthetic evaluation in different countries. Their absence, however, may itself be significant. Art scholars and critics schooled in one esthetic tradition and encountering another do not seem bewildered; apparently they find patterns of evaluation not totally uncongenial. When a work of art is considered by critics of widely varying background, it may tend to be evaluated in a somewhat consistent way.

A similar expectation could well have been derived from humanistic psychology. If, when starting this research, I had been sufficiently familiar with Piaget's theory of cognitive development, that could have provided the starting point for my speculations about esthetic evaluation. Both Piaget's theory, in particular, and humanistic psychology, in general, portray man as an active agent, constantly interacting with the world around him and progressively formulating an understanding based on this interaction. This view of man suggests that his judgments about any aspect of his experience will not be entirely the passive repetition of judgments he has heard others express, and that agreement among individuals will emerge from the similarity of their interaction with the world as well as from their communicating with each other. An esthetic kind of orientation can hardly be expected to be completely uniform among human beings. Some people may not have it at all, interacting with art because of various nonesthetic interests, or avoiding art altogether. But if we consider only people who do have an appreciative or esthetic interest in art, humanistic psychology would lead us to expect their evaluations of art to be greatly influenced by their actual experience of art. Since their experience will in some important respects be a product of universal human characteristics, there is reason to expect some degree of resemblance among the evaluations that result.

Humanistic psychology would, on the other hand, like a modern view of the history of taste, reject the old tradition of absolute and uniform value inhering in a work of art. Humanistic psychology leads us to expect that a competent person observing art will arrive at an evaluation based in considerable part on his own experience of it. Since one observer differs from another and art is observed in varying situations, a single work of art will give rise to varying experiences, and this alone is sufficient to guarantee variations in its evaluation. The assumption that each work of art possesses one true absolute value is just as alien to a humanistic psychology as is the assumption that the characteristics of the work of art have no relevance to value.

Whatever the origin of this expectation that esthetic evaluations will be neither absolute nor completely relative, can the research tradition make any contribution? Can it test the expectation against fact? In doing so, can it lead toward improved general understanding of what the arts mean to their appreciative audience?

A suitable starting point for studying esthetic orientation toward art is to take as an initial standard the responses of people who devote themselves to creating or appreciatively studying some particular art. This is where we might most dependably expect to find an esthetic orientation. To extend the study to other people as well, it is necessary to find or to construct suitable materials and methods for observing their responses to the art in some standard way that will facilitate comparison with the esthetic responses of artists or art experts. I decided to start with visual art, and to construct pairs of pictures to be shown side by side as projected slides. The pairs were constructed by a number of advanced students or former students of art or art history, who among them had a very broad and diverse knowledge of visual art and who each felt able to make confident judgments about quality in art. Each pair consisted of two works of art generally similar to each other in type or subject, and in style, but differing greatly from each other in esthetic value—in goodness as works of art—according to the opinion of the person who paired the two works for me. The pairs were extremely diverse. Some, for instance, paired two Persian miniature paintings of a ruler and his court; some paired two abstract paintings. Some paired two Renaissance paintings of the Annunciation, others two Chinese vases; some, two ancient Greek sculptures, and so on. In each instance the person assembling the pair felt that one work was decidedly superior to the other.

All this material would have been of no use for my project, of course, if these feelings had been just the individual response of the person assembling the pair. To check on this possibility, and to identify pairs especially useful for the research, I had each pair judged independently by 14 people chosen in the same way as those who had constructed the pairs. A first rule about esthetic judgment, not needing demonstration by psychological research, since it can be established by reading art criticism in any of the arts, is that esthetic evaluations are typically not unanimous. Something in the spirit of responding to art seems always to leave open, even in the most competent—perhaps especially in the most competent—the possibility of finding great value in experiencing a work that others dismiss as poor or trivial. Some of my expert judges considered the uniqueness of each person's response so central to esthetic value that they doubted I would find any agreement.

In fact, unanimity among the 14 judges was certainly not typical; it occurred for only about 10 percent of the pairs. In these instances of unanimity, however, the direction of judgment—which of the two works was considered superior—agreed with the original selector 100 times as often as it disagreed. For the vast majority of the pairs, more than half of the 14 judges made judgments which agreed with that of the original selector. To use only materials likely to be truly relevant to esthetic judgment, I eliminated from further use all of the pairs on which fewer than 12 of the 14 judges agreed with the original selector.

A very desirable further test of these materials would be to have them judged by art experts in a number of quite different cultural settings. This would be a major undertaking, and it has not been done on a large enough scale, nor early enough in the research program, to use the results in a further selection of pairs—that is, in identifying a set of pairs on which art experts in a number of cultures agree about which work is better. Several researchers, however, have by now used some of these pairs in other cultural settings, and tentative conclusions can be drawn about similarity of esthetic judgments by people experienced in differing art traditions.

It is perfectly clear that cultural variation is very great, and I think that will surprise no one today. It is also clear that there is some tendency toward systematic agreement among experts or art students schooled in somewhat different traditions. Artists and art teachers in Greece, potters in remote Japanese villages, art students in Pakistan, for instance, all show some definite tendency to agree with the original selectors of these pairs; the agreement varies widely in degree, but in each group is statistically significant. This agreement cannot be any simple result of exposure to art through international communication. It is quite certain, for instance, that the particular Japanese potters had seen far less of Western European art than have American high school students, yet their agreement with the United States judges was far greater than that of the American high school students. To the extent that these transcultural comparisons have been carried, then, they confirm the expectation to which I feel a modern humanistic viewpoint would lead—that independent discovery of the same values in art, in relation to universalities of human nature, would produce some transcultural agreement in esthetic judgment, but that variations in discovery, and genuine variation in what is esthetically valuable (resulting from culturally and individually determined variations in human nature) would limit the degree of agreement.

A second way I used these pairs was to study the personal significance of sensitivity, or lack of sensitivity, to esthetic values. Showing a set of pairs to a group of unselected students in school or college, I could ask each person to indicate his preference within each pair, and I could subsequently count up the number of pairs in which his preference was for the work found esthetically better by experts. This count could then be used as an index—an imperfect, but still a useful index—of a person's sensitivity to esthetic values in visual art. People who tend to prefer consistently, through a great variety of pairs, the art that experts consider better might be presumed to have a high degree of esthetic sensitivity—that is, to be attuned to or interested in the same aspects responsible for the experts' distinctions of esthetic merit. Those whose preferences decidedly do not agree with expert judgment might be said to be relatively insensitive to esthetic values. The scores would certainly reflect other variables as well—sheer amount of familiarity with art, for example—but I thought it worth the risk to assume that sensitivity to esthetic values would be a useful and possibly major component of what was being measured. To what other personal characteristics would this measure of esthetic sensitivity be found to be related? Predictions about this relation could be derived from the humanistic ideas about esthetic value with which I had started, and these predictions could be tested against observed fact.

In working out these predictions and in testing some of them, the Berkeley research on creativity was very useful. Especially pertinent was a measure of independence of judgment that Frank Barron had developed in connection with Solomon Asch's experiments on social conformity. Each of Asch's college student subjects judged the relative length of certain lines after hearing several other apparent subjects (actually confederates of the experimenter) give judgments that contradicted the evidence of his own perception. Many subjects responded to this social pressure by giving a false judgment that could only have come from deferring to the stated judgment of others. Some subjects, however, trusted their own experience and gave the correct judgment. Barron constructed a questionnaire that could discriminate reasonably well between subjects who in this experiment yielded to social pressure and subjects who held to their own independent judgment. A high score on this questionnaire suggests a tendency to make up one's own mind and to trust the judgment reached. A low score suggests distrust of one's own judgment, susceptibility to influence by the judgments of others, and perhaps even a tendency to seek an external authority from whom one can take over judgments already formulated.

This questionnaire seemed directly pertinent to my inquiry. Why do some people agree with the judgments of art experts? A major reason, I thought, is that they have looked at the art carefully, with an esthetic interest, and have found in it the same qualities, good or bad in relation to esthetic interest, as the experts find. This reasoning led me to expect esthetic sensitivity especially in people scoring high on Barron's measure of independence of judgment; it is they who should be most likely to look at art independently and to form a judgment on their own. To be sure, their independence of judgment would not necessarily lead in that direction; there is nothing about independence of judgment that seems to guarantee a person's taking an esthetic orientation toward art, or even looking at art at all. But among those who do look at art, being high in independence of judgment should increase the probability of arriving at judgments resembling those made by experts.

A view more common among psychologists—perhaps among the general public, too, and even in the art world in recent years—would lead to a directly opposite prediction. This view holds that esthetic standards are nothing but arbitrary social conventions, with no basis whatever in the nature of human beings or in the adequacy of a piece of art to satisfy any general human interests. The measure I have called esthetic sensitivity is on this view, of course, not appropriately labeled esthetic sensitivity. It is simply a measure of the extent to which a person responds to art in the way he knows to be conventional among people knowledgeable in art. Among college students, in an intellectual atmosphere where the arts are generally valued, one would expect on this basis that agreement with experts should be found closest in those people who most defer to expert judgment, are most conformist, are most inclined to try to find out what the qualified people in a field believe and then to adjust their own beliefs into agreement. The correlation to be expected on these grounds between the measures of esthetic sensitivity and of independence of judgment is exactly opposite to what I was predicting.

The correlation between these two variables has been the most consistent finding of various pertinent studies. In nearly every group tested thus far, the outcome has been strongly in favor of the prediction to which a humanistic approach had led me. That is, persons high in esthetic sensitivity are found to average high in independence of judgment; persons low in esthetic sensitivity differ from them in the low, or conformist, direction of the independence-of-judgment scale. This relationship, originally found in several groups of American college students, was confirmed in American secondary school students, and in several student groups in Japan, Greece, and Pakistan. My inference is that a person's art preferences are, indeed, greatly influenced by his own genuine interaction with the art, and that persons strongly independent in their mode of judgment are especially likely to find in art the same sources of esthetic satisfaction or discontent that experts are likely to find.

Esthetic sensitivity was also found related to a number of other measures of personality characteristics. Persons high in esthetic sensitivity tend, in their answers to questionnaires, to show high tolerance, even a positive liking, for complexity, for novelty, and for unrealistic experience. Some of these characteristics are touched on in the broad set of items Barron included in his *independence of judgment* measure. When separately measured, however, they were each found relevant to esthetic sensitivity.

Even a semi-behavioral measure was applied. In two studies, each subject was asked to put on a special pair of lenses (aniseikonic lenses). These lenses alter the pattern of the visual field in such a way that everything might appropriately be seen as quite distorted in shape. Some people see a distorted world when they first look through the glasses, and continue to see it distorted as they keep the glasses on for several minutes. For some, the surroundings at first keep their normal appearance, but after a minute or two distortions begin to appear. For others, finally, perception remains entirely normal and stable all during the experience. This variation had been utilized by Riley Gardner and his colleagues as a measure of a person's tolerance (or even liking) for unrealistic experience. The lenses were used in the research on esthetic sensitivity to see whether this measure would be related to esthetic sensitivity in the same way as was the questionnaire measure of tolerance for unrealistic experience. And indeed it was. Persons high in esthetic sensitivity tend, with the lenses on, to have a distorted view of their surroundings, and to find it interesting or amusing; those low in esthetic sensitivity are more likely to report that everything continues to look entirely normal. The same opportunity for unusual and unrealistic experience is open here to all who take part in the experiment; esthetic sensitivity is related to the probability of being flexible and exploratory enough about visual experience to take advantage of the opportunity. Strange visual experience, and the complex and the novel in form, color, and texture seem to be the visual parallels of Wallace Stevens' "flawed words and stubborn sounds." This aspect of the research tends to confirm the generality and wisdom of Stevens' insight into the nature of esthetic sensitivity.

Where this research measures variables also measured in the Berkeley studies of creativity, the findings are generally parallel. That is, individual differences in esthetic sensitivity are related to some of the same personality characteristics as are individual differences in creativity. This outcome can hardly come as a surprise to readers of the Berkeley studies, for esthetic sensitivity was one of the variables measured there and found related to creativity. But the new evidence has value of its own; the measure of esthetic sensitivity used in the Berkeley studies was not, I believe, as satisfactory as the one I prepared and used, and I was able to relate esthetic sensitivity to pertinent variables not considered in the Berkeley studies.

The agreement between these two sets of research, the one focused on creativity and the other on response to art, indicates that the appreciation of art is itself an active process that has much in common with artistic creation. Both are the outcome of an active mind exploring its world and seeking to realize the potentialities afforded for personal growth or satisfaction. Research both on creativity and on appreciation of art joins with humanistic psychology as a whole, I believe, in sustaining Wallace Stevens' view that for those with esthetic interests, "The imperfect is our paradise." Only the imperfect offers the challenge an active mind demands; and the imperfect especially invites, perhaps, the juxtaposition of opposites.

Humanistic psychology, however, readily recognizes the great variety of ways in which different individuals develop and express themselves. Art is only one, though a very important, channel. If we bear that point in mind, the recent research on creativity and on response to art, when compared with the early beginnings of psychological study of art, may be considered to have an important implication for psychology generally: We learn more about man by assuming him to be an active agent than by assuming him to be a passive victim of external forces.

My heart leaps up when I behold
A rainbow in the sky:
So was it when my life began;
So is it now I am a man;
So be it when I shall grow old,
Or let me die!

—WILLIAM WORDSWORTH

6

Hypnosis

Hypnosis may seem a topic unlikely to attract humanistic psychologists. The popular conception of hypnosis suggests rather that they would be repelled. In hypnosis, a person seems to lose whatever control he has over himself. He may renounce it willingly, offering to be hypnotized for his own or others' purposes. Or, in fiction, at least, he may lose control without wish or knowledge—as in du Maurier's novel Trilby becomes the foremost singer of Europe while never aware of singing, her lessons and performances being confined to long hypnotic trances induced by her master, Svengali. From distant recollections of my own childhood introduction to hypnosis through the silent-screen version of *Trilby*, I think a public nurtured on such exaggerations must take for granted that hypnosis has a victim, and that his behavior while hypnotized is dictated by someone else's wishes and not his own.

If humanistic psychologists find hypnosis interesting, then, perhaps it is because they sense a challenge. Is this one situation where a person becomes a mechanism entirely controlled from outside? Or is there more inner control here than appears on the surface? One of the first to confront this challenge was Robert White. More than 30 years ago, considering hypnosis in the light of the humanistic view that a person's actions are always to some extent controlled from within, he speculated about what motives might lead a person to abandon internal control so completely as appears in hypnosis. Later humanistic research has amply sustained White's confidence that this was a fruitful question to ask, and I will describe later some of the knowledge that has resulted.

Hypnosis has been a challenge to behaviorists, too, for different reasons. The appearance of external control is no challenge to them, of course; it is consistent with a characteristic bias of behaviorism. The challenge arises in some of the beliefs associated with hypnosis. Popular tradition, and the beliefs of some hypnotists in earlier centuries, connect hypnosis with a notion of spirit or soul distinct from the body, and with a flow of spiritual energy directly from person to person. To embrace hypnotism within scientific psychology would, then, mean one more victory in the struggle to extend a scientific approach to topics formerly thought inaccessible to it.

This is a type of challenge any psychologist might eagerly take up. The psychological research tradition had tended, however, with its behavioral bias, to narrow the definition of a scientific approach in ways which seriously hamper its application to many phenomena of hypnosis. Only slowly has this narrowness given way to the inexorable pressure of scientific advance. Hypnosis provides a good illustration of the limitations of the conservative research tradition in psychology, the advantages of adding an explicitly humanistic point of view, and the inevitable modifications introduced into the conservative tradition when an effort is made to continue applying it in the face of difficulties.

Behavioristic Approach

A major series of investigations of hypnosis were carried out by Clark Hull, the most influential figure in behaviorism between its founder, John B. Watson, and its present leader, B. F. Skinner. These studies were undertaken around 1930, in the years immediately preceding the development of his behavioristic theory of learning. Hull's work on learning was brilliantly original, and became a major influence for many years on studies of learning and of many other phenomena of human life. It even influenced many psychologists who, like me, were more attracted by psychoanalysis or other theories with humanistic qualities. As a graduate student in his seminar, I admired what I saw of his mind at work, and I greatly appreciated many of his ideas even though I was unable to agree with his fundamental approach. Hull's learning theory, which he was developing at that time, was later a valuable guide to me, along with psychoanalysis, in research on children's free choices between two goals, and in seeking to understand the relation between child-training patterns and magical beliefs in primitive societies. From Hull's learning theory many psychologists drew rich and diverse implications. In comparison, Hull's work on hypnosis seems far less innovative and influential. The difference cannot, I think, be ascribed to any change in the man. During the pursuit of his hypnotic investigations,

Hull was already a mature and highly competent scientist, and indeed the preparation of the book culminating his hypnotic research overlapped by several years the start of his work on learning. Since the two undertakings were the work of the same person at very nearly the same time, the contrast in their outcomes seems likely to depend on the relative pertinence to the two topics of a single approach that he made to both.

Central to Hull's approach was rejection of conscious experience as a part of the subject matter of psychology. This may have been a handicap even in his study of learning, but there it did not prevent his making an outstanding creative contribution. In the study of hypnosis, unwillingness to deal with experience seems to be a handicap that not even Hull's brilliant inventiveness could overcome.

Among the major phenomena of hypnosis are *anesthesia* and *hallucination* induced by the suggestions of the hypnotist. These terms refer to experience. A person's skin is pricked and he feels no pain, or a light is flashed and he does not fully or confidently perceive it; these are instances of *anesthesia,* and the word would be inappropriate if the person were only pretending to feel no pain or see no light. A person is told that he smells a musky perfume which, in fact, is not present, and he smells it, or he sees a flash of light only because he is told he will and not because a flash occurs; these experiences are *hallucinations,* and again the word would be inappropriate if the person were misrepresenting his experience rather than reporting it truthfully. It is very difficult to know when anesthesias or hallucinations genuinely and fully occur under hypnosis, yet their occurrence does not seem to be doubted by anyone who seriously considers experience as well as behavior. Hull's writings give me the impression he did not doubt their reality. Yet he could not fully admit them to his research; he could consider only behavior admissible as an object of scientific inquiry. He used the words *anesthesia* and *hallucination,* and often supplemented them with simpler words from the vocabulary of conscious experience. Yet he was uncomfortable in doing so, and tried to give these words a completely behavioral meaning. The effort was not wholly successful; describing hypnotically induced hallucination, for example, he says that "through suggestion the subject behaves as if sensing stimuli which do not exist."

Hull would not acknowledge the possibility of determining whether a subject has actually hallucinated by asking him to describe his experience; he explains that "the introspective approach here, as usual, is out of the question because suggestion is just as operative on the introspective (speech) reactions as on any other." But if he fully accepted this reason, why did he not take advantage of it by suggesting to his subjects that they would faithfully describe their experience? Hull was not able to be consistent here, because of the atomistic or segmented quality of his scientific model; he did not see that an integrated person, as in the humanistic model of man, was implicitly assumed in his reasoning. Let me explain. The only suggestion Hull makes to his subject is that he is having a certain experience. He is sure this suggestion will affect the subject's speech, and so he prevents or disregards any statements by the subject. Yet the simple mechanical model Hull thought he was using does not provide any connection between the experimenter's suggestion and the subject's utterances. The connection between the two arises only from the implied assumption, so commonsensical it goes unnoticed, that the subject is an active living person formulating sentences under the influence either of his own experience or of what he understands to be the wishes of the hypnotist. But Hull did not recognize that the person is an implied part of his discussion, and thus missed the possibility of suggesting to the person that he devote his speech entirely to accurate description of his experience. I do not mean to argue that such a procedure would immediately solve all the problems of getting at hypnotic experience—only that Hull's dismissal of the problem as insoluble, because lacking a simple and absolute solution, is in no way faithful to the realities of human life, and that when difficult tasks are confronted with appropriate tools the probability of a useful though imperfect solution is greatly increased.

Unable to see any possibility of getting trustworthy accounts of experience, the only criterion of genuineness Hull could set for "experiential" aspects of hypnosis was a physiological criterion. A suggestion to feel pain, for instance, can be believed to produce pain if it results in physiological responses ordinarily evoked by pain and not normally capable of voluntary control. (Even in trying to be completely objective via the physiological route, Hull speaks of voluntary control, though he cannot speak of the will.) I am led to wonder what his subjects thought if they realized that, in pursuing his interest in the genuineness of their hallucinations, Hull trusted the very imprecise apparatus available for measuring one or two physiological indexes, but would not trust his subjects enough to ask them to describe their experience.

Hull's mistrust of the obvious sources of evidence for alterations of consciousness, and his unwillingness to speak of conscious experience, did not prevent him from recognizing some facts that would ordinarily be expressed in those terms. He concludes, for example, that "we find reason to believe that hypnotic anaesthesia is a genuine phenomenon in the sense that painful stimuli will often be endured without the usual outward signs of suffering." In this admission, though, he does not fully face the facts of hypnosis; he places together as a single category the instance where the subject has no conscious experience of pain and the instance where the subject is conscious of pain but restrains successfully the usual outward signs of suffering. Vastly different experiences these are for the subject, and in the long run they may have very different behavioral consequences.

Not only in method was Hull restricted by the preconceptions he brought to the study of hypnosis. He was also hindered by limitation in the ideas that he could allow himself to use. This is shown in his comments on the notion of dissociation. In discussions of hypnosis, *dissociation* refers to the apparent fact that various mental activities go on simultaneously without being brought into the same conscious context. It is often used as a descriptive term difficult to dispense with in an account of what happens. Yet because the term is associated with the concept of consciousness or mind, Hull was troubled by the threat of "survivals of outworn metaphysics" and tried to avoid all reference to dissociation.

In his positive effort to account for hypnosis, Hull was eager to show the relevance of concepts that he was sure could be stated in a completely objective manner. The one he hit on is habit or conditioning. When reference to the subject's conscious experience has been dispensed with, hypnotic hallucination can be seen to have much in common with the conditioned response. Hull explicitly drew the parallel to Pavlov's dogs. Pavlov presented a buzzer or other stimulus just before placing food in a dog's mouth. If, after doing this a number of times, he sounded the buzzer without placing food in the dog's mouth, the dog would salivate just as though the food were there. In experiments on hypnosis or ordinary suggestion, Hull says, "the words of the experimenter presumably are merely performing the function served by the arbitrary sounds, temperatures, et cetera, in the conditioned reflex experiments." The parallel is certainly there. But does it help us much in understanding hypnosis? If we scan the publications on hypnosis in the nearly 40 years since Hull wrote, the implied judgment of most who have written on hypnosis seems clearly to be negative. The analogy Hull noted has greater promise, I think, if applied in the reverse direction; an understanding of hypnosis might have greatly facilitated a proper understanding of what goes on in some conditioning experiments. It took a long time for students of human "verbal conditioning" to suggest that their subjects may at times be seeking to please or displease the experimenter, rather than having response tendencies automatically strengthened or weakened by rewards and punishments. The analogy to hypnosis might well have led to this possibility's being put forward much earlier.

Humanistic Approach

What can a humanistic approach contribute to an understanding of hypnosis? An especially good example, in answer to this question, is provided by another series of explorations of hypnosis done during the last 10 or 12 years by Ernest and Josephine Hilgard. I think their work carries us very much further toward a good understanding of hypnosis than did Hull's, and that the reason lies in their having created an effective fusion of the psychological research tradition with the humanistic model necessary for adequate study of hypnotic phenomena. The Hilgards assume that they are studying a person's experience as well as his behavior. I think they even assume that experience should be especially an object for attention, since it has been so often neglected in earlier studies of hypnosis.

And the method by which they seek to learn of the person's experience? Basically it is by asking him, and by accepting the general view that a person's descriptions of his experience, provided in the context of scientific study, will on the whole be useful indexes of his actual experience. They evidently place some basic reliance on their own experience as hypnotic subjects, for they mention this as one source of confidence without elaborating on it. They also make use of physiological indexes as supplementary evidence, sometimes strengthening or weakening the confidence to be placed in the subject's own description of his experience.

Are their findings, then, because they depend on a method that extreme behaviorists would reject, a flimsy structure of deception? I myself find it hard to imagine how any careful reader of Josephine Hilgard's book reporting this side of the research could arrive at such a conclusion. The fact that the Hilgards infer from a person's description of his experience to his actual experience makes them no credulous believers of statements suggested to the subjects by the experimenters. On the contrary, they carry to this as well as to other aspects of their procedures the whole of their scientific training, with the result that they have a much better understanding of the possible sources of error, and are much better prepared to take account of them, than a behavioristic approach alone would have permitted.

For Hull, the problem was quite simple: the speech behavior of the hypnotic subject, like his other behavior, was subject to suggestion from the experimenter. Speech, to him, was a mechanical response to external stimulation. This is a very incomplete account, and yet for Hull it seemed to justify or require neglecting what a subject might say. The Hilgards' use of what their subjects say is based on a humanistic model of man. The subject is seen as a person. What he says is some kind of creative outcome, produced by him under the influence of a variety of circumstances; it is no simple mechanical effect of some one cause. One difficulty, to be sure, is that the subject may be reporting falsely what he thinks the experimenter wants him to report. If the subject is being treated as a human being—often, in truth, he is a human being just as much devoted to the canons of science as are the experimenters—it may be possible to conduct an interview in such a way that the subject will admit when he has made a false report. The Hilgards aim to conduct such interviews; drawing on clinical tradition, they use interviewing systematically and at length. Through serious attention to what their subjects say, the Hilgards find it perfectly feasible to make the subject's experience a part of their subject matter. The difficulties to be faced are less absolute and more varied than Hull supposed. Not only the hypnotist's suggestions but the subject's desires and total situation need to be considered. Some subjects, for instance, bring to their first session a preestablished interest in experiencing the full effects of deep hypnosis, and report in their first session deeper effects than they really experience, hoping that exaggerated representation of present reality will favor future actualization.

Alterations of experience in hypnosis are found to be more variable than might be imagined in advance. Suppose that the hypnotized subject is shown, as in the Hilgard studies, a piece of wood with an electric light bulb mounted at one end and turned on, and is told that he sees a light at each end. Can subjects be divided into those who see the clear reality of a light only at one end, and those who see identical lights at the two ends? No, there are, instead, a great variety of experiences reported. The two lights are often seen differently. The hallucinated light, for example, may have no contact with the wood, or it may be less substantial looking. Or the subject may note that when he closes his eyelids one light produces a glow through them and the other does not. In any event, the subject often reports an experience not precisely like that of experiencing a real light at either end of the board. Even while having a realistic hallucination, he knows that there is something unreal about the experience. He is experiencing in two different ways at once. This fact might be difficult to demonstrate other than through the subject's description of his experience, yet it seems very characteristic of the hypnotized state. Here is one reason that Hull could regard the concept of dissociation as misleading, as a pseudo-difficulty, whereas the Hilgards consider it a fundamentally apt description of what is experienced in hypnosis.

Personality and Hypnosis

The Hilgard study is not just an exploration of what occurs in hypnosis. It is also a study of how variations among persons in what happens in hypnosis are related to preexisting differences among them. The main purpose of the study is not, of course, to facilitate predictions of who will be a good hypnotic subject and who will not. Hypnosis is not likely to be of such great practical concern as to justify lengthy research into methods of prediction, whose practical application would be principally in selecting subjects for future research. The Hilgards' purpose in exploring individual differences in hypnosis is to increase the understanding of hypnosis through learning why some people become deeply hypnotized and others do not.

In their study of individual differences a first requirement, of course, was a satisfactory way of measuring or classifying differences among individuals in their experience and action as subjects of hypnosis. The Hilgards worked out a standard procedure for inducing hypnosis and then a standard procedure for testing the depth of hypnosis. The measurement is based on a series of 12 items arranged in order of increasing difficulty—that is, increasing depth of hypnosis. The easiest item is a person's lowering his outstretched hand when the hypnotist suggests that it is being lowered; if the subject lowers his hand at least 6 inches in 10 seconds, he is judged to have passed the item. The twelfth and most difficult item deals with posthypnotic amnesia; in a standardized procedure for getting the awakened subject to remember what has occurred during hypnosis, he is scored as passing this item if he can recall no more than three facts about the hypnotic experience before being told that he can now remember everything. The measure of how susceptible a subject is to hypnosis comes from counting the number of these 12 items that he passes. It is a good measure by the usual criteria that are applied to methods of psychological measurement.

A further requirement, of course, for the Hilgards' intended research was the development of methods for assessing the differences in personality and background that might be related to this measure of hypnotic susceptibility. They used two general methods: the somewhat objectified and standardized procedure of personality tests and questionnaires, and the interview procedure patterned on psychiatric interviewing. The two methods complemented each other. The interview procedure is the more clearly humanistic; therefore, I would like to stress the results obtained with it, and then come back to the questionnaire findings. The topics explored in the interview were partly determined by the assumption that conscious experience is a central part of the subject matter; even more, the way in which those topics were pursued was determined by that assumption.

The major finding from the interviews provides the basis for the subtitle of Josephine Hilgard's book *Personality and hypnosis: A study of imaginative involvement.* The finding is that people more susceptible to hypnosis have a history of greater imaginative involvement of various kinds. Involvement in seven different areas were found to be related to hypnosis. In each area the interviewers probed to try to identify just what aspect of the involvement was relevant, and then to formulate theoretically why this should be related to hypnosis. Involvement in no one of these areas is especially critical for hypnotizability. By adding together ratings of a person's imaginative involvement in all seven areas, a much better prediction of his hypnotizability is obtained than by attending to any one area alone. About an equally good prediction is obtained, however, by considering for each person only the area in which he has the greatest involvement, shifting from one area for one person to another area for the next. Perhaps what is important for hypnosis is whether a person has had some experience of deep involvement in something outside himself, rather than how general a propensity he has for deep involvement.

One of the seven areas where involvement was found related to hypnosis is reading. This, like the other areas to be considered, was inquired into through the interviews with each subject that preceded the hypnotic phase of his participation in the research. Not related to hypnosis are the amount of reading, either in childhood or in college, nor various preferences among types of reading that were inquired into, nor absorption in the sense of concentration. What was related to hypnosis was degree of emotional involvement. The emotional involvement might be expressed only in what Josephine Hilgard calls "empathic identification"—thorough participation in the emotional meaning of the story even while not identifying with a character. Exploring her subjects' accounts of their emotional involvement in reading and of their experience in hypnosis, and of the parallels many subjects explicitly drew between these two, Josephine Hilgard arrives at six characteristics shared by the two experiences: active receptivity rather than mere passivity, intense cherishing of the experience of the moment, vivid imagery, suspension of reality-testing processes, the fact that all these are arrived at under the influence of words, and the fact that this experience is confined to a definite time clearly distinguished from normal life routines. She sees possible significance, too, in the fact that people displaying deep emotional involvement in reading usually do so beginning in childhood or adolescence, and that the experience is often related to the great enjoyment of reading manifested by at least one parent with whom the child has a warm relationship.

A second area of involvement is the dramatic arts. For those whose involvement is as a member of the audience, it seems clear that the parallels to hypnosis are similar to those already stated for reading. But the same is true for those whose involvement is as amateur actors. Of the six similarities noted for reading and hypnosis, all of them—with the possible exception only of the element of imagery—clearly apply to deep emotional involvement in acting. Especially conspicuous in the case of acting is the fact that one is not merely passive but is taking an active creative part.

A third area of involvement is religion. Deep emotional involvement in religion was scarce enough among the Hilgards' subjects so that the results are not as certain or as full as for other areas. Especially conspicuous in deep religious involvement is a suspension of the usual processes of reality testing. Hypnotizability appeared to average highest in those whose religion derived from being brought up in a family with firm and deeply felt religion. This point not only strengthens the suggestion that beginnings in childhood or adolescence are important, but also argues, according to Josephine Hilgard, that emotional involvement free of conflict is especially important for hypnotizability. The adult religious convert may be deeply involved emotionally in his religion and yet not be able to free himself entirely from conflict that is based on his earlier attitudes; perhaps it is for this reason that the few subjects who were religious converts showed no special tendency to be susceptible to hypnosis.

Another area of emotional involvement is response to nature. Each person was rated on the extent to which he indicated a history of real involvement in appreciation of nature, as distinguished from intellectual interest in nature. Here some of the elements of similarity between hypnosis and other areas are not pertinent; the person enjoying nature is not responding primarily to words, and is not necessarily enjoying imagery. What is especially conspicuous is intense devotion to the experience of the moment, and devotion in a way that seems active rather than merely passive. From the details of the interviews, Dr. Hilgard also extracts some other points of value in understanding hypnosis. The basis on which a person could be rated as having deep emotional involvement in nature required not only that he have had a highly involving experience originally, but that he be able to recreate some of these experiences for himself in his present description of that experience. This recreation of experience has a certain similarity to the hallucinations of hypnosis. Also, the savoring of recreated experience implies the ability to disregard in its favor the demands of present stimulation, and here is a point of similarity to the anesthesias of hypnotic subjects.

Another area of involvement is adventure, either physical or mental. Some of the hypnotic subjects had been emotionally involved in such physical adventures as mountain climbing, skin diving, skiing, flying, or exploring caves. Others were equally involved emotionally in mental adventures —some through the reading of science fiction, others through meditation or, though rarely at the time the research was done, the use of psychedelic drugs. Not all of those who were adventurous in either of these ways were highly hypnotizable. Among physical adventurers those oriented primarily toward competition, and among mental adventurers those oriented primarily toward intellectual understanding, were not especially likely to be highly hypnotizable. The hypnotizable adventurers tended to show in their experience of adventure some characteristics already noted in other areas of emotional involvement—a special devotion to the feelings of the moment and an active involvement in escaping from the world of reality for a limited time. They also showed, Dr. Hilgard reports, a tendency toward childlike enjoyment of excitement or power in their adventuresome experience.

Two other areas of emotional involvement were less systematically probed in the interviews, yet they also emerged with significant relations to hypnotizability. One is a history of childhood imagination—specifically, a report of imaginative response in childhood to external circumstances; a report of childhood daydreaming, presumably aroused more by internal impulses than by specific stimulation from outside, was not related to hypnotic susceptibility. The other positive result pertains to an involvement in creative activities. The question asked in the interview was simply: Have you had a serious interest in creative activity such as painting, writing, designing and the like? Those reporting such interests were on the average more hypnotizable.

One kind of intense involvement studied and found not favorable to hypnotizability was an involvement in athletics. Above all, subjects greatly involved in competitive team athletics were not likely to be very hypnotizable. In seeking to understand why this kind of involvement was, if anything, detrimental to the possibilities of being deeply hypnotized, Dr. Hilgard locates the difference in three particular features: the athlete is skilled in highly realistic attention to environmental stimuli, and thus is trained against suspension of ordinary reality testing; he needs to appraise accurately conditions inside his own body in order to interact highly successfully with the environment; he places extreme stress on activity, to a degree perhaps preventing the partial passivity hypnosis demands. Hypnotizability is on the average higher among athletes participating in individual rather than team skills. Yet the differences among individual-skill athletes are very revealing. The most hypnotizable among them tend, in describing their athletic involvement, to emphasize enjoying the activity itself more than achieving victory over others. They usually describe their involvement in athletics, moreover, as deriving not only from enjoyment of the activity but also from some additional component of a more passive or contemplative character.

Another kind of involvement is identified as somewhat unfavorable to hypnotic susceptibility: deep commitment to science. Students majoring in the sciences or engineering were on the average less hypnotizable than those majoring in the social sciences or humanities. There were, of course, variations among the science students, and a study of these variations suggested that a carry-over of the high degree of reality orientation characterizing scientific work can interfere with hypnotizability. The science-oriented student able to be hypnotized is one who can set aside his reality orientation for a specified time and reason.

While the Hilgards were interviewing their subjects, they were, as I have indicated earlier, having the same subjects respond to questionnaires. The questionnaires were not planned as a result of what was learned from interviews. Rather they were for the most part constructed or selected on the basis of some initial ideas that guided the planning of the interviews. Thus they do not provide the opportunity to check every aspect of what emerged from the interviews. Yet comparisons are valuable.

The questionnaire results were not as striking as those obtained from the interviews. The central reason, perhaps, is that the interviews provided a wealth of material supplied by the subjects themselves, part of it in response to the invitation to talk about their hypnotic experience and about how they could relate it to other aspects of their life. Hence the picture emerging from the interviews did not have to depend on the investigator's advance formulation of questions.

Especially striking from the questionnaire study were two types of results. One is that hypnotic susceptibility is correlated with similar experiences in everyday life. This finding resembles some of the interview results about relation to emotional involvement. But the experiences asked about in questionnaires are more diverse, not restricted to emotional involvement, and they include more items that have a close and obvious parallel to hypnotic experience. One question, for example, was: Have you ever experienced a part of your body move and have the feeling that it was moving without your volition? Another question was: Have you ever had the experience of telling a story with elaborations to make it sound better and then having the elaborations seem as real to you as the actual incidents? The second finding of special interest is a negative relation between hypnotic susceptibility and reported interest in physical activity, particularly in competitive athletics. This is consistent with the interview finding that deep involvement in athletics is negatively related to hypnotic susceptibility.

Putting these together with all the other results obtained with personality questionnaires, Ernest Hilgard summarized the outcome in this way:

> ". . . a kind of personality description emerges of the hypnotizable person as one who has rich subjective experiences in which he can become deeply involved; one who reaches out for new experiences and is thus friendly to hypnosis; one who is interested in the life of the mind, and not a competitive activist; one who accepts impulses from within and is not afraid to relinquish reality testing for a time."

In the last chapter of his book on hypnotic susceptibility, Ernest Hilgard presents a theory of hypnosis. The theory consists of 17 separate propositions—seven propositions about how hypnotizability is influenced by features in the development of the person through childhood and adolescence, six propositions about the interaction between subject and hypnotist and four propositions about the nature of the hypnotic state. It is directed at understanding the experiences of hypnotic subjects; it recognizes the great diversity of the experiences themselves and of the sources of influence. Throughout, it seems to me, the factors affecting hypnotic experience are seen as influences on a *person,* who is considered as an active agent. All normal people are born, the theory assumes, "with the potential to develop the ability for profound hypnotic experiences." The likelihood that anyone will develop the ability is affected by a variety of childhood experiences such as the Hilgard findings point to. Whether deep hypnosis occurs through a particular attempt to induce it is influenced not only by these developmental factors but by their interaction with the particular induction procedures.

This theory has decidedly a humanistic flavor. To call it humanistic tells us that the theory focuses on the person and his experience, and considers him an active agent. Beyond this general approach, the theory is difficult to characterize briefly; the account I have just given mentions only a few of its major points. The label Hilgard gives it, a *developmental-interactive theory* is not much more informative than to call it a humanistic theory, though it does convey the dual nature of the problems to which the theory is addressed. Perhaps it is fundamental to thoroughly humanistic theories that they should have this character of multiplicity, in conformity to the complexity of man. Hilgard's theory differs here from some earlier theories of hypnosis, which can be easily characterized for the stress they place on one particular element. Much of Hull's theory, for instance, can be summarized in referring to it as a habit theory of hypnosis. Another theory that can be characterized by a name is the *role theory* put forth by Theodore

Sarbin; it generalizes into a theory of hypnosis the fact that the subject is often acting a role—either the role of hypnotized subject as he understands it to be, or a specific role suggested by the hypnotist and the other circumstances of the occasion.

The simpler theories are easier to state and easier to remember. They may each point the way to some important new discoveries. But their simplicity may also lead to error. For example, Hull's emphasis on learning nicely fits the fact that a subject comes to develop the hypnotic state more rapidly in successive sessions with a hypnotist. But it also can lead us to believe that in successive sessions a person will through practice learn to go into ever deeper states of hypnosis. This expectation, as Hilgard summarizes the evidence from several studies done in recent decades, is not confirmed. Or Sarbin's role theory, while it produces new discoveries, may lead one to believe that hypnotized subjects who report unusual experiences never actually have them—a belief belied, I think, by quite adequate and varied evidence. The more complicated humanistic theory cannot offer us simple elegance, but it can more adequately describe and account for the complexities of human behavior and experience.

Movement of Behavioral Research Toward the Humanistic Viewpoint

Another leading researcher on hypnosis in recent years, Theodore X. Barber, shows a mixture of humanistic and anti-humanistic elements. He seems to consider his work completely in the behavioral tradition; but I believe it illustrates how far that tradition has moved, in the 40 years since Hull's work on hypnotism, toward a humanistic orientation.

Barber aims to follow a narrow definition of science that is accepted by many psychologists—a definition restricting it to studying the dependence of certain observed variables (called the consequent variables) on other observed variables (called antecedent). Variables that cannot be directly observed can enter into the scientific enterprise, on this view, only as explanatory links between the observed antecedent and consequent variables. When Barber states this general position, he seems to place variables of the subject's experience entirely in this third category, giving them the status not of fact or probable fact but of explanatory fiction to be used only when absolutely necessary.

Barber seems to start, then, from the same philosophical position as did Hull, one generally associated with the extremes of behaviorism. In one respect he goes even further than Hull in considering the hypnotic subject as controlled by external factors: he practically disregards personality characteristics as an influence. Hull had been interested in demonstrating that variations from one person to another in hypnotizability were related to variations among them in general suggestibility. Perhaps because facts of this kind cannot easily be viewed as a relation between an antecedent and a consequent variable, Barber seems little interested in them. His interest in hypnotizability, or in general susceptibility, is as a consequent variable, to be studied in relation to various antecedent variables that can be manipulated experimentally.

In his very effective pursuit of this interest, Barber does not hold to the behavioristic tradition as consistently as did Hull. Through these last several decades, serious attempts to apply the behavioristic approach to human phenomena have characteristically led to the redefinition of words so that the subject's experience can in effect be made a part of the subject matter, can be shifted in status from explanatory fiction to fact-to-be-explained. Barber's approach to hypnosis differs from that of Hull some 40 years ago in just this way.

A good illustration is provided by the chapter on hypnosis and pain in Barber's book, *LSD, marihuana, yoga, and hypnosis.* It is written very largely from an experiential point of view. It concludes "that some degree of reduction in pain experience can at times be produced by suggestions given under hypnosis," and it distinguishes between this reduction and two other conditions that may be confused with it: "unwillingness to state directly to the hypnotist that pain was experienced and/or an apparent amnesia for the pain that was experienced." Barber has not come fully to the humanistic position that under some circumstances a subject's description of his experience can be taken as exactly that. He differs from the humanistic position in two ways: (1) When variables of experience are evidenced only by a person's description of his experience, Barber denies them the status of probable facts. He grants them factual status only if they are inferred from distinctive physiological responses or from realistic instrumental responses; for example, if surgical patients stop asking for analgesics, Barber seems willing to believe that they are experiencing less pain. He does not seem to carry out this policy with perfect consistency, but he states it as a policy. (2) He is obviously happier about accepting the idea of reduced pain experience when he can believe that the reduction occurs in something he can call a reaction (in anxiety about the pain, for instance, rather than in the actual feelings of pain).

Barber thus modifies his explicit principles enough to consider the phenomena of hypnotism with much greater clarity and much less embarrassment than was possible for Hull. I feel that in studying these phenomena he could gain in clarity, reduce embarrassment and, perhaps, even gain in scientific adequacy and propriety by getting rid of his original principles altogether, in the sense of recognizing the great variety of procedures necessary for the scientific enterprise. His narrow conception of scientific activity limits his research and makes it less valuable in sum, in my opinion, than it would otherwise be. Excessive distrust of people's reports of their experience is one factor, I think, leading him not to concentrate on people who definitely manifest hypnotic phenomena but to study, instead, unselected subjects. It also leads him to selective inquiry into those phenomena that can be most objectively studied, and to study them only by the most objective techniques, regardless of how central or typical the resulting data may seem to be. Such points provide some justification, as a general criticism of the behavioral approach Barber makes, of the reproach Paul Wachtel has expressed in the phrase, "wanting nothing and getting nothing." The researcher who wants to convince himself that certain phenomena do not occur may easily fall into the trap of not looking for them in the right place—in this instance, of failing to look hard enough at the experience of hypnotized subjects.

If Barber relaxes his principles in admitting specific variables of experience, such as pain, he does not relax them in confronting the more global terms *hypnosis* and *hypnotic state.* His positivistic principles are most consistently directed at denying the reality or usefulness of these constructs. His principles lead him here, I feel, to exaggerate somewhat the extent to which *hypnosis* is an explanatory term. I have never thought it to be principally explanatory; it is for the most part just a useful term to refer to a variety of phenomena, behavioral and experiential—a set of phenomena particularly calling for explanation.

From his position that *hypnosis* or *hypnotic state* is an unnecessary term Barber is led to doing research, and to reviewing previous research, showing that many of the phenomena of hypnosis can be duplicated without using the procedures of hypnosis-induction. Many hypnotized subjects, for instance, can on order suspend themselves rigidly between two chairs, supported only by head and heels; but so can an approximately equal proportion of subjects who without being hypnotized are given the same orders. This is just one of many examples of behavior or experience sometimes thought to be distinctive of the "hypnotized state" which, in fact, prove to be continuous or identical with phenomena of normal waking life.

This aspect of Barber's work seems to me especially valuable in working toward an understanding of hypnosis. I am struck, however, by its close parallel to the humanistically oriented work of the Hilgards. Both lines of research proceed from an assumption that a hypnotized subject is first of all a human being, not a strangely distorted creature. Uniting this assumption with his general bias toward analyzing phenomena into very specific variables, Barber is led to find many specific similarities between waking and hypnotized life. The Hilgards are more willing to consider general aspects of experience and behavior, such as an altered sense of reality or a sense of involvement; they, too, are led to study the similarity of these aspects as they characterize waking and hypnotized life, especially stressing the continuity of individual differences between hypnosis and normal life. Barber is very sceptical, and is inclined to reject as improbable anything not known with confidence; the Hilgards are more open or tolerant toward a variety of possibilities. This difference marks another way in which the Hilgards are more representative of the humanistic tradition. Stressing similarity between the hypnotized and nonhypnotized, Barber tries for the most part (as Hull did) to reduce the phenomena of hypnosis to familiar phenomena of daily life. Stress on the same similarity leads the Hilgards to point out in daily life the many remarkable features it shares with hypnosis.

On the presumption that a person when hypnotized and the same person not hypnotized are truly the same person, the humanistic researchers and the behavioral researchers are united. The presumption may fairly be regarded, I think—despite its very different source—as a humanistic element even in the thought of the behavioral researchers, and an important element in making their research valuable. The more open attitude of inquiry that already characterizes the more thoroughly humanistic researchers may also come to be wholeheartedly adopted by the researchers who start in the behavioristic tradition. When it is, the research will, I think, become more penetrating, since the open attitude encourages the study of all aspects of hypnotic behavior and experience, without neglect of those most difficult to study.

Openness to considering experience is especially crucial to the adequate understanding of hypnosis. Much of what goes on in hypnosis is not as distinctive as was once thought, but what is distinctive pertains to experience rather more than to behavior. This is well illustrated in Charles Tart's account of a subject able to experience unusually deep hypnosis. Great changes were found in his sense of time, his feeling of relation to the universe, and other broad aspects of his state of consciousness. There is no suggestion of change of comparable importance in his overt behavior, and the very occurrence of an unusually deep trance might well be missed by anyone who defines his inquiry behaviorally. Small wonder that this contribution to our understanding of hypnosis, and of variations in it, comes from a humanistic psychologist—from one most devoted to unifying the approaches of humanistic thought and the research tradition.

How Can Hypnotizability Be Increased?

Hypnotic subjects, we have noted earlier, cannot be depended on to become more deeply hypnotizable in successive sessions. The theory that serving as hypnotic subject is a role one performs seems to run into difficulty here. With most roles, there seems to be some truth in the old saying, "Practice makes perfect." But if there is not much gain from sheer practice in being hypnotized, are there other ways in which hypnotizability may be increased? Charles Tart has made an important beginning in the study of this question, providing yet another illustration of the fruitfulness of the humanistic approach to understanding hypnosis.

Tart begins by reviewing earlier research in which hypnotizability has been increased through special training. The kinds of training usually tried seem to be focused on the abilities or skills involved in being successfully hypnotized. Training of this sort has been shown repeatedly to produce some change, statistically dependable but not usually large enough to be of any practical consequence.

In only two studies has a really large increase in hypnotizability been found. In one of them, the training was focused sharply on permitting each subject to become "able to experience those hypnotic effects that they had failed" in an initial session. In the other study, training was more varied, but again was directed at encouraging the subject to be able to have experiences new to him. The most effective technique seemed to be the presenting of hypnotic suggestions during extended periods of partial sensory isolation. In both of these studies, then, the training was of a kind especially compatible with the humanistic point of view—accepting the importance of the person's conscious experience and encouraging him to increase its diversity.

From this background Tart went on to new research, in which changes in hypnotizability were assessed in relation to a training program that did not itself have anything to do with hypnosis. The training was nine-month diversified experience in techniques for developing human potentialities—the Esalen Residential Program, conducted at the Esalen Institute. It included a variety of techniques developed by humanistic psychologists for psychotherapy and for achieving altered states of consciousness. Hypnotizability was assessed before and after the training, both by the behavioral scale developed by the Hilgards and by detailed self-ratings of what was experienced during the administration of the Hilgard scale.

The subjects in this study were few, only seven altogether, and the procedures were far from those that would give us great confidence in the results. As an initial piece of evidence about a topic of great interest, though, the results are important. They suggest that for some people, though not all, hypnotizability can be greatly increased by procedures directed only at achieving a generally greater openness and creativity.

What Tart makes of this outcome is directly in line with the developmental aspect of the Hilgards' theory of hypnosis. People are innately equipped, he argues, "to experience a variety of altered states of consciousness," but this ability is inhibited by socialization in a society that accepts only a few states of consciousness as normal. General reduction of this inhibition, by training not at all concerned with hypnosis, through restoring the person to his natural capacity for varied experience, will as one specific consequence increase hypnotizability. Needless to say, it should also be expected to increase creativity. Tart reports that Frank Barron, whose work on creativity in writers I mentioned in an earlier chapter, did extensive testing on this same group of people participating in the Esalen Residential Program, and we may in time hear through him of its effects on creativity.

On the whole then, hypnotic experience is not the imposition from without that has commonly been supposed. Theories associated with recent research suggest that hypnotic experience is part of the repertoire of future experience potentially available to everyone at birth. A person's eventual susceptibility to it has to do with his openness to varied experience and to personal involvement, rather than with helplessness. Wordsworth's feelings about nature make me believe that he would have been a good subject for hypnosis, and would not have needed the help of an Esalen Institute. But he was aware of the inhibiting influences that would have reduced the hypnotizability of many of his contemporaries, as of many of ours.

The world is too much with us; late and soon,
Getting and spending, we lay waste our powers:
Little we see in Nature that is ours;
We have given our hearts away, a sordid boon!
This Sea that bares her bosom to the moon;
The winds that will be howling at all hours,
And are up-gathered now like sleeping flowers;
For this, for anything, we are out of tune;
It moves us not.—Great God! I'd rather be
A Pagan suckled in a creed outworn;
So might I, standing on this pleasant lea,
Have glimpses that would make me less forlorn;
Or hear old Triton blow his wreathed horn.

. . . Now I ask you: what can be expected of man since he is a being endowed with such strange qualities? Shower upon him every earthly blessing, drown him in a sea of happiness, so that nothing but bubbles of bliss can be seen on the surface; give him economic prosperity, such that he should have nothing else to do but sleep, eat cakes and busy himself with the continuation of his species, and even then out of sheer ingratitude, sheer spite, man would play you some nasty trick. He would even risk his cakes and would deliberately desire the most fatal rubbish, the most uneconomical absurdity, simply to introduce into all this positive good sense his fatal fantastic element. It is just his fantastic dreams, his vulgar folly, that he will desire to retain, simply in order to prove to himself—as though that were so necessary—that men still are men and not the keys of a piano, which the laws of nature threaten to control so completely that soon one will be able to desire nothing but by the calendar. And that is not all: even if man really were nothing but a piano-key, even if this were proved to him by natural science and mathematics, even then he would not become reasonable, but would purposely do something perverse out of simple ingratitude, simply to gain his point. And if he does not find means he will contrive destruction and chaos, will contrive sufferings of all sorts, only to gain his point! He will launch a curse upon the world, and as only man can curse (it is his privilege, the primary distinction between him and other animals) it may be by his curse alone he will attain his object—that is, convince himself that he is a man and not a piano-key! If you say that all this, too, can be calculated and tabulated—chaos and darkness and curses, so that the mere possibility of calculating it all beforehand would stop it all, and reason would reassert itself—then man would purposely go mad in order to be rid of reason and gain his point! I believe in it, I answer for it, for the whole work of man really seems to consist in nothing but proving to himself every minute that he is a man and not a piano-key!

—FYODOR DOSTOYEVSKY

7

Attitudes, Opinions, and Motives: Recent Social Psychology

Recent social psychology developed partly out of practical efforts in World War II to manipulate attitudes. Social psychology does have a longer and more varied history. Experiments had been done in the 1920s on how people's task performance is modified by working in groups. Other questions began to be studied at about the same time, and the discipline had progressed to the point where in the 1930s a large textbook and an even larger handbook could be devoted to reviewing it.

This background, and the reputation of the experimental method in psychology, led to the participation of research psychologists in coping with practical problems in the war. What feasible steps could be taken to improve the morale of United States troops, and to reduce the morale of enemy troops? Experiments were done to test the effects on American soldiers of ways of presenting information, and of alternative policies on administrative issues that might affect morale.

In the years after the war, as social psychologists vigorously pursued their study of attitude change, a similar orientation continued. How can external factors be manipulated to shift people's attitudes in a desired direction? How can the manipulator take account of existing differences in personality, attitudes, and beliefs so as to achieve his aim as dependably as possible? The interests of the investigators were those of the abstract scientist, rather than those of the advertiser or political manipulator. But still, the questions they pursued were dictated by a view of the human being as a passive object to be manipulated from outside, with his personal characteristics recognized only in order to achieve more effective manipulation.

A discipline with this history must seem unlikely to provide an important meeting ground for the research tradition and humanistic thought. Yet social psychology has become a major area for such a joining of interests, although the humanistic element in this development was not at first clear and is still not widely recognized.

The humanistic slant in experimental social psychology developed out of work that proceeded from a more subjective point of view than was characteristic of American psychology. The subjectivity probably required a European influence such as the one from which this development came—the influence of Kurt Lewin. Lewin was a German psychologist who in the

1920s had begun applying to human motivation ideas that he had derived from Gestalt psychology—itself a German movement in the study of perception, emphasizing the *organized* character of experience. Lewin moved to the United States in 1933, and eventually had a powerful direct impact on American social psychology by bringing his Gestalt emphasis to invigorate the study of group dynamics. A less direct influence of Lewin came by way of his student and colleague, Leon Festinger. The theory of cognitive dissonance, developed by Festinger out of his Lewinian background, has given rise to some of the most provocative research in social psychology, research instrumental in rehumanizing our understanding of how attitude change occurs.

Cognitive Dissonance

Festinger's approach clearly proceeded (though he called no special attention to the fact) from consideration of the conscious experience of the individual human being. Here is the argument as Festinger developed it. A person experiences at any one time various items of knowledge, opinion, and attitude. He strives for consistency in the total pattern of these experiences. When he finds some of them inconsistent with others, he is said to experience cognitive dissonance. The source may sometimes be simple logical inconsistency, when a person notices that one belief that he holds really implies the contrary of another. Dissonance may in other instances arise from a sense of discrepancy between general and specific attitudes or beliefs which are not logically incompatible (as when a person considers himself a Democrat yet favors the Republican candidate in a particular election); it may depend on reasoning from past experience (for example, if a person pushes a doorbell button and fails to hear the ring that past experience leads him to expect); or it may even result from a person's feeling that his actions are inconsistent with the cultural definition of a role he is assuming (as when "a person at a formal dinner uses his hands to pick up a recalcitrant chicken bone"). Whatever its origin, Festinger assumed, dissonance is uncomfortable, and the person experiencing it tries to reconcile the seemingly inconsistent elements. Among the ways by which he can achieve this reconciliation is to change one of the elements so it is no longer inconsistent with the others. In discussing the choice of elements, and the choice between this and other means of reducing dissonance, Festinger used language very similar to that of behaviorists, although dealing with experience as well as actions; his analytic, even mathematical, mode of thought seemed to lead him in that direction. Despite this manner of speaking, however, he in effect portrayed the person as an active searcher for, or creator of, a solution to the problem confronting him. His theory thus fits my general definition of humanistic psychology in two important ways; it proceeds from including conscious experience in the subject of inquiry, and it treats the person as active agent. Yet neither of these characteristics is explicitly stressed, and they can both be easily overlooked.

Festinger developed his theory of cognitive dissonance while trying to integrate the whole body of knowledge then available about communication and social influence. Cognitive dissonance, he argued, accounts for surprisingly varied aspects of this knowledge and suggests, moreover, future research likely to contribute to our knowledge. Dropping his original plans to attempt a general survey of communication and social influence, he devoted himself to exploring four topics for which cognitive dissonance seemed to be a particularly suggestive idea.

1. *The consequences of making a decision.* A person who has just resolved a conflict (deciding to buy a station wagon rather than a sedan, for example, or to enter law rather than medicine) has committed himself to one possibility and has removed himself from others, whereas he has just previously considered them about equally attractive. Here is a possible source of dissonance, and Festinger is able to show that decisions tend to be followed by just such consequences as might be expected if dissonance is, indeed, characteristic. A decision is often followed by actively seeking information with which to support the wisdom of the decision. Even in the absence of new information, a decision is often followed by increased confidence in its wisdom and by appropriately reordering the relative desirability of the chosen and the rejected alternatives.

2. *Consequences of exposure to information.* Encountering information that is inconsistent with his beliefs and attitudes, a person may experience dissonance. If forewarned of this possibility, he sometimes reduces dissonance by misperceiving the information or denying its validity. If not forewarned, he may still be able to reduce dissonance in these ways, but may find the information convincing and attempt to reduce the dissonance in other ways, perhaps by shifting his preexisting attitude.

3. *Alterations in social support.* A person usually derives support for his beliefs and attitudes through the assumption that they are shared by the groups with which he feels himself most identified. Open expression of disagreement within a group, therefore, tends to create dissonance and varied attempts to reduce it. Sometimes the shared beliefs of everyone in a group are threatened, as when an apocalyptic sect that had predicted the end of the world on a given date found the world still intact. Those who are interacting with the group at the time dissonance arises are likely to reduce their dissonance in a way doing least violence to the group rationale. Those who are alone, needing to reduce dissonance on their own, are likely to do so in a way that cuts them off from the group.

4. *Effects of forced compliance.* Especially influential on subsequent research in social psychology were some experiments Festinger and his col-

laborators devised in applying cognitive dissonance theory to the effects of forced compliance. Festinger's ideas, and the findings of the first experiments, are summarized in the following extract:

> "Dissonance almost always exists after an attempt has been made, by offering rewards or threatening punishment, to elicit overt behavior that is at variance with private opinion. If the overt behavior is successfully elicited, the person's private opinion is dissonant with his knowledge concerning his behavior. . . . If forced compliance has been elicited, the dissonance may be reduced by changing private opinion to bring it into line with the overt behavior or by magnifying the amount of reward or punishment involved."

Typical of forced-compliance experiments is the following: a student subject, after performing boring tasks for an hour, is asked to persuade the next subject that they are interesting. The request is justified by telling the subject that he was in a control group not given any advance expectation, that the next subject is in an experimental group which must be led to expect interesting tasks, but that the helper scheduled to present this message has not yet arrived. Most subjects agree to substitute for the missing helper. The authors of the experiment—Leon Festinger and Merrill Carlsmith—assume that for a person to find himself presenting opinions contrary to those he really holds creates cognitive dissonance. They attempt to reveal the effect of the dissonance by manipulating experimentally a factor that should influence how the dissonance is reduced.

If the subject is very well paid, absurdly overpaid, he will probably be led to reconcile the discrepancy between his statements and his beliefs through explaining it by the extraordinary financial gain it brings him; he thus eliminates the dissonance while leaving his original attitude intact. So some of the subjects are paid $20 for giving misleading information, but some are paid only $1.00. A typical student subject, the experimenters suppose, cannot satisfactorily explain to himself why for a payment of $1.00 he makes statements contrary to his beliefs; he cannot attribute his action to so slight an incentive as $1.00. A subject in the $1.00 group, they hold, will tend to resolve the dissonance by persuading himself that the statements he is making are really not so far from his own attitude after all—in other words, by changing his own evaluation of the boring tasks in the direction of believing that they really have some interest. This prediction is opposite to what might have been made from a simple reward theory, holding that the more a person was rewarded for making a statement the more he would be inclined to repeat it in the future. The prediction from dissonance theory was confirmed; attitude change, it was found, is produced by the small reward and not by the large reward. Interviewed at the end of the experiment, the subjects paid $20 rated the enjoyableness of the tasks no differently from control subjects who had never been asked to participate in a deception, whereas the subjects paid $1.00 gave on the average a dependably higher rating.

Dissonance theory has been used to predict a variety of novel experimental results, as well as to summarize or explain many observations that are less surprising. As research proceeded, however, the concept of dissonance changed somewhat, and in a way that brought it closer to the heart of a humanistic orientation. It had from the outset, as I have said, something of a humanistic flavor, but this began to be more explicit in the experiments and the theoretical writing of Jack Brehm and Arthur R. Cohen, gathered together in a book they published in 1962.

Brehm and Cohen note that most of the experiments prompted by the theory of cognitive dissonance have dealt with dissonance that occurs in connection with a commitment. The four topics Festinger outlined, for example, all suggest commitment: in making a decision, the person commits himself to one rather than to another alternative course of action; exposure to information is usually relevant in relation to attitudes or prospective courses of action to which the person is already committed; alterations in social support are significant because a person is committed to the implications of group membership; and the effects of forced compliance revolve around the person's having committed himself to undertaking a course of action alien to his normal behavior. In relation to the theory of cognitive dissonance, Brehm and Cohen at first state the significance of commitment as lying in three facts: (1) instances of commitment are well suited to studying cognitive dissonance, because the person's explicit commitment facilitates identifying the dissonance; (2) a commitment to an action or attitude affects the relative likelihood of various ways of reducing dissonance, because commitment is tenacious; (3) theories competing with that of cognitive dissonance have not tried to deal with the effects of commitment, and thus in exploring the topic guided by the theory of cognitive dissonance it will be possible to make new discoveries.

As they review their experiments and reconsider their theory, Brehm and Cohen end up by giving commitment a much more important place than this, suggesting that it is probably essential for the occurrence of dissonance. There can, of course, be cognitive discrepancies about matters involving no personal commitment; but they create no discomfort and lead to no change. The application of the term dissonance, they suggest, should be confined to instances where the discrepancy has some meaning in relation to self-esteem. It is when the personal commitment to some action or attitude is discrepant with pertinent information, that dissonance occurs, creating discomfort that the person seeks to reduce. Brehm and Cohen go on, finally, to suggest that the concept of volition may be essential, too: *voluntary* commitment to a course whose wisdom may now be questioned is the source of discomfort.

Here, then, is a considerable change from Festinger's rather mathematical and almost disembodied picture of the abstract cognitions whose inconsistency could give rise to cognitive dissonance. The person is fully restored to the picture: a motivated person concerned with his conception of himself, discomforted not just by information but by a threat to his ordinary assumption that he is able to make sensible choices.

This change in dissonance theory has not gone unchallenged. Brehm and Cohen's theory would itself lead us, indeed, to predict that many psychologists would hold it in low regard. The research tradition in which experimental social psychologists are participating is traditionally committed to the dogma of determinism, and to the rejection of models of man that recognize his freedom. In a paradoxical way, moreover, many psychologists probably feel thay have voluntarily adopted this dogma through insight into its truth. Thus a theory that proceeds from a model of man as free agent threatens those psychologists who have freely committed themselves to rejecting the idea of freedom.

Despite the opposition that the theory itself predicts, and which may, of course, be warranted on more objective grounds as well, the essence of Brehm and Cohen's version of dissonance theory seems gradually to be gaining acceptance. Elliot Aronson, one of the social psychologists most active in dissonance research, for example, writes in 1968 that

> ". . . although we may not have been fully aware of it at the time, in the clearest experiments performed to test dissonance theory, the dissonance involved was between a self concept and cognitions about a behavior that violated this self concept."

Reviewing the Festinger and Carlsmith pattern of experiment, described earlier as an example of forced-compliance experiments, Aronson now views it quite differently from the way that he had at the time it was done. The dissonance, in his original view, was between "I believe the task is dull" and "I told someone that the task was interesting." These two elements would not even be dissonant in everyone, he now points out, and the true dissonance is between these elements: "I am a decent, truthful human being," and "I have misled a person; I have conned him into believing something that just isn't true."

One of the recent experiments by Aronson and his collaborators tests more directly the relevance of the self concept. Subjects opposed to legalization of marijuana were induced to deliver, some for one audience and some for another, speeches favoring its legalization (the speech was videotaped, purportedly for later showing, but in fact was not shown to any audience). A dissonance effect—change of their own attitude in the direction of their speech—was found only in subjects who were told that their speech would be presented to fellow students not committed to a position on the issue. Subjects who were told that their speech would be presented to students already committed to a definite position showed no dissonance effect. Only if a person sees his actions as likely to have a bad effect

—in this case, sees his actions as likely to influence others toward a position he supposedly considers evil—is discrepancy between action and belief productive of dissonance. What is threatened, it seems, is the person's view of himself as a responsible and moral citizen; one way of alleviating this threat is by changing his attitude so that the action he has taken no longer seems so evil. (This mode of dissonance reduction may be likely, of course, only on an issue where the person is uncertain whether his is the only acceptable position.)

This type of interpretation is found in some of the applications of dissonance theory to more newly devised kinds of experimental situations and to newly recognized problems. It is also found in other theoretical approaches that compete with dissonance theory or seek to complement it. Robert Abelson, for example, has developed a theory of "psychological implication," elaborated and modified from an account of "psycho-logic" that he and Milton Rosenberg worked out several years ago. In applying this theory to attitude change he seeks to give an account of the thought processes that create dissonance and resolve it; the account is of an active person who attempts both to understand correctly events important to him and to have and to justify an acceptable opinion of himself. A recent experiment on children—by Mark Lepper, Mark Zanna, and Robert Abelson—provides an apt example. Each child was told by the experimenter, before being left alone for a while, that he must not play with a particular toy that he found very attractive. As dissonance theory predicts, if the child respects the prohibition he is likely later to rate the toy less attractive than before. This effect, it was found, could be prevented by giving the child in advance a good reason for not playing with the toy; giving him the same reason afterward left the dissonance effect intact. Here is a sort of irreversibility of the dissonance effect, and the authors interpret it by viewing the person as an active agent seeking to justify the action to which he has committed himself.

> "The individual must confront and resolve a "How come?" question, usually of the form, "How come I did not behave in a way that I ordinarily would?" In the absence of obvious justification for the behavior, the individual is faced with a puzzle that may require considerable cognitive effort and invention to solve. If the effort bears fruit, the individual will not then likely abandon the result even when given palatable alternatives."

They suggest, moreover, that the tendency to maintain positions once arrived at may, in general, be attributed to "this assumed process of self-congratulation for figuring something out well."

In some recent social psychology, the person is shown as an active agent even when his activity is seen as purely cognitive, aimed at understanding his world rather than at justifying his position in it. This is true of ***attribu-***

tion theory, which concentrates on how a person makes inferences about himself and other people, especially about purposes or causes influencing their present action. Attribution theory originated in the work of Fritz Heider, like Lewin a former German who brought to his social psychology the fundamental orientation of Gestalt psychology. Heider published in 1958 a magnificent analysis of interpersonal relations, in which attribution plays a major part. Several experimental social psychologists (notably Edward E. Jones, Harold Kelley, and Ivan D. Steiner) have since used attribution theory to integrate the results of various experiments and to guide further research in social psychology.

Especially pertinent for my concern here is a behavioristic version of attribution theory, presented by Daryl J. Bem in an ingenious attempt to explain without dissonance theory some of the findings to which dissonance theory has given special attention. The experimental subject who is induced to give a speech opposing his own attitude, and then changes his own attitude, does so (according to Bem's argument) because he observes his own behavior just as he would another person's and makes appropriate inferences from it. If he observes another person stating opinions contrary to those the same person stated earlier, and knows that the person has been paid $20 for making his present statements, the observer will not have to infer a change in attitude to explain the change in behavior. But if he observes a person stating a new opinion in the absence of external pressures that could explain the change, he will infer a real change in attitude. Just so, he observes his own behavior and makes the inferences necessary to account for it. This theory is based on an extraordinary complication, disregarding any capacity of a person to know directly what goes on inside himself while endowing him with an extremely mature ability to study himself objectively as though he were an outside observer. It offers a model of the human being as simultaneously idiot and genius, instead of the middling muddler he seems generally to be.

Bem's argument seems at first glance like a revival of a very simplistic behaviorism, and in his first accounts of it he employed the terminology of Skinner's radical behaviorism. What is noteworthy is that social psychology has advanced in understanding to a point where such a revival can now be put forth seriously only if—as Lepper, Zanna, and Abelson point out in discussing Bem—it ascribes to man cognitive processes so complicated that the theory is difficult to distinguish from cognitive dissonance theory. Bem recognizes the person as a very active agent—purely a cognitive agent, as in Festinger's original version of dissonance theory, and curiously deprived of inner vision, but still far from a reflex responder to external stimuli.

Bem's theory has led him to some very interesting new experiments, whose results suggest that observation of one's own actions, as though from outside, is much more important, and internal observation is much less important, than I would have thought. I believe that many other people would also be surprised and challenged by his findings. I find it impossible, however, to view his experiments as offering any real support to the radical behaviorism with which he started, since they depend on viewing the person as a complex thinker, not as the empty organism specified in radical behaviorism. Perhaps Bem has come to feel the same way. In a recent textbook, he has abandoned the behavioristic framework of his early articles; he now speaks consistently about how a person makes inferences, not—as in his first article—about how utterances are controlled. In a recent and pertinent experimental report, too, he has omitted the behavioristic framework. I feel that in this same paper he is indirectly acknowledging the complexity of his model when he concludes, along with some of his critics, that his theory and the dissonance theory in actual application are so similar that the choice between them may have to be made on grounds of taste rather than of evidence.

Bem's movement in a few years from a predominantly behavioristic to a largely humanistic model illustrates in a single psychologist the change I am in this chapter tracing on a social scale. Psychologists may use a simple mechanistic theory when sketching a program of research on the complexities of human life. If they carry the program out seriously, they seem inevitably to change the approach into a more appropriately humanistic one. But humanism, like mechanism, is diverse, and it may usefully incorporate insights that originate in any point of view. Bem's view, originating in radical behaviorism, that significant self-observation is essentially observation as though from outside, plays an important part in his current more humanistic theory of beliefs and attitudes. It has led, moreover, to discoveries that must be dealt with by other humanistic theories; in seeming to deny the ample and direct self-knowledge that those theories often assume, Bem's discoveries constitute an important challenge.

The Embodied Self

From the writing of R. D. Laing I borrow a phrase to express a related development in social psychology that is representative of another aspect of the humanistic model of man.

In the original formulation of cognitive dissonance theory, attention was centered on purely cognitive elements—beliefs, opinions, and attitudes. It was, indeed, a theory of *cognitive* consistency, as are some of its rivals in the explanation of attitude change. With the more humanistic formulation of dissonance theory at which Brehm and Cohen arrived came attention to processes other than just knowing, and consideration of these other processes as also implicated in dissonance and its reduction. Experiments were then begun to test whether a person's motives are also subject to his control in the interests of reducing dissonance. The first experiments were done with two of the motives traditionally used in experimentation because their strength can be so readily controlled by altering the physical interchange with the environment.

Jack Brehm did an experiment with hunger; Philip Zimbardo and several colleagues followed with a similar experiment on thirst. Here is the pattern of the experiments: A subject is made very hungry or very thirsty—in the first case by agreeing to go without food for a number of hours as a preliminary to experimental participation, in the latter case by being given some thirst-inducing food as a part of the experiment. After his required participation in the experiment is over, a second experimenter asks him whether he would be willing to volunteer for another experiment that would involve continuing his state of hunger or of thirst. The invitation carries no external compulsion, and yet is put in such a way that a large majority of people voluntarily agree to take part.

The subject now finds himself in a continuing state of unpleasant hunger or thirst. There is, at least potentially, a state of dissonance here. A person does not ordinarily allow himself, if he can help it, to get unpleasantly hungry or thirsty. Here he certainly could have helped it. Why didn't he? Well, of course, he may explain his action to himself as altruistic cooperation in the scentific pursuit of knowledge, or as helpfulness to a deserving graduate student, and may find these explanations altogether sufficient. But not everyone can be satisfied with them, and the experimenters suppose that these explanations pose problems to many a subject, even to the typical subject. The subject may feel that in accepting these explanations he would be placing too high a value on intellectual pursuits, or would be too submissive to the interests of others and not sufficiently assertive of his own interests. Dissonance may remain. For my part, I suspect dissonance theory ascribes too little ego strength to the typical college student. If I am right, predictions from it should be quite wrong for many individuals, yet they could still show through in group means because of holding true for some fraction of the subjects.

One possible way the subject might reduce the remaining dissonance is to view his hunger or thirst as less intense than it had seemed to be. If he were only mildly hungry or thirsty, there would be nothing very remarkable in his being willing to tolerate the slight discomfort for a while longer.

The striking outcome of both these experiments is that conditions of this kind do lead many subjects to experience a lessened hunger and thirst. If the evidence came only from people's statements about how hungry or thirsty they are, it might be thought that only their choice of words was changed and not the way they really felt. But there is additional evidence; when freed to eat or drink as much as they wish, persons who have been subjected to the dissonance conditions are found to eat or drink less than control subjects who have been similarly deprived of food or water but without being put in a situation to arouse dissonance.

A further experiment by Zimbardo extended the same sort of finding to electric shock. His subjects, in the preliminary part of the experiment, were given a painful electric shock. A second experimenter then solicited the voluntary help of the subjects in an experiment that he was conducting with exactly the same physical setup, producing exactly the same shock. Again, a large proportion of the subjects voluntarily agreed to participate in the second experiment. Their reaction to this further shock could then be compared with those of control subjects who had been subjected to a comparable series of shocks without the element of voluntary commitment to continuation.

The outcome paralleled those of the hunger and thirst experiments, but was even more convincing because of additional kinds of evidence. One source of evidence was the subject's rating of the strength of the shock. Subjects who had voluntarily chosen to subject themselves to electric shocks rated the second shock as less painful than they had, only a few minutes earlier, rated an identical shock; they also considered it less painful than did control subjects who had not made any voluntary choice. The subjects also were measured on the adequacy with which they could perform a memory task in the course of which the shocks were introduced. The painful shock served as a disrupter of the memory task. If the voluntary subjects actually felt the shock less painful, it should disrupt their performance of the memory task less than the control subjects' performance. This was exactly the outcome. Finally, the strength of the shock as felt by the subject could be measured physiologically, by finding how strong was the physiological response measured by skin resistance. Here, again, the same difference was observed.

These experiments demonstrate, then, effects on the strength of hunger, thirst, or pain as experienced and as acted on—effects astonishing from a common-sense point of view yet suggested by a humanistic form of dissonance theory. Their prediction from dissonance theory depends on only two assumptions: the obvious assumption that a person's finding himself acting contrary to his usual wishes will create dissonance, and the more novel but plausible assumption that a person has some degree of voluntary control over feelings of hunger, thirst, and pain, so that change in these feelings is available as one possible means of reducing dissonance. The self of dissonance theory is no longer a disembodied self of cognitions alone; but a fully embodied self in which cognition and motivation are interrelated.

In recent experiments, Zimbardo has carried this line of thought quite outside the context of dissonance theory. Having, as I have shown, found evidence that people act as though they ordinarily expect to be doing what they have willed to do, and can successfully will remarkable changes in their perception of internal events, or even in the internal events themselves, he looked for parallels in other psychological phenomena. One parallel he noted was in the facts of self-hypnosis. In self-hypnosis a person is willing himself to do something he would not ordinarily be able to do, or not ordinarily realize he would be able to do. He can, for example, become unaware of perceptions from some part of his body. Or he may produce changes in a part of his body that he does not ordinarily know he can produce. In particular, Zimbardo has experimented with attempts to have a hypnotized subject, while lying down and keeping his hands quiet in a constant position, alter the temperature of a hand. He finds that some of his subjects can successfully will to make a hand warmer or colder—and in some way not simply resulting from a general physiological state produced in the body as a whole, since a person can simultaneously make one hand warmer and the other hand colder.

In the chapter on hypnosis we have seen that the study of extreme external control is surprisingly useful in forming a humanistic understanding of man. We now find that considering the special case where hypnotist and subject are the same person becomes a useful tool to the same end, leading to the demonstration that a person's command over his own actions and experiences can be much greater than was generally supposed.

An integral relation of various parts of experience is also seen in the fascinating theory of emotion developed by two social psychologists, Stanley Schachter and Jerome E. Singer. They develop and justify the theory in relation to a beautifully planned experiment on how knowledge and physiological arousal interact to produce emotional experience. The experiment was complex; the logic of the study, when combined with the high ethical requirements of the medical and psychological professions, required several control groups and procedures to ensure that no subject would be hurt either physically or psychologically. A very brief account will show its relevance to our present concern but cannot do justice to these various necessary complications.

Schachter and Singer created physiological arousal in their subjects by an injection of epinephrine. The substance was introduced and explained as one whose effects on vision were being studied; it was correctly described as mild and harmless and was administered by a physician, but only if the subject was willing and if his medical records had given no contraindication. Some subjects were given, as an account of probable side effects, a correct description of the aroused state epinephrine usually produces. Other subjects were misinformed, being given a description contrary to fact. Others were given no suggestion that the injection might produce noticeable sideeffects. Those who were given the correct information were expected, when they experienced arousal, to attribute it to the injection. The other two groups of subjects experienced the same arousal but were not likely to be able to attribute it to the injection.

After the injection, all subjects were asked to wait for the 20 minutes presumably required for it to take effect, so their vision could then be tested. During the wait, each subject was exposed to one of two social situations likely to induce a particular emotional state. One of these situations was intended to arouse happy feelings. A stooge, pretending to be a fellow subject waiting in the same room for the same reason, engaged in a carefully rehearsed series of seemingly spontaneous joyous actions, providing ample opportunity for the subject to become involved in them. The other situation was intended to arouse anger. Subject and stooge were both set to work on a questionnaire that was insulting and grossly intrusive, and the stooge expressed very overtly the anger that the subject could also be expected to feel. The kind of emotional state subjects experienced was inferred from covert observation of their behavior during this period with the stooge, and from later direct questioning.

Subjects who knew in advance that arousal was likely to follow from the injection did, as expected, attribute the arousal to the injection and did not experience it primarily as an identifiable emotion. Subjects lacking this expectation, on experiencing arousal, tended to interpret it as an emotional state. Those in whom a happy feeling was being induced tended to interpret it as euphoria; and those who were being irritated, as anger. Each emotion was much stronger in those who had been aroused by epinephrine than in control subjects who experienced the same situation but whose injection had been a completely ineffectual placebo. The nature and strength of emotion is thus shown to be a joint outcome of physiological state and knowledge of the situation. The person is shown as putting together his external information and his bodily condition and making the best inference he can about the state of his total self in relation to his surroundings.

The model of man emerging from these studies by social psychologists seems to be essentially the model of man implied in a naive common-sense point of view. Applying this familiar model in a context of scientific observation and systematization can lead, however, to really novel understanding. An excellent illustration of this is provided by the recent work by Michael Storms and Richard Nisbett on placebos.

The experiment by Storms and Nisbett was disguised as a study of dreams for which, it was said, people who have trouble sleeping were desired as subjects because they remember their dreams better. To study the effects of the level of bodily activity on dreams, the insomniac subjects were asked to take a pertinent nonprescription pill on going to bed, for the two nights of the experiment. The pill was in fact a placebo, a bit of sugar. Half the subjects were told that it would produce arousal, half were told that it would produce relaxation. In the interview after the two experimental nights, the subjects were asked as indirectly as possible about their sleep; comparable information had been obtained earlier about their sleep on the two nights preceding the experiment.

The subjects who had been told that the pill was arousing got to sleep faster after taking the pill than they had on the preceding two nights. Subjects who had been told that the pill was relaxing showed just the opposite effect; they took longer to get to sleep than they had on the preceding two nights. These are the effects the experimenters had anticipated, basing their expectations on dissonance theory and Kelley's attribution theory. On the average, presumably, the subjects went to bed on the experimental nights just as aroused or relaxed as on the preceding two nights. If a subject believed a pill he had just taken was arousing, however, he could attribute part of his arousal to the pill and believe himself to be basically more relaxed than usual; this assurance could then itself be relaxing and permit him to get to sleep more readily. If a subject believed the pill he had just taken was relaxing, he would have to suppose that to be as aroused as usual he must basically be more highly aroused; this evidence of internal upset could then lead him to feel still more aroused and to have more than usual difficulty in getting to sleep. Exactly what internal processes occur, in what sequence, we can of course not know until future studies of a different character give us more detailed knowledge about what is going on inside a person under such circumstances.

The striking novelty in these findings is that they directly contradict the usual expectations, based on a notion of suggestibility or direct external influence, which give rise to the use of placebos in drug-evaluation experiments. Whenever subjects know or may guess the purpose of a drug that is being evaluated, some of them are, without knowing it, given a placebo instead; the effect of the placebo alone is taken to measure how much effect is produced by suggestion, and a superior effect of the true drug will be taken to evidence a genuine effect. The placebo is usually assumed, and often found, to have some positive effect in the direction suggested by the instructions or circumstances. In the experiment by Storms and Nisbett, the placebo has an effect in exactly the opposite direction. Why the difference?

Storms and Nisbett argue that the effect they get should in general be found wherever the subject has precise expectations about the internal condition under study and can compare his actual experience with these expectations. Only if he lacks this precision of expectation will his experience be shaped directly by the suggestions that surround the administration of the placebo. Their insomniac subjects know well their usual feelings while trying to get to sleep each night. Some of the standard experiments on drug evaluation might provide similar circumstances, and they suggest the following parallel: "Experiments designed to test the effectiveness of tranquilizers must have a control condition in which subjects are given placebos which they believe to be tranquilizers." Reviewing published research of this pattern, they report that the paradoxical effect they themselves have identified has, indeed, occurred there and has been considered a puzzle, since the notion of external control through suggestion offers no clue to its meaning. Not only in psychology itself but in allied sciences dependent on human subjects, the mechanical model of man as controlled by separate external causes needs to give way to a more adequate humanistic model.

Some of these experiments demonstrating the embodied self seem far afield from the special subject matter of social psychology. They certainly are not intended to erect boundaries between this discipline and the rest of psychology. The social psychologist is also a psychologist, and when his specialized work leads to suggestions of great value for general psychology he does not hesitate to pursue these suggestions wherever they may lead, but we may be left wondering why these suggestions depend on so special a source. As I indicated at the beginning of the chapter, social psychologists began with a topic that lends itself to a manipulative and exploitative attitude toward interpersonal relations. The methods used may be seen from some of these examples, moreover, to involve offensive manipulation of people, to the extent that a part of each experiment is a "debriefing"—a full explanation of the experiment to each subject at the end of his participation, to reduce the chances of his carrying away even a mild bad effect on himself and a hostile attitude toward research. Why, we may ask, have such valuable suggestions for general psychology arisen, as I think they have, rather more in this improbable specialty than strictly within the tradition of systematic research in general psychology itself? I think a part of the answer is that social psychologists, feeling themselves to be pioneering in a new discipline, have been less rigidly confined by the conventional restrictions of thought that have developed in the psychological research tradition. They have been freer to go where common observation of man as human, when linked with a scientific approach, leads them, freer to develop in the novel directions suggested by a humanistic approach even though, perhaps, not thinking of themselves as humanistic psychologists.

Personal Freedom

In the humanistic model of man that emerges in the developments I have thus far reviewed in social psychology, the emphasis is on activity and integration of the person rather than on his freedom. Yet the concept of freedom appears, as in Brehm and Cohen's suggestion that voluntary commitment may be essential for dissonance to appear. Freedom, which Dostoyevsky made paramount in his humanistic portrait of man, is also given explicit predominance in certain other developments in social psychology.

Jack Brehm has been the leading figure in this movement. In 1966 he published a book with the rather formidable title, *A theory of psychological reactance,* describing a theory and experiments that could have been prompted by reading Dostoyevsky. By "reactance" he means a person's arousal by threatened reduction of his freedom, arousal directed at reestablishing any freedom already lost and preventing further loss. He devised a number of experiments to test the idea that loss or threatened loss of freedom does produce arousal. The experiments employed several techniques of kinds familiar in social psychology and in the study of child behavior.

Several experiments concerned the attractiveness of various choices offered to subjects. One study, for instance, had the appearance of a market survey by a record company. The subject listened to four records and rated their attractiveness, and was promised his choice among the four as a reward the next day. The next day he was told that the supply of the records to be given out as rewards had arrived, and that one of the four was missing. For each subject, the particular record third in his preference order was the one he was told was unavailable. This day he was again asked to rate the four records. The researchers expected that the record that had been removed from the subject's scope of free choice would now seem more attractive, since his arousal by this loss of freedom had no other easily available channel of expression. A large proportion of the experimental subjects were found to consider this record more attractive than they had previously considered it, whereas control subjects for whom all choices had been left open showed no tendency to increase the attractiveness of the record that they had originally rated third.

Another group of experiments concerned attitudes on public issues. The most informative of these was reported later in an article by Stephen Worchel and Jack Brehm. The issue used for the experiment was the appropriate treatment of the Communist party in the United States, chosen because there was a wide variation of attitude in the college where the study was conducted, most students holding one or the other of two opposite extremes. Two weeks before the actual experiment, the relevant attitude had been measured by part of a questionnaire that had been administered in an introductory psychology course. In the experiment proper, each subject read one of several prepared speeches, distributed among subjects so that half would read arguments favoring their own position and half would read arguments advocating the opposite extreme. In each case, half the speeches included statements attempting to limit the subject's freedom of choice, for example, "you cannot believe otherwise," or "you have no choice but to believe this." Afterward, the attitude questionnaire was filled out again.

One group of subjects stood out in the results of this experiment—those who had read arguments favoring their own position and were told that they had no choice but to accept them. A large majority of this group came to reject their own initial position, as did only a very small minority of any other group. This finding seems to be consistent with the view that threat to freedom was the main source of attitude change in this setting, for freedom appears to have been threatened only in this group. Subjects who read arguments opposed to their own position and are told that they have no choice but to accept them are not threatened, one may suppose, because they have the evidence of their own preexisting attitude to convince them that they can, indeed, feel otherwise than they are told they must. Subjects who are not given any freedom-limiting communications, of course, seem unlikely to sense a threat to their freedom regardless of whether the arguments they read agree or differ with their own attitude.

Brehm's suggestion that interference with freedom of choice forms a potent source of change in attitude and action is leading to diverse efforts at experimental test. As Brehm recognized in his original account, this theory may account for some of the same facts that dissonance theory accounts for. In deciding which theory is more adequate, social psychologists must try to find instances where the two theories lead to opposite predictions for the same experiment. The first experiment that claims to meet this requirement, one by Robert A. Wicklund, has now appeared. It creates a situation where, if a person regrets a choice that he has made between two objects, the regret can be detected by giving him an opportunity to reverse the choice. The subject was permitted to choose as a gift one of two items. After choosing one, he was told that if he had chosen the other he would have had to pay something for it instead of receiving it for no charge; later, he was told that he could now have either item at no expense. The question is, will the subject now be inclined to hold to his original choice or to reverse it? Wicklund argues that dissonance theory would predict a strengthening of the original preference; the unexpected fee would be dissonant with a shift, and maintenance of the original choice would reduce dissonance and thus be strengthened. For reactance theory, on the other hand, the fee is a threat to the person's freedom to choose the initially rejected object; so the fee should increase the desirability of that object and, hence, the likelihood of choosing it when the fee is later removed. The outcome was the one predicted by reactance theory, so that Wicklund claims his experiment argues for the predominance of a need for freedom over that of a need for consistency. Psychologists know well from experience that the issue between competing theories is not decisively resolved by single experiments, and the final outcome here will only be determined in the future.

Meanwhile, other psychologists have studied freedom in situations where its absence is to be expected and the special effect of its presence is noted. One such situation is that of an experimental subject who has agreed to take part in an experiment involving painful or very annoying stimulation. The typical subject in such an experiment must know that he has an ultimate freedom to stop the experiment. But he feels strong pressure to go through with what he has committed himself to, and knows that the experimenters are not going to allow anything to happen that is really dangerous. So, in effect, he may feel no real control over the discomfort he is experiencing. What would happen if his sense of freedom to stop it were substantially increased?

The most pertinent set of studies is one where noise is the source of discomfort. In a first experiment, David C. Glass, Jerome E. Singer, and Lucy N. Friedman, compared a predictable and an unpredictable noise. They measured tolerance for the frustration of working on an insoluble puzzle, and quality of performance on a proofreading task that required careful attention. Both showed interference from an unpredictable noise but not from a predictable one. The authors believed that feelings of control might be an important element here; faced with predictable noise the subject can, for example, adjust his work to the schedule it affords, but faced with unpredictable noise he can make no adjustment. They decided on a second experiment to explore directly the role of feelings of control—in this instance, sense of freedom to discontinue the noise. One group of subjects were shown a button and "told that they could at any time terminate the noise for the remainder of the session by pressing the switch. They were further informed that the experimenter preferred that they did not press the switch, but the choice was entirely up to them." A control group was not provided with a button, nor with any comparable instructions. Otherwise, the two groups were treated identically, and both received the unpredictable noise which in the earlier experiment had been disrupting. Although none of the subjects made use of the button, the sense of freedom it provided led to a large difference in performance. The subjects who were encouraged to feel they could stop the noise showed much greater tolerance of frustration and performed the proofreading task with much greater accuracy.

As social psychological research has come to deal more directly with man's sense of freedom, with man as agent or initiator as well as responder, it has come to be related to other fields of psychology in new ways.

Some social psychologists, their interest aroused by these discoveries in their own field, have gone on to study parallels in a person's relation to his physical environment. Stanley Schachter and Richard Nisbett have both studied human obesity in the light of a dimension to which their attention was called by these advances in social psychology—variations among people in the extent to which their actions are initiated from within or by stimulation from outside. It is easy to suppose that obese people have eaten too much because they have an especially strong craving for food and seek it out too often. Schachter and Nisbett both report evidence that what is distinctive about obese people is, rather, that their eating is primarily determined by cues from outside. Whenever attractive food is present, they are inclined to eat; in its absence, they may not seek it, but in its presence they cannot easily refrain or stop. In the nonobese, external conditions have less influence; when they eat, and when they stop, are determined primarily from within. Something often considered to be a basic psychological feature of man—potentiality for autonomous initiation and control of his own behavior—is thus shown to be realized in varying degree by different persons. Within each person, too, different kinds of behavior doubtless vary in the extent to which he controls them from within. The degree to which internal control pervades any given person's interaction with food is shown here to be an important influence on his physique.

It would obviously be premature to conclude that the inner control pertinent to avoiding obesity is found only in fully developed human beings.

In research by Schachter, Nisbett, and others, the same pattern of relationship—desirable weight being associated with internal rather than external control of eating—has been found in newborn infants and in lower animals. This fact might suggest that the pattern can be produced by relatively simply mechanical processes, and that humanistic concepts are superfluous even for explaining its presence in adults. It might suggest, instead, that concepts rooted firmly in the study of man are needed, as was held by many psychologists of an earlier era, even for the adequate understanding of lower animals. There are still other possibilities, but of these two suggestions I find the second especially intriguing to explore, while many of my fellow psychologists would prefer the first. Here is an indication, I think, that psychology is an actively progressing science, with its various parts interacting to generate the tension of uncertainties such as we know in the history of other sciences. The outcome of this particular uncertainty lies in the future. What is important for my argument here is that only through boldly and directly facing the complexities of human life did these social psychologists generate ideas that laid bare more general issues. A humanistic approach, when applied in the framework of the research tradition, can be influential far beyond its own original limits.

Social psychological attention to man's sense of freedom is related also to recent research initiated by the clinical psychologist Julian Rotter. He prepared a questionnaire to measure the extent to which a person feels himself subject to external as against his own internal control. Rotter's original description of the questionnaire used the terminology of his "social learning theory," a somewhat humanized version of learning theory which allows for an inner look at expectations, for instance, though it still speaks of "inner control of reinforcements" rather than more broadly of "sense of freedom." Subsequent research using the questionnaire—showing a strong sense of inner control to be related to nonsmoking and the ability to stop smoking, active participation in programs of social change, and other diverse forms of action—has tended to make less use of the original formulation in terms drawn from learning theory. One influence in the constructive broadening (as I see it) of this concept of inner versus outer control may have been the users' awareness of the various movements in social psychology that suggest the value of a more humanistic model in which sense of freedom is explicitly considered. The change in social psychology is well illustrated by Charles Kiesler's recent discussion of the earlier term, "illusion of freedom"; depending on how this tendentious phrase is interpreted, he argues, it is either meaningless or misleading. Both the person's testimony of his own experience of freedom, and experimental demonstration of important effects produced by that experience versus its absence, combine to make the unqualified word, "freedom," more appropriate.

Systematic evidence for the importance of a sense of freedom is by now diverse and persuasive enough that alternative explanations of the evidence must, in disagreeing with Dostoevsky's view that a need for freedom is the basic element, proceed from a very complex and human psychological model. This is apparent in a very ingenious paper on cognitive dissonance by James Tedeschi, Barry Schlenker, and Thomas Bonoma. They note that a person's perception of his freedom to choose appears to be critical in understanding why "dissonance" is sometimes aroused and sometimes not, why "reactance" occurs and why "commitment" is an important influence on attitudes. Additional facts, they argue, not so clearly pertinent to freedom of choice—such as differences between attitude change in public and in private situations—can be brought into relation with these by viewing them all as special cases of a more general principle: that people working as subjects in social psychological experiments typically devote themselves to "managing the impressions that the experimenter forms about them." In certain contexts a subject typically becomes interested in giving an impression of freedom, in some an impression of consistency, and so on. A decidedly human model is here being proposed for understanding experiments in social psychology. As its authors say,

> "The impression management theory does not view subjects in experiments as passive targets of the subtle or clever manipulations of the experimenter. Rather, subjects have been the originators of influence attempts directed at the experimenter. The effectiveness of subjects in manipulating the impressions that experimenters have of them has been made evident by the fact that social-psychological theory reflects the lack of awareness by experimenters about how they have been manipulated."

Social psychology is far from establishing as yet the extreme position on man's striving for freedom that Dostoyevsky put so eloquently. Social psychology does, however, make a clear case for rejecting a model of man accompanied by metaphysical dogma that leads researchers to avoid consideration of man's sense of freedom. A picture of man as completely under external control can succeed, it now appears, only if it is at once so complicated in form and so vague in application that it, in effect, acknowledges the importance of strivings for freedom. A simpler model, and one more faithful to observation, directly accepts the sense of free choice, regarding man as an active agent. Such a model is consistent with the generally humanistic direction of movement that I have traced in recent social psychology.

If the doors of perception were cleansed every thing would appear to man as it is, infinite.

For man has closed himself up, till he sees all things thro' narrow chinks of his cavern.

—WILLIAM BLAKE

8

Extrasensory Perception

Aldous Huxley drew on this passage from Blake in giving a title to the first book in which he tried to describe the experiences that he had obtained through psychedelic drugs. With at least equal accuracy, we can see it as expressing the feeling some people have about extrasensory perception and its importance in their lives.

Most of us suppose that our knowledge of the world comes entirely through the known senses. Yet many believe, and others suspect, some of their knowledge has come through other channels. Personal experiences that seem to prove extrasensory communication are the enduring basis for some persons' belief in its reality.

No events in my life have ever even half-persuaded me that I was experiencing extrasensory perception (which I shall follow custom in calling ESP). If you, too, are in the same position—and especially if you have not even talked with people who have experienced such events—you may not appreciate the strength of conviction that they can produce. Hence, I think it is relevant to start this chapter by citing such an experience. It is one among several which gave me at an early age a lively sense of the possibility of channels of communication other than the obvious ones. It was an experience of my maternal grandfather, for whom I had special respect in my childhood, seeing him as a very sober and practical businessman who was yet very warm toward people. His testimony was the more impressive because he seemed to lack any of the religious beliefs or interests that might have given rise to it. As far as I could see, a vigorous need for correct and adequate understanding was the only motive for his persistent interest in puzzling experiences. As a young man he had gone from his native Pennsylvania to Mexico, where in the 1890s he managed a mining and lumbering operation. Some years after his retirement he wrote a book of memoirs, entitling one chapter, "Some things which have happened to me in life which are hard to explain." He began the chapter with the most impressive of these experiences:

> "A few months after starting to work the Preseña mine, Mr. Andy Urquhart and myself had been down the mine all the forenoon working with the pumps. We came out for lunch very tired and hungry. There was a terrible wind storm raging and the air was full of dust. We had an old Portuguese cook named Tom Dios. This particular day he had a nice big roast of beef, which he had flavored by drawing young onions through it. We sat there eating our lunch, enjoying it very much, and remarking from time to time how nice the beef was that day, when suddenly I jumped up from the table, ran to the door, called the coachman out of the kitchen and told him to hitch up the mules quick, as I wanted to go to Parral. He immediately started to hitch up the mules. I went back to the table to try and finish my lunch while he was doing so; but I could not eat nor even drink my coffee, I was so nervous.
>
> "I put on my hat and went out to help hitch up the mules. Mr. Urquhart followed me out, asked me if I was sick and begged me to go in and lie down, and not try to go during the storm. I told him no that I was not sick, but that I was needed in Parral and that I was going just as quickly as possible. He followed me down to the foot of the hill and helped hitch up the mules, but still begging me all the time to not go to Parral but to go back to the house and lie down. (He afterwards told me that there was not a trace of color in my face, and he was thoroughly satisfied that I had suddenly lost my mind.) When we got the mules hitched up, and the driver was in his seat, I got into the back seat and told him to drive just as fast as he knew how, and not to stop for anything or anybody. We had a lively pair of mules, and when he saw anybody ahead in the road, he would commence to shout for them to get out of the way. When we had gone two-thirds of the way to Parral I saw a workman coming over a little rise in the road, with the red mill dust on his shirt. I said to the driver: "Stop when you reach that man, as he is after me." The man, the moment he saw us, signaled us to stop. When we did so, he climbed into the wagon and motioned for us to go on. He was out of breath from running, but as soon as he recovered his breath he said to me: "The place is on fire and they sent me for you." I then told the driver to stand up and whip the mules in turn to keep them on a gallop. We drove the seven miles in thirty-five minutes.
>
> "When I reached the mill I found the large wood pile containing probably five hundred cords of wood, which was located between the mill and mine, a raging furnace of fire.

> "There were nine Americans working for the company on the ground; but they had all lost their heads, and had not started the fire pump, nor given the fire alarm. My first act was to run into the boiler room, tie the whistle down, and hand the fireman a stick of wood with instructions to use it on anyone who tried to stop the whistle. I then grabbed the different Americans and gave each one quick orders what to do. Probably in less than five minutes from the time I arrived, I had two streams of water pouring on the wood, one on each side. Inside of thirty minutes there were probably five hundred or six hundred men from town on the ground ready to help; so we soon got the fire at a safe distance from both the mill and the mine, thus saving both plants. We lost most of the wood. Had I been thirty minutes later in reaching the place, the company's property would all have been destroyed. We got the fire under control, and practically out by midnight. When we had time to think and could compare watches, as near as we could tell I jumped up from the table at the exact moment the fire started. The question is, what made me do it, as there were no means of communication between the mine and the mill, except by messenger."

Some humanistic psychologists are especially likely to give serious attention to accounts like this one. Possibly the explanation is that the humanistic emphasis on individuality can lead to expecting that different persons may have had very different experiences. If these psychologists have had no anomalous experiences themselves, they will not necessarily be extremely skeptical of the possibility that another person might have had them.

The bias in this direction is not necessarily shared by all humanistic psychologists. Some purported incidents of extrasensory communication are, doubtless, pretenses by skilled people who wish to entertain or deceive. Many others may well be coincidences, regardless of how remarkable. The uncertainties of human memory, moreover, and distortion in a direction of greater distinctiveness and interest, must make many incidents more remarkable in the retelling than they would have appeared on direct observation. A humanistic approach does not require one to be gullible, nor to abandon ordinary standards of critical judgment. One of my grandfather's stories tells of his getting off a train for several hours for no good reason, in order to take a later one, and learning during his wait that the train he had abandoned went on to have an accident in which several passengers were killed. He was obviously inclined to believe that he had been prompted by advance knowledge (called, by students of ESP, precognition) of the accident that was about to occur. His account reminds me of an experience that I once had, while attending a weekend scientific meeting, going with four other colleagues in the car of one of them. The night before our return, I had a terrifying nightmare of our all being killed the next day in a head-on collision. Had I been inclined to believe in precognition I might have determined on returning by train and trying to persuade my friends to change their plans as well. The dream was so vivid that even though I had no such inclination I found myself somewhat nervous the next day. But we all arrived home safely, with not even a suggestion of danger along the way. The many experiences of this sort that go unreported need to be set beside the few where fear coincides with reality; they suggest that what seemed like precognition may have been pure coincidence.

Most experiences that seem to witness ESP are strange and evanescent. With some justice, perhaps, we may suspect that subsequent accounts often exaggerate the brief experience and misinterpret it. Of those who have such experiences, some few seek to catch them on the wing and fix them for subsequent inspection. The American novelist Upton Sinclair and his wife tried to do this. She seemed often to receive impressions of his thoughts from a distance, and they sought to test the reality of this occurrence by a series of carefully planned observations, including some with other senders. Upton Sinclair published an account of them in a book, *Mental radio*. It provides remarkably strong evidence. Typically, the sender concentrated on a diagram while Mary Craig Sinclair tried to keep her mind open to visual impressions and drew whatever came to her. The frequently close correspondence does not require statistical evaluation for confident rejection of the idea that "chance" was responsible.

When a humanistic psychologist has himself had experience persuasive of the reality of ESP, then I think there may be some special inclination for him to trust the judgment he arrives at from his own experience, and not to suspend judgment while he awaits evidence objective enough to persuade others. Carl Jung is an instance. His autobiography indicates that he was a believer in extrasensory phenomena because of his own experiences, and it makes no reference to systematic research (though in other writings he showed familiarity with pertinent research).

Some other humanistic psychologists who have either believed in the reality of extrasensory perception or had a very vital sense of its possibility seem to have been influenced more by their openness to conviction from external evidence. This seems to have been true both of William James and of Gardner Murphy. As humanistic psychologists, they were acutely aware of the complexity of a human personality and of the multiple possibilities to be encountered in human experience, and thus were more open than most psychologists to persuasion by accounts of the experiences of others and by the outcome of systematic research. For my part, I was in this respect a humanistic psychologist from the beginning. I read Sinclair's *Mental radio* when I was in my teens and was greatly impressed. My opinion of Upton Sinclair, from knowledge of his novels and his life, prevented my accepting the possibility that he was intentionally deceiving his readers; the inconsistency was too great with his career of unmasking deceptions that corrupt our society. The only remaining possibility other than ESP seemed to be self-deception, and the experiences he recounts could be explained only by very intricate and improbable self-deceptions. Acquaintance with Sinclair's book and with my grandfather's experiences made me long ago more interested in ESP, more sympathetic to the case for it, than most psychologists. Lacking personal experience of my own, and knowing of no experimental procedure that can be depended on always to give objective evidence of ESP in research subjects. I have not been solidly convinced of its reality. But the evidence long available clearly suggests the presence of phenomena important to study.

Many psychologists, and fellow scientists from other fields, have been more strongly attracted to this study than I and have engaged in research on ESP, some led to this work by humanistic thought such as I have described. In recent years, an additional relation has appeared between humanistic psychology and the issue of extrasensory perception: the systematic research on this question has itself taken a decidedly humanistic turn. First, we must look at the general pattern of the earlier research, and the response to it.

Experiments on Extrasensory Perception

The standard pattern of experiments in extrasensory perception is essentially in the laboratory tradition. The subject sits in a laboratory or office —usually with greatly reduced stimulation, to ensure the quiet that might facilitate concentration. He is carefully isolated from possible perception at the time, or knowledge from the past, of the sequence of targets he is trying to know by extrasensory channels. If the targets are physical objects or events, not now being perceived by anyone else, *clairvoyance* is the term used for possible ESP. If the targets consist of another person's thoughts, *telepathy* is the term used. Most often the two possibilities are both left open; a set of symbols in a list, or on successive cards in a deck, serve as targets, but a second person is watching and concentrating on them, hoping his thoughts can be grasped through extrasensory channels. This person is for convenience called a sender or transmitter; the term is not intended to imply any theory about how ESP might work. The sender (if there is one) and the targets are in another room, sometimes in another building, carefully isolated from any possible channels of sensory communication to the subject. By prearrangement of times or by controlled signals, if necessary, the subject can make and record guesses about the successive symbols in the target list and his guesses can later be compared one by one with the entries in the target list.

The targets are often of the particular sort used by J. B. Rhine, the longtime leader of extrasensory research in the United States: a deck of 25 cards, made of five cards bearing each of five standard symbols. A subject with no source of information about which of the five symbols is on each successive card as he tries to guess it, should on the average be able to guess correctly one fifth of the time, or five times on each run through the deck of 25 cards. The question about any set of guesses is, then, does the proportion of correct guesses differ from one fifth too greatly to be explained as the product of random variation? In some protracted series with single subjects, the proportion of correct guesses reported exceeds the chance value enough so that the possibility of random origin is less than one in many thousands or even millions. The same is true of some large bodies of data obtained by pooling of guesses made by a variety of subjects.

Neither individuals nor groups are consistently found to do very well at this task. The margin of correct judgments, in most studies showing any margin, is so small that it might go unnoticed except through the application of precise techniques of statistical analysis. Yet whenever the experiments as a whole have been carefully surveyed, the judgment seems always to have been that there is very decidedly evidence of something systematic, a genuine departure from random judgments.

Must one conclude, then, that extrasensory perception is a reality? Reluctance to arrive at this conclusion has led to a great variety of alternative explanations for the departure from random results. Were statistical procedures wrongly applied? If not, and the departures from chance were genuine, could they be due entirely to scoring errors, reflecting a tendency to make errors systematically in the direction that favored ESP? Or could they be due to other kinds of errors committed by well-intentioned experimenters and well-controlled subjects? Each of these questions suggests an alternative explanation that could explain some of the positive results of earlier years and, despite improvements in ESP research, perhaps some in recent years. But they all seem to have been eliminated, either separately or together, as satisfactory explanations for the totality of positive findings.

Passionate opponents of ESP seem finally to be left with only one alternative: that positive results not explicable in other ways are due to fraud on the part of the experimenters or the subjects or both. This position was finally advanced explicitly some years ago in an article in *Science,* and seems to have remained the only alternative explanation that could not with complete confidence be rejected.

Should this alternative be accepted? Widespread practices in fortune-telling, in supposed communication with spirits, and in other claims to occult transactions, certainly show that very clever forms of deception can be devised and put into practice and that many of us are easily fooled even by deceptions that are not very clever. The circumstances under which fortune-tellers or mediums operate are very different, however, from the circumstances of experimentation on extrasensory perception. The scientific setting of the research weakens financial incentive for dishonesty at the same time that it strengthens moral and intellectual support for honesty. Incidents of fraud in the sciences, such as the hoax of Piltdown man, show that dishonesty can occur even in this setting. For my part, I am skeptical enough to guess that some of the published evidence may, indeed, be the result of fraud. But that the sum total of it could be—that so many people with scientific training working in a field whose history makes them alert to the dangers of fraud and error, could be so grievously duped or dishonest, and that enough of the subjects would be both dishonest and sufficiently motivated and skillful to deceive successfully in the face of difficulty—this I find highly implausible. So I consider it more probable that there is some real phenomenon here, although I have no preconception about what it could be.

Many other psychologists have arrived at the same conclusion, though they may well remain a minority. Why then has there been no great burst of research directed at understanding this mysterious phenomenon? The most important reason is that no method has been found for dependably demonstrating ESP, so that anyone can readily obtain for himself evidence comparable to that he can read about. Procedures that have yielded highly significant results with one subject or one group may with another subject or group, or at a later time, yield nothing significant. A great deal of time can be wasted in unproductive research, and active researchers are usually attracted to topics that they can feel confident of pursuing to an interesting outcome. Yet for most other topics of interest, I think, leads such as we have about this one would have been pursued much more thoroughly. Had extrasensory perception received its reasonable share of scientific attention we might by now have arrived either at dependable techniques for studying it, or at a justified conclusion that there is nothing here to study.

Reluctance to pursue these leads has its roots, I believe, in the fact that ESP is disturbing to most of us, since we cannot confidently assign it a general place in our view of the world. Yet the threat is not to our psychological conceptions so much as it is to our physical conceptions. For psychology itself, why should it matter how many means of access to knowledge the individual has? Many more than the original five senses have been discovered and psychology is not threatened. The difference is that for all the means of access that we call senses we have some understanding of the physical processes involved. That we can feel radiant heat on our skin or contractions of muscle within us offers no challenge to our scientific understanding of physical processes, nor to the kind of priority that we ordinarily give to the physical sciences.

The claim that ESP is a reality offers a two-pronged threat. On the one hand, it might involve stimulation of the organism by some physical process either unknown to physics or not yet understood as a potential medium for transmitting information to a human being. The threat here is of intolerable presumption. Do psychologists, participating in their ill-developed and so often maligned attempt at science, presume to discover a challenge to the most advanced and respected science? The worlds of practical affairs and of ancient myth join in prompting visions of the humiliation that might follow on this presumption. On the other hand, extrasensory communication might seem to be a phenomenon of a completely nonphysical nature. Such an idea is, of course, readily acceptable within the context of many religious traditions, but it seems almost nonsense to those whose understanding of the world has been shaped primarily through the modern European scientific tradition. The respect we psychologists, like most of our contemporaries, have for physical science and for the naturalistic tradition tends to make us feel that considering ESP a reality would be impossibly presumptuous, and to make us not really want to press the question further, for fear an attack on the very temple of science might come to be required by that part of our scientific conscience that insists on respecting facts.

Adherence to the humanistic point of view in psychology might make for a little less fear on this point. It would free us to center the study of man on what is observed about man, with physical and biological knowledge providing a helpful background rather than determining conclusions. Psychological research with a humanistic orientation would use the general approach and hold to standards of evidence that psychology shares with the other sciences; but it would insist that the substance of its conclusions be based directly on the study of man. To a humanistic psychologist, the accumulated research on ESP poses a challenge instead of a threat.

Today, as I have already indicated, a further claim can be made for a humanistic orientation. Important developments in extrasensory research itself have emerged from a humanistic approach recent investigators have made to their problems. One trouble with the classical kind of demonstration of ESP is that it so often does nothing but exhibit a puzzling phenomenon, without helping to solve the puzzle by informing us of conditions that influence the phenomenon. The older pattern of research on conditions that might influence ESP was first of all to vary physical factors, and the results were on the whole negative. That is, even where the puzzling phenomenon seems to be demonstrated it is found not to be greatly influenced by distance, by time of day, by physical surroundings, and the like. Thus the research defining the problem as a physical one has not yet led to much positive knowledge of how various factors influence ESP. The recent humanistic research seems to be producing more of that positive knowledge. Some of it confirms suggestions appearing already in the earlier research, which in general tenor was not at all antihumanistic. In his 1934 book, for instance, which introduced experimental parapsychology to the world, J. B. Rhine had stressed individual differences and the importance of the person's general state. Humanistic leads derived from the earlier research, joined in recent years with other sources of humanistic thought, have proved extremely profitable. The person who comes to ESP, as I have, with a great deal of doubt may still remain less than totally convinced that ESP is a real phenomenon. But the recent research is ever more challenging to that skepticism, because at the same time that it presents the puzzle anew it also seems to offer possible steps toward a solution of the puzzle.

Individual Differences in ESP

The classical experiments on extrasensory perception strongly suggest large individual differences. A few subjects give scores rather consistently above the chance level, occasionally remarkably far above. But most subjects seem to give scores that are close to the chance level, and some perhaps consistently below it. There has been a tendency, of course, for the few subjects who give high scores to be used at greater length than the others, and especially for them to be the subjects in experiments trying to get at the variables that influence score. After all, unless the phenomenon is present, there is no way of studying what factors influence its magnitude.

Yet in these classical studies there had been no direct utilization of the fact of individual differences itself—that is, no systematic study of what distinguishes high scorers from others. A good proportion of the work on this question has been done by a single psychologist, Gertrude Schmeidler. She began with studying the relation of individuals' ESP scores to their attitude toward ESP and collected data on this question systematically over a period of years.

Gertude Schmeidler followed the pattern of the classical experiments on clairvoyance, generally using as materials the five-symbol decks of cards popularized by Rhine's work at Duke University and asking the subject to guess which of five symbols was on each successive card of a 25-card deck. After describing to the experimental subject the procedure he was about to go through, she always proceeded by asking him how he felt about the possibility that extrasensory perception might be demonstrated through this procedure. The subjects' responses to this question were recorded and were used later to classify subjects into two groups. The rejectant subjects were those who had altogether denied the possibility that ESP could be demonstrated in the experiment—often, of course, because they considered the entire phenomenon to be impossible. The acceptant subjects were those who had expressed varying degrees of tolerance toward the possibility that the phenomenon might be demonstrated. (The names Schmeidler applied to these two categories of subjects—"sheep" and "goats"—have been generally adopted, but in a book on humanistic psychology how could I go along with the practice?)

In individual experiments Schmeidler tested a total of 151 subjects; each subject made guesses for many 25-card decks. The average score to be expected by chance was five correct guesses in a single run through a deck. In Schmeidler's whole series of individual experiments the average score of acceptant subjects was about 5.23, while the average score for rejectant subjects was 4.86. The difference is not large, yet statistical analysis shows it to be highly consistent. The probability that the difference between the two bodies of data could have arisen by random variation is six in 100,000. Another way of looking at the data, more suggestive of a phenomenon of importance than are the very small deviations of the average scores, is to ask how many subjects of each kind had average scores above and below the chance value of 5. Of the acceptant subjects, 67 exceeded the chance value and 34 fell below. Of the rejectant subjects, only 13 fell above the chance value and 26 below it. The evidence clearly indicates that tendency to score above or below chance differs between the two groups.

Schmeidler also did group experiments in psychology classes through the years. Here she had many more subjects altogether, a total of 1157, but with each subject generally making fewer guesses than in the individual experiments. The mean scores show the same kind of departure from random results—a mean of 5.10 for the acceptant subjects and a mean of 4.93 for the rejecting subjects. The departure is smaller than in the individual experiments. Yet with the larger body of data the difference between the two groups is even more significant. Here the probability of so large a difference occurring on a random basis is only three in 100,000.

In a 1958 book by Schmeidler and McConnell, in which the results of Schmeidler's various separate experiments were brought together and analyzed as a whole, the authors were also able to review several follow-up studies by other experimenters. Since these other experimenters used varying ways of determining attitude and classifying subjects, their results cannot be put together in a single body as could Schmeidler's. Despite some exceptions, however, they tend as a whole to confirm Schmeidler's finding, and to extend it by showing that it is not obtained only under the very specific conditions of Schmeidler's procedures.

In the years since, ESP score has continued to be studied in relation to attitude or belief. In a recent review, John Palmer finds the results falling into the same pattern as previously, suggesting a small but real difference in score between those who accept and those who reject the possibility of ESP. To me, Schmeidler's work remains the most persuasive, because if I have understood correctly it is the only long series of separate experiments done by a single person who is committed to reporting all the data. Here we can be especially confident we are not being misled by a tendency—very common among psychologists and probably not entirely avoided by those studying ESP—to fail (or be unable) to publish research with negative results.

Schmeidler and McConnell, in their 1958 book, also reviewed several studies that explore the more general personality characteristics to which ESP score might be related. Personality might be pertinent as an origin of the attitude toward extrasensory perception that Schmeidler and others find to be related to score. Or it might be pertinent independently of attitude. Either possibility is compatible with what Schmeidler found in studying Rorschach test performance: suggestive evidence that high scorers on ESP are generally acceptant of new experiences and are flexible rather than rigid.

Several separate studies of ESP and personality, more recently, seem in a variety of ways to confirm the general tenor of Schmeidler's suggestive results. One set of studies pertain to artistic interests and to creativity, both consistent with flexibility and a liking for novelty. Charles Honorton used two different measures of creativity, and found each positively related to ESP score. Researchers at UCLA, in two studies to be described in the next section, found ESP scores higher in artists than in nonartists. Psychological research on the personality of artists suggests, as might be expected, that artists tend to be high in creativity, so that this finding seems consonant with Honorton's.

A second kind of result pertains to flexibility in the face of stress. Martin Johnson and B. K. Kanthamani found ESP score positively related to evidence of high tolerance for stress, as measured by the lack of distortion in a person's description of threatening pictures that he is shown for a brief fraction of a second.

A third and broad set of results pertains to extraversion versus introversion. The British psychologist H. J. Eysenck has argued that many findings on personality and ESP suggest that ESP is favored by extraversion rather than introversion, since the correlates of ESP are on the whole more consistent with extraversion. Direct evidence from studies using measures of introversion-extraversion seems to support this idea. Eysenck reviews the relevant research and reports that:

> ". . . in no case where there is evidence of psi [ESP and similar phenomena] in the total record has there been found a tendency for introverts to score better than extraverts, and in practically every case examined has there been a significant or near-significant tendency for extraverts to do better than introverts."

Eysenck argues that the apparent superiority of extraverts in ESP is also consistent with some findings that in themselves have nothing to do with personality. Evidence for ESP has sometimes been found at the beginning of a session and not later, or only during the first of a series of sessions, as though the performance involved is interfered with by monotonous repetition, and favored by novelty. Extraverts, Eysenck asserts, differ from introverts in showing generally more decrement from monotony, and more benefit from novelty. The way ESP is influenced by repetition of the task, then, joins with some of the personality studies in suggesting that ESP involves an especially positive and receptive attitude toward novelty.

The research on individual differences, considered all together, shows enough uniformity to add substantially to the evidence that ESP is a real phenomenon, and also offers leads to be followed up in future research. Yet here, too, no one has yet discovered a pattern of relationship so dependable that it can be counted on to appear in every study. A humanistic approach that takes full account of individuality may in time permit the predictable demonstration which would lead to general acceptance of the reality of ESP, but it has not yet done so.

Bringing Emotion into the Experimental Study of ESP

The bulk of experimentation on extrasensory perception has followed closely the pattern of laboratory research on ordinary perception. Both the would-be transmitter and the would-be receiver of telepathic messages are sitting quietly in a laboratory or similar place, undisturbed by strong emotion and concentrating on the stimuli or on impressions that might come to mind. In real-life incidents where extrasensory perception has been claimed, the circumstances are usually quite different; the mood is more often one of passionate concern, of strongly aroused emotion.

A humanistic point of view might well suggest a different line of experimentation as perhaps more profitable in uncovering any real phenomenon that is here. If extrasensory perception exists at all, it is generally weak and uncertain. From ordinary life experience, the most frequent claim for ESP is that it tends to appear in special circumstances; perhaps ESP can be dependably demonstrated in experiments only if they duplicate some of those circumstances. This is the reasoning followed by Thelma Moss and Joseph Gengerelli in a notable recent experiment at the University of California at Los Angeles. They do not attribute their plans for the experiment to any systematic background of humanistic thought, and Gengerelli is a psychologist of long experience in the experimental research tradition. Their approach is, however, especially consistent with a humanistic point of view.

The basic innovation of Moss and Gengerelli was to use emotionally meaningful stimulus material. There were six sets of stimuli, of which five consisted of a series of projected slides with a synchronized tape recording emotionally appropriate to the slides. One set dealt with President Kennedy's assassination, a second with relaxed and serene views of ocean and water, a third with the discord and horror associated with the Nazi regime, a fourth with jazz and exposure of the body, a fifth with the gaiety of Disneyland. A sixth stimulus consisted of keeping the left foot in a bucket of ice and water for 40 seconds to produce cold, tingling, and pain. The would-be sender, at the end of each of these six experiences, was asked to describe his reactions, and his description was preserved on a tape recorder. The would-be receiver, located in another room isolated from the first, was notified each time when the sender was undergoing an experience; he was asked to describe the impressions that came to him during each period, and these, too, were recorded on tape.

The subjects were people who believed that they had telepathic ability, and usually the sender and receiver at a given session were people who were well acquainted with each other. These two conditions, like the character of the stimuli, were intended to increase resemblance to the circumstances under which extrasensory experiences are most often reported in everyday life.

The test of whether extrasensory communication appeared to be present was made by a matching procedure, undertaken separately by 12 professional psychologists and psychiatrists. For each session of the experiment —that is, one sender experiencing each of the six stimuli and one receiver reporting his impressions, the judge was given the six reports by the receiver and was asked to try to match them with the six target stimuli, as described in a written document prepared in advance by the experimenters. For half the sessions, the experimenters' description was accompanied by the sender's recorded description of his reactions.

The overall record of accuracy in matching was extremely significant statistically. The particular standard of correctness with which the authors chose to work was for a judge to match target and stimulus correctly at least two times out of the six in a given experiment. The chance probability of so good a matching is .26. Each judge dealt with 30 sessions, so that on the average he would by chance have so good an outcome $30 \times .26$, or in about eight instances out of 30. So good an outcome instead appeared, on the average, 13 times out of 30. Every one of the 12 judges exceeded the chance expectation. Two of the judges had individual records that were separately significant at the 1 percent level, and five more at the 5 percent level. More than half of the twelve judges, then, gave individually significant results, even though the body of material consisted of only 30 sessions with six stimuli each.

Compared with most of the experiments that have reported positive evidence for extrasensory perception, the level of accuracy found in this experiment is phenomenally high. It may be that a technique has been developed by which telepathic phenomena might appear in certain people with a magnitude high enough to permit effective study of how it is influenced by experimental variables.

But can we be certain? Obviously not, unless this experiment is followed up repeatedly with similar outcome. Too often, in psychology generally as well as in the study of ESP, we encounter very promising leads which then are not confirmed in further experimentation. There is, moreover, one difficulty with this experiment that makes it less convincing than might thus far appear.

The difficulty is that the experiment does not altogether exclude the possibility of deception by the subjects. If a sizable proportion of the subjects had learned the details of the experiment from earlier subjects, the results might be explained by their having used this knowledge of details to deceive the experimenters. This is unlikely on two grounds. First, the subjects were obtained from diverse sources rather than from a single course or campus, and were therefore not likely to be in contact with earlier subjects. Second, the experimenters report that nothing in a critical review of the results provided any suggestion of collusion. For example, the sender-receiver teams whose results were the best from the point of view of matching did not exhibit the greater accuracy of detail about the stimulus material that might have been expected from their having prior knowledge of the experiment.

Four follow-up experiments have now been published. In one, Moss and Gengerelli tightened their control of possible deception by subjects, and used a different set of stimuli and a different criterion of ESP. There were three pairs of potential stimuli, and only one of each pair—selected at random—was shown to the sender. The receiver was subsequently shown a sample from the two stimuli of each pair (one of nine slides about space travel shown to the sender, for example, against one of eight slides about drunkenness), and was asked to guess which was a sample of what had been shown to the sender. The experimenter who showed the slides to the receiver did not himself know the answer to this question.

For the overall average of all sender-receiver teams, there was no significant evidence of extrasensory perception. We might now be inclined to consider this line of experimentation a trail to nowhere. But two striking findings argue against that conclusion. One is that subjects who believed they had previously had ESP experiences showed highly significant evidence of it in this experiment. The other finding, already mentioned in the previous section of this chapter, is that a large difference was found between teams that included at least one artist and teams that did not include an artist. The latter were somewhat below chance expectation in their performance. The former, however, gave evidence of ESP which was highly significant statistically; 24 out of the 26 subject pairs that included an artist showed above-chance results. This experiment, then, confirms in a very different setting Schmeidler's results about attitude toward ESP, and adds impressive evidence that ESP might be especially compatible with personality characteristics artists tend to share.

Further confirmation comes in a third study, planned in advance to test the difference between artists and nonartists. Procedures were similar to those in the research just described. A large ESP effect was found in artists (largest in artists who believed in ESP), and no appreciable effect in nonartists. Testimony that the methods used in these studies are very successful in producing large effects is that highly significant results are obtained with a relatively small number of subjects; in this instance, only 73 subjects altogether took part as would-be receivers.

Another follow-up experiment, by Thelma Moss, Alice Chang, and Marc Levitt, uses a technique similar to the experiment just described. Wishing to compare ESP at various distances, however, the experimenters found it necessary to present the stimuli in a single order for all subjects, to permit simultaneous group sessions. This procedure permits common guessing sequences, if present, or social interaction within a group, to be a basis for deviation from chance in either direction. The fact that overall results again were significantly above chance can, therefore, not in itself be taken as strong evidence, as Alan Baron and Thomas G. Stampfl have pointed out in a critical note on this study. The qualitative evidence, though, suggests that ESP was involved; as in the previous experiments of the series, some of the receivers' written impressions show striking resemblance to the material witnessed by the senders and to the senders' accounts of their experience. The fifth UCLA experiment, which shows very large effects arguing for ESP, I will describe in the following section, to which it has a special relevance.

The five experiments thus far reported by this group of psychologists at UCLA suggest, then, that ESP may be a reproducible phenomenon if we introduce into the experimentation some of the emotional intensity frequently appearing in spontaneous ESP reports. By bringing this aspect of a humanistic approach into ESP experimentation, these psychologists appear to have identified an important aspect of the conditions on which the ESP phenomenon depends. If this identification is confirmed in the subsequent experimentation that is sure to follow, we may have taken an important step toward understanding the ESP phenomenon.

This inference is strengthened by the outcome of two other types of experiment that have been done elsewhere in the last several years, independently of the UCLA experiments and in a manner somewhat closer to the classical ESP experiments.

One line of research grows out of experimenting with the type of target, testing whether evidence of ESP appears more often with one type of target than another. Some of these experiments find that evidence of ESP varies according to whether the targets are emotionally charged. In one instance, a set of personally significant names, chosen by the individual subject, were compared with standard ESP cards as targets. In another, the comparison was between the standard cards and erotic stimuli. A simple effect on ESP has not been found in all the experiments. Sometimes the effect interacts with personality characteristics that might influence openness to emotional stimulation. On the whole, these experiments are sufficiently variable in outcome, and small in scale, that I feel they would not in themselves carry strong conviction. But their general congruence with the more striking experiments I have described, in indicating that emotional significance of the target is an important variable, adds to their importance.

The other line of research relevant to this point is concerned with the mood of the subject at the time that he participates in an ESP experiment. Gertrude Schmeidler has recently asked subjects to rate their mood during an ESP experiment on a mood adjective list that two psychologists, Vincent and Helen Nowlis, had previously assembled and used in studying drug effects on mood. She has found ESP significantly related to mood, but not in a constant way. The effect seems to vary with other circumstances—perhaps with personality and group atmosphere, for instance. These studies provide additional evidence that ESP is a real phenomenon, in showing that ESP scores are consistently related within a given setting to variables that can be measured, and that they include variables of emotion.

The same point can be made about a specific piece of research where mood may be involved, though not directly measured. With the consent of three patients in psychotherapy, John Hudesman and Gertrude Schmeidler explored how ESP scores might vary with the state of mind that is associated with relative success of therapeutic hours. At the end of each day's therapy session, a brief ESP trial was conducted, with emotionally neutral targets (clock faces, with the position of the single hand to be guessed). The 25 percent of sessions judged most successful as therapy were followed by guesses that gave overall evidence of ESP, while the other 75 percent of sessions were not.

ESP and Dreaming

In that portion of every person's daily life spent in dreaming, he fantasies a great deal that seems important emotionally. Observing the apparent relation between emotionality of context and evidence of ESP, then, we might guess that dreams provide a special opportunity for studying ESP. There have, indeed, been many specific claims of telepathic influence on dreams. Some appear in reports from clinicians who are impressed by the apparent intrusion into a patient's dreams of thoughts strikingly similar to incidents in the therapist's current life of which the patient could have no knowledge by ordinary means. Other clinicians have been impressed by other evidence patients have offered for ESP in dreams. Sigmund Freud seems to have been in this latter group, though with considerable conflict. In 1922 he delivered a paper on dreams and telepathy. He began by telling the audience they would not learn whether he believed in telepathy, and he ended by saying he had no opinion. Yet in between he spoke of "the incontestable fact that sleep creates favourable conditions for telepathy." Other reports appear in a variety of laymen's accounts. L. E. Rhine compiled information about more than 7000 accounts of ESP and similar experiences outside the laboratory, and 65 percent were found to be of dream experiences. Analysis of these cases shows, moreover, that reception of full information about the target is much more often claimed for dreams than for waking experiences.

The discovery a few years ago that dreaming is accompanied by specific patterns of eye movement and brain wave permits the experimental test of this as of so many other problems related to dreaming. It is now possible for an experimental subject to sleep in a dream laboratory while records are being continuously made of his eye movements and brain waves. An experimenter watching the records as they are produced can tell when the subject is dreaming and can awaken him well along in each period of dreaming and obtain an immediate report of the dream. Thus dreams and the time of their occurrence can be much more fully and accurately known than was possible before.

The modern dream laboratory has been used by a group of researchers at the Maimonides Hospital in Brooklyn for studying telepathy. Their intial report—published in 1966 by Montague Ullman, Stanley Krippner, and Sol Feldstein—describes a preliminary experiment with 12 subjects, conducted as a screening device in the hope of locating an especially good subject, and a follow-up experiment with the most promising subject found. In the preliminary study, the 12 subjects each took part for a single night. Twelve reproductions of paintings were used as the target material, only one for each subject. The would-be sender, thoroughly isolated from the dreamer, devoted several 30-minute periods during the night to looking at the target picture which had been selected at random for that night, and to writing down the thoughts it suggested to him. An experimenter monitored the brain waves of the subject and asked for a dream report well into each of the dream episodes. At the end of the night's sleep the subject was asked for elaboration of the dreams and for his impressions of the experiment; he was also shown the 12 pictures and was asked to rank them in order of degree of correspondence with his dreams.

The test of ESP included a test of whether the dream reports, and the dreamer's accompanying impressions and associations, could be successfully matched with the pictures. That is, a judge was given the 12 protocols and the 12 pictures and tried to match them up (also making some more detailed judgments). The outcome was inconclusive in that the matching was done with significant accuracy according to some statistical techniques that could be applied and fell short of significant accuracy according to other techniques that might have been thought at least equally appropriate. The rankings by the subjects themselves gave just barely significant results.

Two research assistants had served as would-be senders in this experiment, each for half of the sessions. There was a statistically significant difference between the accuracy of matching obtained for sessions with the two assistants. The one for whom there was the greater evidence of success was therefore chosen as the agent for the individual experiment to follow. It was conducted with the one subject whose dreams had shown the most striking similarity to the target picture.

The individual experiment was planned for 12 nights, one in each of 12 successive weeks, but it was terminated after seven weeks because the subject became ill. Judges who tried to match the seven sets of dream protocols with the pictures on which the sender concentrated during the particular night did so with a highly significant degree of accuracy. The authors present excerpts from some of the dreams. The content of the pictures never appears very fully, yet the correspondence of some elements is very striking. On the night when Dali's "Last Supper" was the picture on which the sender concentrated, for instance, the subject's dreams included references to the ocean, a chair, a table, and a glass of wine as well as to a group of people of whom one was not good. On a night when a Degas painting of a ballet class was the target, on the other hand, the dreams included reference to a large house with high ceilings (corresponding to the physical setting of the Degas painting), to a class with a woman instructor in which "at different times, different people would get up for some sort of recitation or some sort of contribution," and to "one little girl that was trying to dance with me." The dream material is not published in full, but I think anyone familiar with dream protocols will feel that the extracts presented argue strongly for a correspondence very impressive in detail.

The same carefully selected persons who had served as sender and receiver in this experiment took part in another similar experiment two years later. Eight sessions were carried out and yielded the number of dreams that had been set in advance as a minimum. Several changes were made in procedure. Some were designed to render any normal communication between sender and receiver even more improbable. Others were designed to heighten the emotional meaning and actuality of the target; the sender was awakened whenever the physiological monitoring of the receiver indicated that he was beginning to dream; thus the sender could think about the target picture throughout each dream. The sender had instructions, too, for acting out some of the ideas expressed in the picture.

The outcome of this second individual experiment was even more impressive than that of the first. Three judges rated the materials. A judge looked separately at each of the 64 combinations of target material and subject's response (a typed copy of all his dreams for the night and of an interview at the end of the night, including the subject's guess as to what the target might have been). The judge rated each of the 64 combinations for the degree of correspondence between target and response. For six of the eight nights, the average rating for correspondence to the true target was higher than that for any of the seven other targets. For the remaining two nights, the true target ranked second or third out of the eight targets.

Here, then, an approximate repetition of the first startling study led to an even more startling confirmation. With a different subject, selected on grounds of successful participation in a similar study conducted elsewhere by other researchers, Krippner and Ullman did a third individual experiment. It, too, produced extremely impressive evidence that the target material—paintings, as before—influenced the content of the subject's dreams. The evidence was again very strong both by statistical analysis and by common-sense consideration of qualitative correspondence between picture and dream.

A great advantage of this series of studies is one that they share with

Schmeidler's attitude research; they were conducted as a single program by a single team of researchers who have reported all their experiments, not just those yielding significant positive results. Up to the time of the most recent summary they have published, two group experiments and two individual experiments, comparable to the one group and three individual experiments I have already described, apparently failed to yield any statistically significant results. The experiments with significant results were not, then, rarities; they constituted half of the experiments done. Even the experiments lacking in statistically significant results, moreover, provided some impressive qualitative findings, a number of very striking similarities between dream and target.

In these experiments in the dream laboratory, the researchers several times noted striking similarities between dream content and a future event, suggesting the phenomenon that has been called *precognition.* This is the kind of ESP my grandfather thought was responsible for his getting off a train which soon after had a serious accident. Evidence of precognition may be considered threatening to humanistic thought in particular, for it suggests complete determinism, in seeming to imply that the future somehow exists now to be perceived. The Maimonides researchers have responded by developing, more fully than have most ESP researchers, ideas about the processes that might underlie ESP. They seek to reconcile a person's foreknowledge of what is probable with genuine pliability in the actual working out of events.

Their fortuitous observations of possible instances of precognition have led these researchers recently to a unique experiment. They used as the subject a person who had often reported spontaneous precognitions. On each of eight nights in the dream laboratory, his dreams were recorded. In the morning, a theme was randomly selected, around which an experimenter (who had spent the night in isolation) constructed a multisensory experience. After he had written a description of the planned experience, he then met with the subject and led him through the experience. The subject's dreams for various nights were systematically rated for correspondence with the descriptions of the various morning experiences. The dreams showed remarkable correspondence with the experience of the following morning rather than that of later or earlier mornings. The evidence, both on statistical and on qualitative grounds, seems to be about as strong as for the earlier individual experiments on telepathic influences on dreams. For those who, like me, find precognition especially implausible, it is comforting to note that telepathy or clairvoyance, as the authors point out, might indirectly explain the results of this particular experiment. For example, the experimenter planning the details of the morning experience might conceivably have been influenced by telepathic awareness of the subject's dreams. An elimination of telepathy and clairvoyance as possible explanations requires very complicated controls, which were not considered essential to introduce in this first experiment. It stands, meanwhile, as one more impressive reason to believe that the dream laboratory may prove to be the locus in which ESP may be consistently demonstrated in subjects who are appropriately selected in advance.

ESP and Other Alterations of Consciousness

In speaking of dreams, I have cited their frequent emotionality as a reason for considering ESP in relation to them, since ESP in ordinary life is often said to occur in events of great emotional meaning. The same general reasoning—that ESP should be sought in circumstances similar to those in which its occurrence in ordinary life is claimed—provides another justification for considering ESP in dreams, and it is a justification that also suggests additional possibilities. Dreaming is an altered state of consciousness, and ESP has been asserted to occur not only in dreams but also in other altered states. The term, "altered states of consciousness," has only recently come into general use, but descriptions antedating the term often make its relevance clear. A good instance is provided by Mary Craig Sinclair's account of her experience as an extrasensory perceiver, and by the advice she offers to other would-be perceivers. People who meditate, and those who have read modern research on meditation, will find that both the state she describes and her techniques for inducing it sound familiar. The American psychologist, Richard Alpert, who has now adopted the name Baba Ram Dass, describes remarkable evidence of telepathy and clairvoyance in an Indian guru, presumably associated with his long and effective use of meditative techniques. Similar accounts have often been given in the past; certain alterations of consciousness are claimed to be accompanied by a great expansion of ESP.

Can experimental study of ESP, then, be favored by inducing meditative states of consciousness or, perhaps, the somewhat similar hypnotic state? Hypnosis was, I think, the first technique to be widely used in research on this question. Two summaries of the work done thus far have been published recently, and both conclude that the evidence tends to confirm this hunch. R. L. Van De Castle, the author of one of these summaries, brings together the quantitative results of all experiments in which the same subjects were tested both in a normal state and while hypnotized. In the normal state, their total performance showed no significant departure from random guessing. Their performance while hypnotized exceeded the random level with great consistency, although the average difference was not large. The average score of the hypnotized subjects, working with the five-symbol deck of 25 cards, was about 5 5 correct guesses out of 25, instead of the 5.0 average expected by chance.

A much higher level of accuracy, with the aid of hypnosis, is suggested in an experiment by Thelma Moss and her co-workers at UCLA, with her technique of emotion-laden targets that I have described previously. The experiment was laborious, and only three of the hypnosis teams persisted through all of the six sessions planned. For the 75 guesses made by these teams, of which 50 percent correct would be the chance value, 76 percent were correct. My astonishment at the performance here is but slightly tempered through recognizing a bias whose influence cannot be precisely measured; subjects were told their ESP score after each session, and high scores in early sessions were doubtless an influence motivating certain teams to persist.

In an experiment published more recently, posthypnotic suggestion was used in an effort to heighten ESP; the hypnotized subject was told that after awakening he would be especially sensitive. The experimenters (William McBain and several collaborators at the University of Hawaii), while using rather simple symbols as the target material, chose symbols somewhat more significant emotionally than those traditional in ESP study. They selected symbols for each team of sender and receiver, and matched the two people, so as to use for each team symbols of dependable emotional meaning. They did not experiment on the efficacy of any of these devices, nor did they compare performance under posthypnotic suggestion with performance in its absence. Using all these devices together, however, they arrived at one more instance of significant departure from random guessing.

A beginning has been made in exploring ESP in states of meditation. Karlis Osis and Edwin Bokert obtained the cooperation of a number of experienced meditators, willing to come to weekly sessions, each time rating the subjective qualities of their meditative experience, and participating in ESP trials. The research was, as the authors say, designed to produce leads rather than to test definite ideas formulated in advance, and its outcome does, indeed, leave us in complete uncertainty. We may expect, though, that the exploration will be continued in the coming years.

Hindu tradition claims meditative states induce or favor ESP. In this period when meditative practices and scientific skills are often united in the same person, this claim will surely be widely studied. This expectation is strengthened by the burst of recent research on ESP utilizing the minor alterations of consciousness produced by brief training in self-control of brain waves. A few years ago the psychologist Joseph Kamiya discovered that many people could achieve deliberate control of their alpha waves, the brain waves characteristic of states of relaxed alertness, by arranging a machine to monitor their brain waves and sound a buzzer whenever alpha waves were present. This device has now been used by several researchers in studying ESP. There seems to be no simple relation between alpha waves and ESP. But statistically significant relations of varying sorts have appeared in several studies. Such variations in consciousness as are indicated by presence or absence of alpha waves seem, from these studies, to be important for ESP, but in a complicated interaction with personality, nature of the particular task, and other specific variables. If, as seems quite probable, there is some real relation here, it is going to be ascertained and better understood only if the very best skills of scientific research continue to be applied to its study.

Recent research on ESP, we have seen, has been influenced by a number of procedures inspired by a humanistic approach: the separate consideration of subjects differing in personality or in attitude toward ESP, the use of emotion-laden targets, the consideration of the subject's mood, the inclusion of dreams among the responses analyzed for evidence of ESP, the modification of relevant attitudes through hypnosis, and the testing for ESP as states of consciousness are altered. All of these may contribute to developing dependable ways of obtaining ESP effects so that we can learn more about what is occurring, and the research already done with these variations is an important source of ideas about what may be occurring.

Yet an even more consistently humanistic approach may be needed. As Gertrude Schmeidler points out, we may need to give special attention to circumstances not yet made the subject of study, and to use them in developing new methods of study. One ESP researcher who often gets positive results, she reports, is distinguished for his amiable personality and for the cooperative spirit with which co-workers and subjects respond to him; she suggests that this may be a factor at least as important as any of the others in influencing whether ESP occurs. Dependable ESP effects, perhaps, will be obtained only when the experiments are planned with the full consideration of the personality of each participant, and are carried out in a context of warm personal relations. Yet the possibility of error or fraud must be meticulously guarded against, or the research will be of no definite value. Progress here, it seems, must depend on a real fusion of the humanistic orientation and the research tradition; neither alone is adequate.

Patient (to whom the therapist has just offered a cigarette). It proves that a scientist is one who offers a smoke to another one.

Therapist. If he is also human, maybe—maybe courteous—maybe —call it what you like. You wanted to know whether I was kind or not.

Patient. Are those who say 'go to bed' kind? When it's made out of a locomotive? No—never ever. (pause) The Alaskan railroad was bothered.

9

Schizophrenia

This interchange between patient and therapist is cited by Paul Watzlawick to illustrate schizophrenic communication. It is easy to suppose that a person who speaks so unreasonably as this patient is afflicted with illness —a mental illness—and that the label of *schizophrenic* applied to him refers to a specific disease process analogous to those responsible for mumps or diabetes.

About half the patients in American hospitals are called schizophrenic. This label, by far the most frequently applied of all labels for "mental illness," covers a variety of conditions. A recent book on schizophrenias by the psychiatrist C. P. Rosenbaum considers their description by Bleuler in 1911 to be still the best. The symptoms of schizophrenia are there classified into fundamental and accessory. The fundamental symptoms include changes in certain simple functions—defects in association of ideas, alterations of emotion, difficulty in dealing with contradictory feelings—accompanied by maintenance of generally normal sensation, memory, consciousness, and command over bodily movement. The fundamental symptoms also include changes in "compound mental functions," such as excessive attention to inner mental life, defects of attention and will, and confusions of identity. The acccessory symptoms include hallucinations, delusions, and a variety of postural and other muscular symptoms.

What holds this diversity of symptoms together as a single concept, and sets it off from other forms of "mental illness" ? Bleuler's answer to this question is also his justification for the label *schizophrenia,* which implies some sort of mental split. The various symptoms of a schizophrenic, he says, appear in a way that indicates various functions are split off from one another, the normal integrity of the person being disrupted. According to a passage Rosenbaum quotes from Bleuler, "The psychic complexes do not combine in a conglomeration of strivings with a unified resultant as they do in a healthy person; rather, one set of complexes dominates the personality for a time, while other groups of ideas or drives are 'split off' and seem either partly or completely impotent."

The concept of schizophrenia is now familiar to many, many people who have never heard of Bleuler, and we easily forget that like the airplane it is an invention of the twentieth century. The substantial and distinct meaning it is sometimes given suggests it must point to a condition of frequent occurrence in all societies. We may well be surprised, then, that schizophrenia has not been recognized throughout human history as a definite type of illness. If this fact leads to questioning the specificity of schizophrenia, to doubting whether it points to a single identifiable disease process, other considerations may readily strengthen the doubt.

Some names of categories of "mental illness," such as alcoholic psychosis or syphilitic psychosis, usefully direct attention at a specific factor important in the origin of the condition and essential to consider if the illness is to be cured or arrested. Nothing comparable can be said in defense of the category of schizophrenia. Attempts to characterize what all schizophrenic conditions have in common are so broad and general, overlapping at so many points with characteristics of other conditions, that the isolation of any single and discrete underlying factor seems improbable. The concept seems rather to point to a variety of conditions whose specific characteristics are highly diverse yet overlapping; like *art* or *psychology, schizophrenia* is a term whose boundaries of application are vague and shifting yet clearly include an area usefully distinguished from conditions far outside the boundary.

The concept is sometimes used, however, as though it were a clear and simple unity with definite implications for understanding and for practice. Laymen, at least, are likely to infer from the diagnosis of schizophrenia that a person's abnormalities are all caused by a specific disease process, akin to an infection. They may think that recognition of the presence of schizophrenia has dictated the choice of a drug or of a shock treatment as a therapeutic procedure, or the decision that the patient was probably incurable. Psychiatrists and psychologists dealing with patients have doubtless never gone so far as laymen in ascribing the schizophrenic patient's disturbance to the compelling influence on him of a specific disease process. Yet they may not be able to escape all influence of such oversimplified thinking, and may at times join the laymen in thinking of schizophrenics as a qualitatively distinct kind of being.

The simple disease model of schizophrenia is most likely to be encountered today in discussions that emphasize genetic origins or biochemical correlates. Facts established by research on innate predisposition toward schizophrenic patterns, and on biochemical accompaniments, might conceivably justify in the future a specific disease model for schizophrenia. Even in that event, it seems most improbable that either or both of these biological approaches could so totally explain all aspects of schizophrenia that a psychological approach would no longer be pertinent. I do not wish to get into the issue of biological *versus* psychological or social factors, except to say that I consider it a pseudo-issue; both kinds of factor seem likely to be crucial. Integrating them eventually into the best possible understanding of schizophrenia seems more important than judging their relative importance, and I think a humanistic approach will be useful in achieving that integration. For now, my objective is the more modest one permitted by what has been achieved thus far: the consideration of humanistic contributions to the psychological side of understanding schizophrenia.

What elements in a humanistic approach might be expected to have an impact? One is the emphasis on experience as well as behavior. When we consider only overt behavior we can find at least one thing common to everything called mental illness—some serious lack of fit to the demands of normal social life. It is always tempting, then, to adopt the term "mental illness" and such subdivisions as "schizophrenia," and to exaggerate their usefulness. Against this temptation, descriptions by former patients of what it was like to be "mentally ill" and hospitalized, supply a useful corrective, in exhibiting the common humanity and the individuality maintained throughout in the inner view. But, generally, mental health practitioners have not been inclined to disregard the patient's point of view; a purely behavioral approach to mental illness is rare. So this element in the humanistic approach does not promise as much novelty for the professional as it does for the layman.

Another element I have stressed in the humanistic approach—attention to free choice—promises more novelty here. Let's take the patient to be basically like the rest of us—that is, a person exercising his freedom of choice among alternatives that he sees open to him. No longer, then, can we feel the patient's actions are senseless because he is driven to them by an inexorable disease process. We must ask instead: What is the situation of the patient, that he chooses alternatives that seem so senseless to us? Some early accounts of schizophrenic patients implied this question, and are similar to accounts written by humanistic psychologists and psychiatrists today. The novelty of the humanistic approach seems to lie in the consistency and strength with which the question is urged. Humanistic writers seek to push as far as possible the view that the schizophrenic is an ordinary person in a special situation; they firmly renounce the easier course of regarding him as a special kind of person controlled by a specific disease process.

In the interchange between patient and therapist at the outset of this chapter, the therapist was taking a humanistic point of view (as most therapists presumably always have, whatever their theoretical orientation). His response to the patient's first statement indicates that he understood that statement to be a challenge and inquiry about the therapist's kindliness. His knowledge of the patient also gave him some insight into the patient's second and more mystifying statement: "Are those who say 'go to bed' kind? When it's made out of a locomotive? No—never ever. The Alaskan railroad was bothered." The therapist understood this to have substantially the following meaning: "You're a hospital employee and the hospital says 'go to bed' and treats me like a child for crazy reasons and the whole system works impersonally, inevitably, and coldly. And then the hospital acts like my mother and complains of being bothered if I don't think it's kind of her to say 'go to bed.' " Watzlawick continues, in the recorded lecture in which this interchange is included, with some further passages; their sequence strongly suggests that the therapist was correct in his understanding of these first passages. Along with many other recent writers on schizophrenia, he seems confident that, in general, schizophrenics' statements can be understood.

Why Does a Person Become Schizophrenic?

Extracting some meaning from a schizophrenic's acts and statements is but a first step. The expression of meaning by such wild indirection, almost certain not to be understood, may seem as diseased as does a complete lack of meaning, unless the schizophrenic can be further shown to be in a situation that especially favors inadequate communication.

The humanistic approach leads directly, then, from trying to understand the patient's utterance toward trying to understand the situation out of which it grows.

A group of researchers and clinicians in California—including Gregory Bateson, Jay Haley, Don D. Jackson, Paul Watzlawick, and John Weakland—have sought to understand schizophrenia as an outgrowth of peculiarities of communication within the family. Interacting with the rest of his family, a child may develop responses that are understandable in that context. When he carries these responses over into communication with other people, the context of origin goes unnoticed and the schizophrenic may seem to be acting unreasonably, even when the current meaning of his action is understood.

The peculiarity of communication particularly stressed in this account of schizophrenia pertains to what this California group have termed the "double bind." In a double bind there are three elements: (1) The person is told he must perform (or refrain from) some act, on threat of severe punishment. (2) An opposite command is stated or implied, at or about the same time, and again on threat of severe punishment. (3) Circumstances are such that the person cannot resolve this conflict by just escaping. Bateson and his collaborators provide examples, which other writers have in turn cited so often that there is more value in providing an example from elsewhere. The ease of doing so helps confirm the usefulness of the concept. In a study of schizophrenia and the family which I will mention again a bit later, the authors tell about a girl they call Nancy; as Nancy entered adolescence, her mother

> ". . . had continued to be distrustful and extremely intrusive, wanting to know exactly what Nancy did whenever she was away from home. Nancy began to fight back, and unable to retain some privacy by maintaining silence, because her mother would nag and insist that she tell, she learned to talk but reveal nothing. She purposely became vague and confusing. . . ."

Nancy could not escape her mother; her mother clearly threatened her for silence and, the context suggests, would also have criticized much of the truth had Nancy revealed it. Nancy's resolution of the conflict, gaining some reduction of maternal attack, was one that could be a preliminary sketch for a schizophrenic type of withdrawal.

The double bind is an example, then, of the elementary conflicts that psychologists have recognized, classified, and tried to study in the laboratory. The laboratory research on conflict does not, however, have much direct relevance for this account of the origins of schizophrenia, since the laboratory research has studied the immediate effect of a single conflict, all of whose elements are readily apparent to the person studied. Bateson and his collaborators, on the other hand, very clearly do not in any way hold that schizophrenic tendency can be produced by any one instance of conflict, no matter how severe; and they think that the obscurity of the conflicts to which some children are subjected has something to do with the impact of repeated conflicts. They do not regard one double bind as itself producing schizophrenia. Something more is required—what they call the double-bind situation.

The additional elements they stress in the double-bind situation are several, although for some elements I am making explicit what is only implicit in the original account by the California group:

1. The double-bind pattern is recurrent, even dependable, in the behavior of at least one parent toward the child. It is no accident of momentary circumstances, but a product of the parent's character and the significance of this particular child in the parent's life. It is an outgrowth of conflict in the parent about his relation to this particular child; neither

parent nor child can easily change himself in ways that will terminate the conflict.

2. The severe punishments involved in the recurrent double binds are often very subtle: comments or gestures suggesting that the child is unworthy, for example, or that some greatly desired reward, such as a parent's warm approval, might be withheld.

3. The parent's contradictory communications are often expressed in utterly different ways: one by an explicit statement, the other by a facial expression or slight bodily movement. This discourages the child from bringing them together for rational consideration (if any is possible), and the parent may further this discouragement by denying either or both communications in the language of the other. He may in loving words deny that he intended any gesture of threat or withdrawal, and at the same time in overt action belie the reassertion of affection or admiration.

4. Because of the dependable recurrence of double binds, the child may come to infer them even when the parent is not at the moment actually supplying all the relevant cues. The child generalizes from previous experience with the parent, perhaps correctly anticipating what the parent is likely to be doing in a few minutes. Eventually, indeed, the child's understanding of the world, even the world of his imagination, may be one of recurrent double bind. Watzlawick describes a case in which the imaginary voices heard by a schizophrenic reinstate a double bind such as his parents had repeatedly subjected him to.

There might be diverse views about why a double-bind pattern should tend to result in schizophrenia. The original theory of Bateson et al. dealt with intellectual functioning; a double-bind situation produces an inability to discriminate modes of communication—for example, to distinguish metaphor, literal statement, play, fantasy, sacrament, and the like. A person who cannot make such discriminations cannot adequately understand communications from other people, nor the communications he addresses to others, nor indeed his own private experiences. The theory does hold to something like a disease process, then, and tries to identify its exact nature. Members of this California group—especially Haley—in other articles incorporate the double-bind pattern into a more humanistic view of the schizophrenic as less sharply deviant from other people than this original theory suggested.

Humanistic from the beginning was a research project begun in Connecticut at about the same time as the California study of schizophrenic communication. Intensive clinical research by Theodore Lidz, Stephen Fleck, and Alice Cornelison concentrated on a small number of cases and made systematic comparisons among them. The patients selected for study each had at least one nonhospitalized sibling whose life experience could be compared with that of the patient.

The very intensive study of these patients and their siblings led to a series of papers that focus first on one, then on another, aspect of behavior and experience and of the family background in which it developed. This research identifies, as a major influence on schizophrenia, parent-child relations basically similar to those pointed to by the California studies, but it gives a more detailed picture of their variation from one family to another. The authors draw their theory from Freudian ego psychology. The humanistic character of their interpretation is well indicated by their statement that schizophrenia "instead of being a *process* that has inserted itself into a person and possessed him, depriving him of reason, is rather one of the potential fates to which man is subject in his efforts to find a way of life as an independent person amid the many potential hazards that beset his path from infancy to maturity."

The most widely read of scholarly writers on schizophrenia must be the British psychiatrist Ronald D. Laing. He commands a large audience through combining his insightful accounts of patients with full consideration of parallel problems shared by all mankind, and through expressing his ideas felicitously and inventively. His general account of schizophrenia comes out of the British tradition in psychoanalysis, which readily lends itself to the existentialist emphasis Laing gives it. Like other existentialist writers in psychology, Laing is clearly humanistic in the broad sense in which I am using that term. Laing's account stresses the schizophrenic's feeling of not being understood and of not understanding himself, the divorce between his self and his body, and his lack of a firm sense of power to initiate action. Laing sees these as outgrowths of the special relation the future schizophrenic has developed in childhood, and has continued to maintain, with the rest of his family.

Among Laing's varied writings on schizophrenia, one written in collaboration with a fellow psychiatrist Aaron Esterson, *Sanity, madness, and the family*, is especially pertinent here because like the work of Lidz, Fleck, and Cornelison it is based on procedures approaching the hypothesis-testing research whose value to humanistic interests I wish to show. Laing and Esterson studied intensively about a dozen schizophrenic women and their families through repeated interviews with individual family members and various groups of family members. In describing these interviews and presenting excerpts, they persuasively argue that schizophrenic behavior appears in these patients as a somewhat sensible response to an extremely difficult situation; a double-bind situation in the child's communication with his parents seems to be part of the difficulty, but probably only a part.

These various studies of why people become schizophrenic—and there are others, too, somewhat similar in approach and outcome—all follow a single general pattern: an intensive study of individual cases, followed by thoughtful attempts to summarize, interpret, and integrate what can be most reasonably inferred from them separately and together. In comparison with other modes of research, this approach facilitates fuller understanding of the individual persons studied. This very desirable aim is reached, however, at some expense in objectivity—that is, in the confidence any one study may justifiably give us that other investigators, given the same problem to study by similar methods, would have emerged with similar conclusions. Confidence in the conclusions is, of course, strengthened by the general agreement among these studies. But comparison is not possible on every important detail, and even the major agreement could be challenged by a skeptical critic, who could argue that it may result from the common preconceptions of the researchers more than from objective similarities among their patients.

Despite the great value of this clinical research, then, we need to consider whether a humanistic approach is also supported by more objective research—research that may forego fullness of understanding of the individual person and may concentrate on obtaining highly dependable evidence about limited issues. The origins of schizophrenia do not lend themselves readily to such clean-cut patterns of research. Implicating as they do the whole life history of the person, through years of time and at levels of functioning all the way from genetic transmission of predisposing factors to social interaction with parents and siblings, separate bits of cause-effect relations are not easily abstracted for an objective test. In the face of such difficulties, though, some progress has already been made toward the rather rigorous and objective test of ideas suggested by the clinical research.

One approach here has been to concentrate on the patient's family during his convalescence, when their interaction with the patient is accessible to direct observation. Frances Cheek is one researcher who has used this approach, systematically observing and objectively analyzing the interaction of convalescent patients with their parents, and applying the same procedures to study the interaction of control subjects, nonpatients, with their parents. Contrasts found between the patients and nonpatients in their parental interaction are for the most part consistent with expectations from the earlier clinical research, and provide an objective confirmation of the general thesis that family interaction is significant in the development of schizophrenia. Some findings that are surprising may point to refinements of this thesis, supplying details that will make it more useful, but this single study is not enough to establish any details firmly.

Another approach to checking the clinical research and the humanistic model through more objective procedures is to derive from them some predictions about differences between patients and nonpatients in themselves, rather than in their interaction with parents. The English psychologists Donald Bannister and Phillida Salmon have applied this approach in studying conceptual structure—that is, the patterns of similarity and dissimilarity among various related concepts in one person's mind. A disease concept of schizophrenia might suggest that all sorts of conceptual structures would be equally disrupted by the illness. The clinical research, viewing schizophrenia as an adaptation to aberrant family relationships, suggests that the patient's concepts about people should be more disrupted than his concepts about material objects. Bannister measured stability versus disruption in two ways: by the similarity in patterning of thought when similar concepts are considered on a single occasion, and by the similarity in patterning of thought when a single concept is considered on two different occasions. On both measures, when schizophrenic patients were compared with a nonpatient control group, the schizophrenics did, as predicted, show more disruption in thinking about people than in thinking about things.

These various studies seem to me to offer more promising leads to future knowledge than most of what I have read before in the vast body of quantitative research on schizophrenia. These few studies, obviously, are not yet enough to establish firmly the special value of a humanistic understanding of the origins of schizophrenia. They do not, however, stand alone. During these same recent years a rather larger body of systematic research, also prompted by a humanistic model, has been done on the meaning to schizophrenics of their hospitalization and of their performance on psychological tests. I consider this research now, returning at the end to more general problems about schizophrenia.

Are Hospitalized Schizophrenics Choosing Their Mode of Life?

A humanistic point of view suggests that a schizophrenic patient is making choices about how he wants to live. This notion may be applied even to a wish to enter or to remain in the hospital; I will later mention research pertinent to that point. Here let us just assume the patient's presence in the hospital. What does he do there? Is he a helpless pawn in a struggle between disease process within him and forces of authority and guidance without? or is he to a considerable extent in command of the situation, deliberately choosing for his advantage among the possibilities afforded by his rather limited environment?

Here the way to understanding has been led by the study of the institution as a social system. The sociologist Erving Goffman has been especially influential through his penetrating comparisons of life within a mental hospital, life within other institutions, and life in the normal community. His analysis is based on a universal model of man, rejecting the assumption that initial and basic differences between mental patients, prisoners, and ordinary community members are the decisive source of differences among the three settings—hospital, prison, and community—in the behavior typically exhibited there. Here another research tradition, that of anthropological and sociological field study, supports the findings of clinical research in arguing for a humanistic approach.

On the appropriateness of a humanistic model for understanding the hospital patient's general behavior, I think the evidence provided by these field studies is of prime importance. I want to show, though, that research growing out of the quantitative traditions of systematic psychological research also offers pertinent support. A study by four psychologists—Benjamin Braginsky, Jules Holzberg, Dennis Ridley, and Dorothea Braginsky—serves as a simple but effective demonstration.

One implication of the humanistic point of view is that life in the hospital should be essentially continuous with the patient's life outside the hospital. Though a hospitalized patient is in a special environment, we should not expect his adjustment to it to be identical with that of other patients, and we should expect it to resemble his own adjustment to other environments. We should expect to find a variety of ways of living in the hospital, corresponding to the variety of ways of living outside, and to find that each person might tend to exhibit some continuity in the way of life he chooses. This is the possibility explored by Braginsky, Holzberg, Ridley, and Braginsky in a study of open-ward patients, who have wide freedom of choice in where they spend most of their waking hours. Interviewing patients about how they spent their time, they were able to classify them roughly in three groups: (1) workers, who spent substantial time in employment for which they could volunteer within the hospital; (2) mobile socializers, who spent substantial time in social activity away from the ward in which they lived; (3) warders, who tended to remain in their ward. A patient's choice of one or another of these ways of life was related to similar choices he had made before entering the hospital. The amount of time spent on the ward was highly correlated with the patient's report of the amount of time he spent at home on a typical weekend before hospitalization. It showed little correlation with the amount of time he reported spending at home on a typical weekday. The way of life in the hospital seems to continue the pattern of life at home on leisure days, not on working days.

Among the open-ward patients, who could be studied in this way, their choice among adjustments to the hospital situation was not related to severity of illness ("degree of psychopathology" as judged by the psychiatrist in charge of each patient). Patients who stayed on the ward did not do so because they were too sick to venture out; they did so by their own choice. Mental patients, the authors of the study conclude, are like other people in "utilizing their environment to their satisfaction."

This finding could be greatly surprising only to a person who believed the grip of mental illness to be altogether and always overwhelming. Psychologists proceeding from the humanistic point of view have devised ways to test a number of other implications of their view of patients as reasonable people, and I think some of the other findings that have resulted are less expected, as we will see.

Why Are Some Hospital Patients Inconspicuous?

In a Connecticut hospital where Benjamin and Dorothea Braginsky and Kenneth Ring were working, each psychiatrist had assigned to him a number of patients, and the researchers noted that a psychiatrist was obviously more aware of some patients than of others. It occurred to them to look into the sources of this variation in visibility of the patients. Could it be that some patients are little noticed by their psychiatrist because they are trying not to be noticed, and that others take active steps to make themselves conspicuous? A patient's reasons for wanting to be noticed by his psychiatrist could be diverse, but would surely include his recognition as an important individual to influence if the patient wants to be judged ready for discharge from the hospital. Reasons for avoiding notice, on the other hand, might well include the consideration that if the psychiatrist receives no evidence to change his opinion of the patient he will take no action to change his status; thus a patient who wants to continue his hospitalization may be motivated to avoid his psychiatrist.

The researchers separated patients into more and less conspicuous groups by a simple procedure: they asked each psychiatrist to try to name all the patients currently assigned to him; comparing the outcome with the official list, they divided the patients into those the psychiatrist named and those he could not name. At a later time, each psychiatrist was asked to supply a variety of information and ratings about each patient on his total list. In addition, a number of the conspicuous and of the inconspicuous patients were specially interviewed by the psychologists. The conspicuousness of a patient was found related to the number of times the patient had approached his psychiatrist, and this measure was related to the total amount of contact between psychiatrist and patient. The conspicuousness of a patient was not related to the severity of psychopathology that he manifested. It was related to the way in which the patient spent his time—the division into workers, mobile socializers, and warders—differently for the two sexes, but in a pattern which seemed to fit the assumption that the inconspicuous patients were acting in a way calculated (appropriately for their sex) to avoid bringing them to the attention of their psychiatrist. By checking up some months later, the researchers learned that the patients the psychiatrists could not name had, in fact, proved less likely to be discharged.

Do Patients Exhibit the Same Concern as Other People About the Impression They Make?

A questionnaire about attitudes toward the hospital was prepared for use in a study by Benjamin Braginsky, Dennis Ridley, Dorothea Braginsky, and Kenneth Ring. Of central concern were two kinds of items: (1) Unrealistic, exaggerated statements of praise; an endorsement of such statements, by a person in normal control of his actions, would suggest an attempt to ingratiate himself with the authorities responsible for the hospital. (2) Mildly critical statements about the hospital, generally reasonable and correct; a rejection of these statements would similarly suggest an attempt at ingratiation. The questionnaire was administered to groups of patients under two different conditions. Some groups were asked not to sign their names on the questionnaires. The other groups were asked to sign their names and were told that members of the hospital staff, in reviewing the responses, "would like to know which patients filled out which tests." The somewhat unrealistic, ingratiatory responses were more common in those patients who had been asked to identify themselves. Clearly, in a situation justifying individual concern about the impression their statements might make on others, the patients showed a normal concern. No quantitative comparison with other people is possible, but the patients are clearly shown not to lack awareness of the impression they might make on others. If their responses can be traced to them, rather than being anonymous, then the responses are modified in the light of expectations about the impression they might make.

Do Patients Try To Control Their Hospital Life Through the Impression Their Statements Make on Others?

We have seen that at least some hospitalized schizophrenics are capable of modifying their statements to please others, or to avoid giving offense. But is this just a mechanical carry-over of earlier patterns of social interaction, or can they put their ability to use in the interest of present needs, in adjustment to the present social situation? Do the statements of a schizophrenic patient seem calculated, for example, to influence decisions about whether he is kept in the hospital, and about whether he is permitted the most desired living conditions while there? The same group of psychologists have tested this question in two studies, one concerned with a questionnaire, the other with statements made in an interview.

The first study employed a questionnaire especially prepared by drawing from a standard personality questionnaire 30 items that have no clear implication for mental health. One group of patients were told, by the examiner who was introducing the questionnaire, "We have found that the more items answered True by a patient the more severely ill a patient is and the greater are his chances of remaining in the hospital for a long period of time." The other group of patients were given an opposite instruction about the significance of responses: "We have found that the more items answered True by a patient the more he knows about himself, the less severely ill he is and the greater are his chances of remaining in the hospital for a short period of time." Each group was composed partly of newly admitted patients to the hospital, and partly of old-timers. If patients are, on the whole, able to achieve what they want in relation to the hospital, the old-timers must, for the most part, be people who want to live in the hospital; they should therefore be trying to give an impression that they are sick enough to be kept in the hospital. The newcomers, on the other hand, are likely to include a substantial number of patients who are aiming at getting discharged but have not yet succeeded; they should be trying to give an impression of being well.

Patients do on the average respond differently to this special questionnaire according to the way it is presented, and the effect is in one direction for old-timers and in the other direction for newcomers. The old-timers check "True" for twice as many statements if they have been told that "True" indicates mental illness than they do if told the opposite. The newcomers check "True" more often if they have been told that "True" indicates good mental health.

In the interview study only old-timers participated. As each patient was being brought to the interview, his escort made a comment that was experimentally varied and not made known to the interviewer. Some patients were told, "I think the person you are going to see is interested in examining patients to see whether they might be ready for discharge." A second group were told, "I think the person you are going to see is interested in examining patients to see whether they should be on open or closed wards." In the interview, the patient was asked how he felt, both physically and mentally. The interview was recorded on tape, and psychiatrists later rated each patient's degree of psychopathology and the amount of hospital control he seemed to need. Both ratings were substantially higher for patients who were led to believe discharge might be under consideration than for those led to believe shift to a closed ward was under consideration. The statements a patient made in the interview seem clearly to have been aimed at showing that he was sufficiently ill to be kept in the hospital but not so ill as to be put in a closed ward.

An account of this experiment might arouse some concern for the welfare of the patients. Do the long-run objectives of research justify the risk of upsetting patients by leading them, falsely, to believe that their present status may be in danger of change? The researchers were able to deal with this problem by carrying into their personal relation with the patients the same respect for their individuality that, in a more abstract manner, is embodied in the research. Each interview was followed by an explanation to the patient of the real purpose of the experiment, so the patient would know his status was not threatened. By conducting the interviews all in a single day, it was possible to ensure that patients coming to the interview could not have heard anything about it from those who had already taken part and been informed of its true nature.

Both these studies provide clear evidence, then, that some of the statements patients make about themselves are instrumental acts directed at the goal of maintaining the patient's life in the hospital, or of gaining his release.

An earlier experiment by Stanley Zarlock may be seen to point in the same direction. Zarlock brought hospitalized schizophrenics to one-hour group sessions in each of four different settings created in a special room: recreational, occupational, social, and medical. The procedure was repeated for 10 days, and observations were systematically recorded. Verbal responses indicating pathology were 80 times more frequent, and bizarre responses were 10 times more frequent, in the medical setting than they were in the other settings. Zarlock interpreted this enormous difference as a product of habit and social expectation. It may equally well be interpreted as another indication of the positive value of schizophrenic symptoms, and of their role in ensuring continuation of the mode of adjustment the patient has chosen. In the nonmedical setting, the patient enjoys interaction with his peers. In the medical setting he displays the behavior that he knows to be required for continued residence in the hospital; by this display of symptoms he avoids being returned to the everyday-life situation in which his difficulties first developed and for which he may now feel less prepared than previously.

May the Performance Deficit of Schizophrenics Be Only an Apparent Deficit, Brought about in Their Effort to Create a Particular Impression on Their Examiners?

For many years, research by clinical psychologists on schizophrenics was directed mainly at determining exactly how their performance on various tasks tends to differ from that of various other diagnostic groups and of normal people. This knowledge was sought partly for its value in permitting readier recognition of whether a person was suffering from schizophrenia or from some other "mental illness." It was also sought for a more fundamental purpose, to develop better understanding of the nature of schizophrenia. Schizophrenics were found to perform more poorly on many tasks than might have been expected from their education and preschizophrenic history.

Their poorer performance on many tasks is not surprising when one considers schizophrenics' apparent inadequacy in using their intellect in their ordinary daily life. A person who in ordinary conversation or in an interview speaks as did the patient quoted at the head of this chapter does not surprise us by doing poorly on a formal task calling for rigidly logical use of words. But recent research, we have seen, gives us reason to suspect that some schizophrenics' inadequacy in social interaction is partly illusory, that they want to make a poor showing for themselves in order to justify hospital care or other special attention, and to avoid the fearful challenge of return to a situation that they have already found intolerable. Could the same view apply also to schizophrenics' response to the formal tasks with which they are confronted by clinical psychologists who are attempting to assess their mental status?

This question has been considered by another group of psychologists, Alan Fontana and Edward Klein, in research with schizophrenics in several hospitals. They selected two groups of patients distinguished by the kind of impression they seemed to want to make. The selection was based on the patient's responses to questionnaire statements whose social desirability was clear. The statements were to be marked "True" or "False"; for each, one of these two answers would clearly be more consistent with a picture of mental health and the other with a picture of mental illness. The answers a patient gave were assumed to indicate the way he wanted to present himself to the examiner and to the hospital staff generally.

Patients of both categories, those tending to present themselves as healthy and those tending to present themselves as sick, were then selected to be given a reaction-time test. The task was simply to respond as quickly as possible to an auditory signal every time it was sounded; this is a task on which schizophrenics characteristically show a performance deficit, responding more slowly than normal people. With all patients, the examiner began by explaining that he "had been testing psychiatric patients and industrial employees around the state of Connecticut on a short task" and would like the patient to participate in his study. With half the subjects, the examiner then went on to say that midway in the task he would look over the patient's scores "and tell him how he was doing in comparison to other people already tested." This element in the instructions was omitted with the other half of the subjects, so as not to suggest that they would be evaluated. For these patients who were not given the evaluation-oriented instructions, the initial statement might lead them, about as convincingly as would be possible in the hospital situation, to see the situation as one in which their responses would not be used to evaluate them.

Reaction time was found to vary according to whether the instructions were evaluative or not, and in a different way in two different hospital settings.

Some of the patients were in custodial buildings containing long-term patients who were not actively engaged in therapy and had no reason to expect a change in status. In this setting, the healthy-presenters showed only a slightly shorter reaction time than did the sick-presenters (the difference was not statistically significant) when the instructions made no mention of evaluation. When evaluation was mentioned, however, the healthy-presenters responded more rapidly and the sick-presenters responded more slowly than otherwise. Here the patient's performance on the task was consistent with the tendency shown on the questionnaire; having been led to view their performance as relevant to how sick they were, the sick-presenters slowed down in order to be among the poorest of the group, while the healthy-presenters speeded up to maintain their sense of being among the healthiest in the group.

The rest of the patients were in therapy buildings, where patients were actively undergoing therapy and discharge was a lively possibility. Here the evaluation instructions had an opposite effect; they led the sick-presenters to respond faster, and the healthy-presenters more slowly. Fontana and Klein view this outcome as consistent with the implications of being in the therapy building. For the healthy-presenters, to have too healthy an appearance might lead to discharge, and most of them would presumably prefer still to remain in the hospital; calling attention to evaluation leads them to perform more poorly. For the sick presenters, the threat suggested by evaluation is that of being sent back to a custodial ward, and the result is that they improve their performance. Of special importance is the fact that the best average performances here—the healthy-presenters under nonevaluative conditions and the sick-presenters under evaluative conditions—are as good as the performance of a nonschizophrenic control group. Here, then, it appears that altering the motivation will not merely reduce the magnitude of the deficit shown by schizophrenic, but will altogether wipe it out.

As might be expected of an initial study, this one is far from conclusive. Its interpretation depends on varied assumptions about the relation that questionnaire answers and task performance bear to the patient's other behavior and experience. The assumptions seem reasonable to me but they are not necessarily compelling. In any event, more varied evidence would be needed before we could feel certain that schizophrenics' delay is characteristically deliberate. Reaction time, moreover, might turn out to be a special case, not at all representative of performance on tests in general. Perhaps the deficit of a schizophrenic in more complex test performance will remain as evidence of intrinsic defect brought about by a "disease process" and outside his voluntary control. But we will not know until much further research is done. The humanistic point of view, when combined with systematic research, suggests the possibility of a revolutionary change in our understanding of why schizophrenics react slowly. If this possibility is realized, a more general revolution in understanding schizophrenic deficit might also follow.

Is the Movement of Pateints into or out of the Mental Hospital Partly by Their Own Choice?

Several of the studies I have already described might suggest that patients' getting into the hospital and out of it are both much more under their own control than is provided for in the formal procedures of committal and discharge. The same suggestion emerges from applying a humanistic model. The experts charged with deciding on admission and discharge reach their decision through considering pertinent evidence, and the most pertinent evidence is provided by the patient's behavior. If the patient's behavior is under his own control, he is in a position to influence very greatly the decision as to whether he should be hospitalized or should be discharged (quite apart from the instances where the patient's admission or discharge is explicitly a voluntary decision by him). Those who make decisions on admission and discharge must always, if in varying degrees, have been aware of this influence, even though at times they feel obliged to act against a patient's will or in lieu of a will that is absent. The rest of us, however, are likely to think of patients' being committed almost always against their own wishes, and of remaining in a hospital only so long as authorities require them to stay. The humanistic orientation leads to quite different expectations, and the research and systematic observations made under their influence are quite instructive for those of us who have no experience of our own to go on.

The group of Connecticut psychologists who have done several studies that I have already described—Benjamin Braginsky, Dorothea Braginsky, and Kenneth Ring together with other colleagues—have also followed up two implications of their humanistic orientation for hospital admissions. One study concerned attitudes toward the hospital on the part of new patients admitted for the first time. Attitudes were measured by a questionnaire that the patients were asked to fill out. Two groups of patients were compared: those who had friends who had formerly been patients in the hospital, and those who had no such friends. Attitudes toward the hospital were found to be decidedly more positive in the former group. Presumably, what ex-patients communicate to their friends, then, is on balance a positive view of the opportunities offered by the hospital as an asylum from an unhappy life outside. It seems likely, though it is not proven, that a potential patient who has this attitude is more likely than otherwise to accept voluntarily the suggestion of others that he enter the hospital, and even to take definite steps toward securing admission.

The researchers then proceeded to a more direct test of the idea that committal is partly a choice influenced by contact with ex-patients. They explored hospital records systematically to see whether admissions tend to include a disproportionate number of pairs (or larger groups) of patients who (1) live close together in their home community, (2) are of the same sex and approximate age and thus likely friends, (3) enter the hospital close together in time, and (4) include at least one ex-patient and one first admission. These tendencies were confirmed. The evidence was only the objective sort available from records; it did not include direct evidence about whether the prospective patients were, indeed, friends and were making conscious decisions about the continuation of friendship in a possibly more congenial setting. The study does strongly suggest, however, that considerations of this kind are one influence on the decision to gain admission to a mental hospital.

Pertinent research on discharge from mental hospitals has been especially concerned with careful study of experimental wards directed at increasing the discharge rate among chronic patients. Alan P. Towbin has described a special ward at the West Haven Veterans Administration Hospital instituted as a result of humanistic analysis of the problems chronic patients face. It is clearly demonstrated that the chronic patients prefer to stay where they are, and that a situation is not easily created in which many will reach and carry out a decision to return to life outside. It seems likely, too, that their choice to continue hospitalization is for most a poor choice in the long run. An analogy to drug addiction may be useful here. Being hospitalized, like taking a drug, provides by evasion an easy solution to some of the problems a person faces; it offers great immediate rewards. Yet the longer the person continues to evade problems by staying in a hospital, the more he may become incapacitated for facing those problems realistically; he becomes, for example, further and further removed from the practice of the skills by which he has earned his living, and may become more established in a pattern of economic dependence. The forces leading some patients toward unnecessary hospitalization, and toward its continuance, are so powerful that large-scale change may be brought about only by major changes in our institutional arrangements for coping with the problem of "mental illness." Here this group of researchers are in agreement with Ronald D. Laing, who would also like to supplant mental hospitals with quite different kinds of social organizations that would not be hospitals at all. Both, too, arrive here at a view which converges with that reached by many sociological students of mental hospitals. What is envisioned are homes where a patient can break away at least temporarily from the particular social setting in which his difficulties have developed, can be in daily contact as an equal with patients and nonpatients who also reside there, can receive whatever professional help he wants without having to accept the stigma of an inferior status, and will be free to make any use he can of the normal social and recreational resources of society. In such a setting, it is hoped, troubled people may in a much larger proportion than heretofore find their schizophrenia a period of successful and relatively rapid passage on to a more satisfactory way of living.

The recent effort in the United States to encourage community mental health centers is directed, of course, at producing a sizeable change in the way our society deals with "mental illness." But the community mental health center as so far developed does not differ enough from the mental hospital, Towbin argues; it still requires a person to produce symptoms that will discredit himself, as a condition for admission, and thus works against the best interest of those admitted. As Towbin concludes,

> "A basic redefinition of the hospitalization situation would involve abandonment of self-discreditation as an access condition. Even if mental health professionals endorsed this change, it would undoubt-

edly be appreciated by the public as a fundamental change in the institution-community relationship, and is not likely to be accomplished without controversy."

Application to schizophrenia of a humanistic point of view has led, then, to suggestions for radical changes which may offer enormous benefit to potential patients and to all of society. Yet these changes can be brought about only if the humanistic point of view is carried to the public, replacing the widespread mechanistic views of man which—especially in the form of the "mental illness" concept—breed tolerance of the present system of degradation.

Radical changes in institutional arrangements have been most urgently advanced by writers who believe that the distinctive behavior of hospitalized schizophrenics originates primarily as an effort to maintain their dependent status. The position taken by these writers may well turn out to be much more extreme than the facts warrant. Among the questions needing exploration is how broad an application is justified for the humanistic view of the schizophrenic as essentially like everyone else rather than as victim of a specific disease process. Some of the past research I have not reviewed has prepared the way for this inquiry.

Many researchers have considered especially useful a distinction between "process schizophrenia" and "reactive schizophrenia." The distinction does not pertain principally to symptoms, but to how and when schizophrenia appears and the course it takes. "Reactive" is used to label schizophrenia that appears suddenly, following on events clearly involved in precipitating it, and not typically preceded by any very marked tendency toward schizophrenic adjustment. "Process" is used to label schizophrenia that appears without clear precipitating events, as a gradual aggravation of long-standing tendencies. Although schizophrenics cannot be neatly divided into types, these two concepts seem useful in pointing to patterns accurately describing some persons and useful as an approximation to the more complex facts about many others. The general humanistic model may be altogether adequate for understanding the more rapidly developing "reactive schizophrenia" as the response of a basically normal person to very unusual stress or confusion, whereas the chronic "process schizophrenia" may more often require a disease model.

Future research may ultimately establish, what many clinicians believe, that schizophrenic experience and behavior are partially controlled, in some or all instances, by something very much like illness, perhaps by organic conditions, perhaps by deficiencies of ego functioning that once established can at best be repaired only by slow reconstruction, whether entirely spontaneous or aided by skillful therapy. Some of the extreme humanistic writers seem at times to argue the contrary, and propose a complete change in our understanding of schizophrenia. While the value of a humanistic approach to schizophrenia seems, in general, well established, the value of these extremer proposals associated with the humanistic approach can only be assessed after much further research.

I could not prove the years had feet,
Yet confident they run
Am I from symptoms that are past
And series that are done.

I find my feet have further goals,
I smile upon the aims
That felt so ample yesterday—
Today's have vaster claims.

I do not doubt the self I was
Was competent to me;
But something awkward in the fit
Proves that outgrown, I see.

—EMILY DICKINSON

10 Psychotherapy

Psychotherapy is principally directed at helping people who feel seriously discontented with their present self—seriously enough to lead them to seek professional help. Psychotherapy is an interaction, traditionally between the therapist and a single patient, guided by the scientific knowledge and professional skills of the therapist, who may be a psychiatrist, a clinical psychologist, or a psychiatric social worker. In recent years, practices akin to psychotherapy have increasingly been extended also to helping people who, while not seriously doubting their present self, seek greater personal fulfillment. This recent development, allied with psychotherapy but distinct enough to merit a label of its own—"human potential movement" has been suggested—is especially associated with humanistic psychology. Psychotherapy itself, however, has for the most part always been a humanistically oriented enterprise, devoted to facilitating a fuller realization by more individuals of their own goals in life.

The form of therapy known as psychoanalysis is appropriate to study first, because of its broad and lasting influence since Sigmund Freud devised it in the 1890s. Some forms of psychotherapy developed as modifications of psychoanalysis, and others as radically different substitutes. In one way or another, most present-day therapy is greatly influenced by psychoanalysis. Although any simplification of history is bound to be incomplete, there is relatively little distortion in taking psychoanalysis as a reference point in tracing some of the major developments in psychotherapy and their relation to a humanistic approach.

Psychoanalysis: Freud's Therapeutic Invention

The method of therapy devised by Freud is, like the theories associated with it, known by the simple label of psychoanalysis. It is a lengthy procedure; the patient typically spends several hours per week with the therapist, through many months or even several years.

Freud developed psychoanalysis in his work with neurotic patients. It seeks to effect change through the patient's gaining increased insight into why he feels and acts as he does. This gain is especially facilitated by the patient's reexperiencing in his relation to the therapist the emotional significance that close personal relationships tend to have for him.

Underneath the neurotic patient's conscious life, Freud found evidence of an ongoing current of psychological processes, actively kept from conscious awareness but nonetheless influencing feeling and action, and Freud believed this finding applies to everyone, not just to the neurotic. In particular, there are powerful drives toward sexual and aggressive expression, which to some degree retain modifications of strength and of direction acquired through early childhood experience. In everyone, these drives and the specific wishes they produce are at least partially unconscious, and that condition may be necessary for normal social life. A normal person has found ways to satisfy these drives reasonably well, or he is able to deny them expression; he is to a reasonable degree master of his inner life, and he does not feel greatly threatened by glimpses he may get of tendencies that he is generally unconscious of. A neurotic person lacks this sense of mastery. Perhaps because some of the unacceptable wishes are especially strong in him, perhaps because he is especially fearful of anything unacceptable in himself, he feels threatened by glimpses of these specters and seeks especially hard to remain always unconscious of them. He is less likely than the normal person, therefore, to find indirect ways, acceptable to him, of satisfying these wishes. The unsatisfied wishes are likely to build up to high intensity, and to find an outlet in peculiar behavior that he does not understand. The aim of psychoanalysis is to bring the neurotic patient to something like the normal state of self-understanding, so that he can use his full conscious capacities to find acceptable ways of partially expressing his impulse life, and to restrain the unsatisfied part of his wishes.

This increase in insight cannot be attained by lectures and reading. What the patient needs is not acquaintance with psychoanalytic theory—which indeed, he may have before he even begins therapy. What he needs is a more vivid recognition of his impulses, of the varied feelings to which they give rise, and of the relation his actions bear to these underlying impulses and feelings. The neurotic is used to defending himself in various ways against the threat this recognition would pose. In psychoanalysis he tells of his current experiences, his dreams, his memories, and must try to say whatever comes to mind, as a way of combatting his usual defenses against awareness. Instances of resistance against this rule are likely to be especially instructive, sometimes pointing unmistakably to the nature of a hitherto unrecognized evasion. The patient's relationship with the analyst is a particularly useful topic for study: it is emotionally important and immediately present; yet much of its emotional impact must come from the patient's transferring to it attitudes already established toward parental and other authority figures. The analyst occasionally offers interpretations of the material the patient has produced, but these are generally calculated to go not very far beyond the insights that the patient has already attained. The patient's response to the analyst's interpretations may then themselves be an object of inquiry.

Gradually, in the ideal analysis, the patient develops increasing awareness of his impulses and of his defenses against them, and is therefore increasingly able to make deliberate plans for handling his impulses and to carry those plans into action. Freud's early accounts of analytic technique—after an initial period of exaggerated stress on uncovering traumatic incidents of childhood—emphasized the patient's gaining awareness of impulses, of the threat that they pose, and of the personal history of their modification in childhood experience. Later Freud and other analysts came to place relatively more stress on the patient's gaining awareness of his defenses against impulses and their threat.

Freud's aim was one with which most humanistic psychologists would sympathize. Despite Freud's general emphasis on a rigorous biological determinism, his therapy suggests a somewhat humanistic model of man. Certainly it more closely approaches a humanistic model than does much theoretical writing by experimental psychologists. Yet many later developments in the psychoanalytic and other forms of therapy have come from a feeling that existing psychoanalytic practice was in one way or another not as fully humanistic as it should be. Several different issues arise, and I propose to discuss them one at a time. It would not serve understanding well to think of them as ranging psychoanalysis at one extreme and competing therapies at the opposite extreme. They are all very lively problems for people working within any tradition of therapy. Each issue has at times been stated as part of an argument that psychoanalysis errs in the nonhumanistic direction; but for each issue there are other forms of therapy that are still less humanistic. Even among those trained and working in the psychoanalytic tradition, moreover, there has been since Freud's first years much movement toward a more humanistic position on these various issues. The development of ego psychology by psychoanalysts since the 1920s and their increasing attention to the person's relation to a social system exemplify changes that seem to me clearly in the humanistic direction.

Criticism of the psychoanalytic tradition in therapy has not always been from the humanistic direction. Many "behavior therapists" object to psychoanalysis as being based on too humanistic a model. I will discuss behavior therapy later in this chapter, considering first the humanistic criticisms and modifications of the psychoanalytic tradition.

Psychoanalysis as Insufficiently Centered on the Client

In labeling this criticism of psychoanalysis I have adopted terminology used by the American psychologist Carl Rogers, substituting *client* for *patient* as he did in trying to move away from the medical model. Rogers for some years even used *client-centered therapy* as the name for his particular form of psychotherapy. This label suggests that all other therapies fail to be centered on the client, a suggestion that seems grossly unfair. Therapy, after all, is an outgrowth of the medical tradition of concern for the patient's welfare, and loyalty to professional ethics is no rare occurrence.

Variations in degree of centering on the client must surely occur, however, and three relevant points have been made by Rogers and his fellow critics of psychoanalysis. Each refers to some difficult problem, where well-meaning people may, indeed, vary in their choice, and where therapeutic practice of recent years has tended to become more client-centered.

First—and I think it is the criticism Rogers intended most importantly —what the therapist does may at times be influenced too much by his general theory, too little by his specific client. The psychoanalytic therapist is trained to bring to his work the command of a definite body of theory. Psychoanalytic theory changes through the years, modified through the experience of many psychoanalysts with their patients. Yet at each time it does stand as a relatively consistent body of theory guiding the work of the analyst. A therapist of the highest skill might make only the most pertinent and fruitful use of this theory, not allowing it ever to distract him from empathetic penetration into the experiential world of the patient. With anyone who falls short of this ideal—and I for one would suppose any therapist must inevitably fall somewhat short—the theory may at times give the therapist too strong an expectation of what is coming next, too facile a categorization of what the patient says, too great a readiness to exaggerate how well he already understands the patient. The training of a psychoanalyst is, of course, directed at guarding against just these mistakes which can accompany the advantages of having a definite theory. They could be guarded against also by not using so definite a theory. Such a policy is sometimes chosen because of special doubts about the adequacy of psychoanalytic theory or of any other theory. But even a person strongly convinced of the adequacy of his theory, doubting the capacity of any human being to apply it carefully enough, might feel that the approach to ideal therapy is favored by keeping the therapist more completely set to feel himself into the patient's view of his world, less set to interpret it by even a very adequate theory.

A second problem is a familiar one in the history of medicine. The profession is traditionally committed to helping the individual patient as well as currently possible; it is also committed to trying to improve the possible future treatment of other patients. The second half of this professional commitment requires the doctor to be on the alert, in interaction with each patient, for generalizable knowledge and skills he can acquire and transmit to fellow professionals. Psychoanalysis was founded by a physician strongly impressed with this long-run responsibility of the profession. May the pattern of therapy established by Freud have been too much influenced by this aim? Is psychoanalytic therapy perhaps less than ideal for helping the individual patient, despite or even because of so greatly favoring the therapist's understanding of the patient and of human personality in general? Here is a second reasonable basis for differences of judgment, related to the first problem but going beyond it. Even where the theory is ideally suited to the patient's being correctly understood—whether by the therapist or by himself—has the orientation toward scientific progress created a therapy too much concerned with understanding and too little concerned with other consequences of interaction between client and therapist?

A third, related problem pertains to the general pattern of the therapeutic interaction, and to what other relationships provide the model for it. For Freud and most of his followers it has been easy to accept certain aspects of the traditional relationship between doctor and patient. The physician is an expert, with knowledge and skill he can use in helping the patient if the patient respects and trusts him, keeps back no relevant information, and accepts the rules and restrictions the physician sets. Maintenance of these two very different but complementary social roles has obvious value in the curing of diseases. It helps ensure that the physician will indeed have the specific skills needed to deal with the problem presented by the patient—or, lacking them, will refer the patient to a fellow professional who has them. It helps ensure that the patient will cooperate fully in supplying the necessary information and in doing what he needs to do to get well. But a pattern useful in the treatment of diseases may be far from ideal for helping clients with personal problems. In everyday life people often obtain help by a very different kind of relationship with another person—the intimate encounter with a person of equal status, a close and friendly confidant. The traditional roles of doctor and patient may be far less fruitful for psychotherapy than a relationship patterned on intimacy between equals.

In various ways the different humanistic critics of psychoanalytic therapy differ from psychoanalytic tradition on one or more of these dimensions.

Carl Jung argued principally against applying to every case the same definite theory. With one patient he used Freudian therapy, with its associated emphasis on sexuality, because it seemed correct and useful. With another he would follow Adlerian therapy, with its emphasis on striving for power. Still another patient might suggest to Jung the invention of new techniques. Therapy and associated assumptions should not be set by any one theory, Jung argued; various therapies each work for some patients, and various theories are each appropriate in understanding certain people. The fundamental rule for the psychotherapist, Jung said, "should be to consider each case new and unique. That, probably, is the nearest we can get to the truth."

Jung also differed from psychoanalytic tradition on the third problem I have mentioned—not explicitly criticizing the traditional medical role, with which he seemed to identify himself, but in other ways arguing for greater equality of patient and therapist. Therapy is a social interaction, he insisted, and a more balanced one than the participants may realize. Not only does the patient change in response to the therapist's application of his professional skill; the therapist also changes in response to the patient, just as he would in interaction with a friend. And Jung regarded this as essential for the success of therapy; "you can exert no influence if you are not susceptible to influence." Freudian psychoanalytic theory recognizes this reverse influence in its concept of countertransference. Corresponding to *transference,* the patient's unreasonable extension to the therapist of emotional attitudes toward parents and other authority figures, is the countertransference of the therapist, who may unreasonably feel toward the particular patient emotions more appropriate to his earlier relations to other people. Jung agreed thoroughly with the need for the therapist to understand the countertransference, and pointed out repeatedly that he was the first to insist that analysts must themselves for this reason be analyzed. But the concept of countertransference is not in itself adequate, Jung felt, to handle all the implications for the therapist of his interaction with patients.

Otto Rank was another psychoanalyst who argued that Freudian therapy was insufficiently centered on the patient. He explicitly argued that therapy must be devoted to the welfare of the individual patient alone, and that this devotion is threatened when the analyst seeks to learn from his practice, to increase his own general understanding. Obviously there is just a difference of emphasis here; Rank did not seem embarrassed to acknowledge that he had developed his own point of view through his experience with patients. Rank placed more emphasis on the other two humanistic criticisms, bearing on the role of theory and the kind of interaction.

The therapist should not rely on any theory of personality, nor use a definite technique that derives from a theory; he should listen with full respect to the patient as the person best informed about his problems and most capable of arriving at a decision about how to solve them. He argued that the therapeutic process is facilitated by this open approach, respectful of the patient. If the patient is assumed to have little knowledge of why he acts as he does, he is glad to accept this excuse for evading responsibility, and to appear unconscious of much more than he really is. When responsibility is placed fully on the patient, Rank claims, the patient turns out to know much more than a Freudian therapist would expect. An open and respectful approach, moreover, facilitates adjustment of procedures to the patient's individuality. Specific aim and technique can be less dependent on an abstract theory about people in general. They can be centered instead on the one relevant person, on his discovering how to understand himself, how to accept his general nature, and yet to make those changes he desires and finds possible.

This humanistic argument for greater centering on, respect for, acceptance of the client appears in the writings of many later psychoanalysts, psychiatrists, and psychologists. In the work of Carl Rogers it reaches its peak, being presented there as the defining characteristic of his particular style of therapy. Though Rogers was never a psychoanalyst, his argument for his type of therapy is, like Jung's and Rank's, based partly on the criticism of psychoanalysis on just this issue. Rogers was trained as a psychologist, not as a physician, and addresses himself also to practices in clinical psychology that invited similar criticism. The counseling activities of clinical psychologists, he argued, were built around the particular skills of the counselor—often based, for instance, on the giving of advice rather than on encouraging the client to arrive at an understanding or decision himself. (This aspect of Rogers' critique, indeed, is not pertinent to psychoanalysis, in which the patient often struggles for advice and does not get it.) Rogers also criticized the diagnostic procedures then current in clinical psychology. Tests of intelligence and personality might well improve the psychologist's understanding of the patient, but were often a mistaken application and pursuit of professional skills, being directed at the wrong person. The client is the only one whose understanding really matters, and the therapy should be directed at his arriving at an appropriate diagnosis. He is likely to do so by interacting with the clinician as an equal, not by witnessing the clinician's display of obviously recondite skills.

Psychoanalysis as Based on Too Biological a Theory

Freud laid great stress on sexual drive as an influence on experience and behavior. He argued that it motivates a great variety of actions and thoughts that do not on the surface appear to be sexual. The Freudian stress on sexuality has on the whole, I believe, helped move the image of man in a humanistic direction. Intellectual discussions of man in the preceding centuries had often been of a highly rational sort, picturing man as mind rather than body, as thinking rather than feeling. Ordinary conceptions of man, obviously, had always remained more rounded and diverse, as the literature and visual art of those centuries so well demonstrate. In forcing intellectual discussion to attend more to neglected sides of human nature, Freud was shifting the academic model of man in the direction of man's ordinary self-perception.

But perhaps Freud's emphasis on the biological side of man went so far as to create, when fully accepted, a view of man just as one-sided as the one it replaced. That is the burden of a series of complaints against Freudian psychoanalysis. It formed part of the objections that motivated the early withdrawal of Adler and Jung from Freud's group of close colleagues and disciples. Adler saw man's most important motive as the need for power, to overcome the basic insecurity of human existence. Jung assigned no single motive a predominant position, but argued that Freud had attributed to one truly important motive a ubiquity and general indirectness of influence not justified by the facts. When Otto Rank some years later also became a dissident from Freud's intimate group, rejection of Freud's biological emphasis again played a part. In Rank's view, fear of living and fear of dying had a certain predominance among human motives. Fear of living and dying may sound biological, but Rank gave these terms a metaphorical meaning; "fear of living" included fear of growing into independence and of fulfilling one's personal potentialities, while "fear of dying" included fear of holding back from growth, fear of failure to realize potentialities. To these fears Rank ascribed many of the manifestations that Freud had traced to the sexual drive.

Many of those who have helped spread psychoanalytic thought in the United States have shared this general criticism with Adler, Jung, and Rank. Conspicuous among them was Karen Horney, who viewed sexuality as only one of several foci of conflict inevitably arising for every individual in modern life. Another, Erich Fromm, accepts Freud's general ideas but tries to give them a largely nonsexual meaning. Fromm considers his reinterpretation of Freud humanistic, though to me it would seem more humanistic if it were less desexualized. Especially influential in American psychiatry was Harry Stack Sullivan; he, too, presented a social reinterpretation of the developmental problems that Freud had considered sexual. While sharing with Freud a recognition that early oral activity and toilet training, for instance, are important influences on later personality, Sullivan had a different view of how this influence was exerted. Freud held events of early childhood to have lasting effects if they produced extreme satisfaction or frustration of the strength of the drive or of the direction in which it sought expression. For Sullivan, the same events were important because they involved critical emotional relations between child and parent, and the child's early sense of self and others; the pattern of interpersonal relations was the route of influence for Sullivan, not alterations of a physiological state.

In recent years the existentialist movement in clinical psychology and psychiatry has stressed the cognitive side of life, and especially the general meaning the person finds in his existence. Viktor Frankl, a Viennese psychiatrist, traces his existentialist view to his experience as a prisoner in a Nazi concentration camp. In addition to immediate suffering, including the threat of death, many prisoners underwent a personality breakdown likely to interfere with the successful resumption of normal life should they survive. Frankl ascribes some prisoners' maintenance of well-organized personality to their finding some meaning in their concentration-camp life. Some found meaning in ministering to the needs of fellow-prisoners worse off than themselves; some, including Frankl himself, found meaning partly in the better understanding of man they developed through suffering and could hope to bring to their possible future work in psychology or psychiatry. The American psychologist and psychoanalyst Bruno Bettelheim, who as an Austrian spent a year in a Nazi concentration camp, gives a similar account of how he maintained a degree of stability under extreme strain. For both men, this experience was an important influence in leading them toward an existentialist emphasis in psychiatry or psychoanalysis. In the years after World War II, the existentialist stress on search for meaning in life became increasingly common among clinicians. This departure from Freud's biological emphasis has much in common with the views of Adler, Jung, and Rank. Although using different words, each presented in his own way an existentialist argument against a biological model of man.

Now why should this replacement of early Freudian theory by a less biological theory be pertinent to therapeutic practice? In general, of course, it is relevant because any therapy is likely to be greatly influenced by the theory held by the therapist. In particular, holding a theory that stresses sexual drive as the universal source of emotional disturbance is likely to bias the therapist toward sexual inquiry, toward rewarding the patient by attention and approval when he produces sexual material, for instance, and toward aloofness or negative comment when the patient's thoughts seem excessively remote from sexuality. Where Freud's stress on sexuality is appropriate, so is this behavior of the therapist. But when Freud's early theory is on this point inapplicable to the particular patient, then the same therapeutic practice may distract therapist and patient from more truly critical problems, and give the patient who is unconsciously trying to avoid his problems a tool with which he can deceive the therapist into collaborating in his effort.

Just this is the claim made repeatedly by writers on therapy who criticize the sexual emphasis of Freudian psychoanalysis. Jung, for example, considered the transference of patients working with a Freudian analyst of his time to be with excessive regularity a sexually tinged attitude, for this was the aspect of interpersonal relations to which they were repeatedly led by the analyst's reaction to other material they introduced. In any patient, the humanistic critics argue, excessive stress on sexuality may distract attention from other important elements; in some patients, it may lead to positively erroneous interpretations.

Psychoanalysis as Excessively Rational in Aim and Technique

Psychoanalytic technique, I have said, has been widely criticized by humanistic thinkers for being exclusively rooted in a biological viw of man. Yet humanistic thinkers—often the very same ones—also argue that psychoanalytic technique is excessively rational. These two contentions may at first glance seem contradictory, yet they may both be valid.

The aim of psychoanalysis, as applied to the neurotic problems for which it was first devised, is to help the patient become conscious of biological impulses, of the threats they pose, and of the defenses he has established against them, so that he may deliberately and consciously reach rational decisions about expressing or controlling those impulses. The root of neurotic difficulties is seen to lie in the inaccessibility of those impulses to the conscious self. The assumption is that when the impulses become conscious, relevant plans can be made and executed, and the biological impulses will no longer find uncontrolled expression in ways perhaps detrimental to the person's interests. Rationality—control of one's behavior by plans chosen realistically for their instrumental value in achieving explicit goals—is the criterion of mental health predominant in the therapeutic aims of psychoanalysis.

This aspect of psychoanalytic technique, to the extent that it stands by itself as a full description, suggests an excessively intellectual ideal for the human condition. In the eighteenth century, an exclusive idealization of the rational side of man might have met with general consent. In Freud, whose writings are so much a part of the romanticist movement away from that eighteenth century view, this strongly rational ideal seems to many readers incongruous. Through most of the twentieth century, while rationality may have continued to seem just as desirable as ever, other aspects of life have also gained more recognition as rightful parts of our ideal for man. Therapists, like the rest of us, today more willingly grant to other sides of human nature a part in a balanced ideal. The therapist and his patient, when they view the ideal man as not only rational but also emotional, physical, and perhaps mystical are led to different or additional views about the aims or techniques of therapy.

Carl Rogers provides a particularly clear instance of moving away from a position akin to the psychoanalytic one on this point, for the change came during the years of his writing on techniques of therapy. His early view of the objective of "client-centered therapy" was enabling the client to obtain an understanding of himself. Rogers did not, like Freud, speak of undoing repression. He shared with Rank the view that the patient had readier access to his own motives than Freud believed. He agreed with Freud, though, that therapy works through the patient's attaining clearer understanding of himself. Because the patient becomes more fully and accurately aware of all sides of his actions and their sources, he can act more rationally in his own interest. Later, Rogers came to think that the attainment of understanding is not enough, and that therapeutic technique cannot be adequately based on that single aim. He came to see emotion as much more central. When therapy works, Rogers eventually argued, it is because the client feels himself understood and genuinely accepted and appreciated by the therapist; only then does he become able to appreciate and accept himself in the face of all the things that he regrets or hates about himself. The client's new emotional attitude toward himself, made possible by the attitude of the therapist, is more basic than the clearer self-understanding that generally accompanies it.

The Present Scene in Psychotherapy and the Human Potential Movement

Psychotherapy is itself now practiced in extremely diverse ways. Related practices in the human potential movement—designed to encourage personal fulfillment or growth in persons who present no symptoms other than finding their lives less fulfilling than they wish—further increase the variety of techniques in use. Some of the techniques, whether used in a clearly therapeutic context or in a broader search for personal growth, represent in an extreme degree the humanistic trends that I have described.

The encounter-group movement provides a clear example. It is one of the several ways in which therapy or something akin to it is conducted in groups. Different modes of group practice have different kinds of leadership and, typically, different kinds of members. Encounter groups, specifically, are small groups formed for the benefit of the participants where seriously disturbed persons are ordinarily not included and many or all participants may not even be patients. Encounter groups are for the most part, I judge, relatively little guided by systematic theory nor directed at developing one. The events of a session seem to flow from the personalities and present concerns of the participants, and the emotional relationships established among them; interventions by the group leader seem directed more at facilitating this flow than at structuring it through the leader's command of any body of psychological theory. The leader often strives to take a position of one among equals—something of a catalyst but also a full participant in the emotional relationships that develop, expecting that he may be profoundly influenced by the experience. The model of man that seems implied in encounter groups is a diverse and human one, with no special emphasis on the priority of biological impulses and the establishment of rational control over them. While encounter-group leaders might to some degree share the Freudian emphasis on rational control as an ultimate aim, the techniques used include encouragement of great openness and directness in emotional expression, and of mystical feelings of union with the group.

Another example is provided by the appearance in the human potential movement of techniques that are derived from religious traditions. Pertinent techniques of Western origin include those of prayer and meditation found in the traditions of Jewish and Christian mysticism. More conspicuous thus far in the human potential movement are techniques of Eastern origin, especially the meditative techniques of Hinduism and Zen Buddhism. The Eastern techniques, at least as they are taught in the United States, do not, in general, involve any profession of religious faith, so that they gain readier acceptance than the indigenous techniques often associated with literal theological beliefs which are rejected today by many Westerners of Christian or Jewish background.

Many thousands of Americans—especially college students, but some of all ages and educational levels—have in recent years taken up the practice of these techniques or of the physical exercises associated with them. As in their original settings, these practices are not principally intended as psychotherapy. They are growth techniques, seemingly more apt for inducing new interests than for eliminating problems about old ones. Their advocates do at times, however, also claim for them important therapeutic value.

The exact techniques of meditation vary, but for the most part they involve isolation, quiet, and some restriction of attention for periods each day. They may all be said to turn attention inward, and they throw the person on his own resources, perhaps guided by an individual teacher but not constantly interacting with him; in these two respects they are more completely "client-centered" than any technique of psychotherapy. The discipline involved is often described as spiritual, and the physical exercises merely as aids; here, these growth techniques continue something of the post-Freudian movement away from the strictly biological. Finally, meditation techniques are not generally oriented toward clearer rationality as the main goal (though not necessarily incompatible with that goal). They seem more oriented toward encouraging certain general states of mind—relaxed alertness, perhaps acceptance, and in some instances mystical experience. In these respects, too, they share the general movement of thought and practice I have been tracing, supplementing the goal of rationality with other goals neglected by many rational people.

Meditation, encounter groups, and various other techniques may be combined in comprehensive programs for promoting personal growth, at growth centers such as the Esalen Institute, whose residential program I mentioned when discussing research on hypnosis. These extensions beyond the therapeutic tradition, embracing a much greater variety of aims and techniques than does the therapeutic tradition itself, may be seen as part of a general social change. A better balance between rationality and other aspects of man seems to be part of what is sought in many other forms of social experimentation too. The humanistic developments in psychotherapy and the human potential movement are paralleled by recent efforts to establish new forms of family life, new forms of political action, and new forms of art. The popularity of each of these recent developments may, of course, turn out to be only temporary, a product of special relevance to societal and personal needs of our time. My guess is that the human potential movement has a long future, and that many of the growth techniques associated with it will continue to be used.

The efficacy of these techniques of therapy and growth, in facilitating the personal changes people seek can in the long run be the more accurately assessed the more we are able to base our judgments on pertinent scientific knowledge. Two kinds of scientific knowledge are relevant. One consists of the general psychological knowledge that can warrant some estimate of the validity of specific psychological statements, including those about professional practices. A basic instance is our general knowledge about the origins and the modifiability of human sexual and aggressive urges. Freudian thought tends to be very pessimistic about the possibility of their easy and effective control. Humanistic psychology is sometimes very optimistic, considering these urges less as inevitably strong and insatiable, more as situationally determined. General scientific knowledge about sex and aggression should be useful here, and I believe that it already is. I think it indicates excess and error both in the early Freudian theory of sex and in the easy optimism implied in some humanistic writing. The trend toward humanism in defining the subject matter of psychology should make future psychological research an ever better basis for indirect inferences about professional practice.

The other, more specific kind of pertinent scientific knowledge is the outcome of research on professional practice itself. What happens in therapy, and in the human potential movement, has principally become known through the writings of clinicians and clients, who have summarized their experience or have described particular cases as examples. This knowledge can be valuably supplemented by systematic research. The course of each session can, under appropriate conditions, be recorded and analyzed in detail, permitting an accuracy of description and comparison beyond what anyone's memory can provide. In research, moreover, the outcome can be followed longer and more accurately assessed than it normally can in a busy routine of clinical practice.

Adequate research on therapy and on the human potential movement poses great difficulties, but many of the difficulties can with effort be surmounted. A substantial body of research has now been done, mostly on therapy, and it has recently been summarized in a large handbook edited by Allen Bergin and Sol Garfield. I believe that if I were a therapist I would find knowledge of this research an essential supplement to my clinical experience in reaching decisions about what kind of therapeutic procedure to use in each particular situation. Yet I would be dissatisfied with the state of this knowledge and eagerly press for its further development. On each of the issues I have reviewed above, a wise decision about how far to move from the tradition started by early psychoanalysis, and whether to move toward or away from the humanistic extreme, may vary greatly according to person and circumstance. The clinician's and his client's ability to make good choices among the variety of procedures they might use should be greatly improved when the resources of the research tradition have been more fully utilized to provide relevant knowledge about the procedures themselves and about the basic nature of man.

Behavior Therapy

One major development of recent years in psychotherapy has often seemed to be in a direction quite opposite to the humanistic, toward a rigid external treatment based on a strict machine model of man. This is the development that is allied with the experimental study of learning; to it are applied such terms as behavior therapy, conditioning therapy, and behavior modification.

Dependence on a mechanical model is most thoroughgoing in the writing of Wolpe, Eysenck, and Skinner. Many other advocates of behavior therapy are content to leave theory aside or else to apply a simple mechanical model only to the process of therapy itself, making no assumptions about how the behavior to be changed has come into existence. Wolpe, Eysenck, and Skinner are among those who advocate a mechanical model of man; they argue vigorously for the origin of personal problems in the conditioning of inappropriate responses, whose replacement by other responses should then be the obvious aim of therapy. To people who are true believers in the conditioned-response theory as a complete account of personality development, the position these authors take must seem to have all the advantages of clear and correct thinking. To those who like me find the conditioning account completely inadequate as a general theory of personality development, their position seems a very unfortunate and confusing mistake. It obscures the real values to be found in the therapeutic procedure that they advocate and in some aspects of their theory accounting for why these procedures work.

Behavior therapy has been more the subject of systematic research than any other form of therapy. There are, I think, two main reasons for this. One lies in the fact that behavior therapy draws on the tradition of experimental research in which the study of conditioning originated. Some behavior therapists have been trained as experimental psychologists before turning their attention to therapeutic application. This background of training or of knowledge tends to make a person unsatisfied with claims of knowledge for which he does not have very adequate evidence, and it acts as a strong pressure for checking claims of therapeutic efficacy by the closest approach possible to the ideal pattern of laboratory experimentation.

A second reason is that the nature of behavior therapy affects (like other therapies) the choice of problem to which it gets applied, and does so in a direction that facilitates research. Behavior therapy is based on reasoning about how to eliminate an undesirable response or how to establish a desirable response. It is thus most likely to be applied to problems where a person has a clearly defined external symptom; the patient's complaint may be, for example, that he drinks or smokes immoderately, that he trembles when called on to speak, or that he is unable to make sexual responses he considers desirable and appropriate. When the nature of what is undesirable, and the objective of a program to achieve change, are so clearly defined in terms of the individual's relations with the external world—changing his typical response in some definite class of situations—it is very easy to assess the success or failure of the program. Research on the outcome of therapy becomes much more feasible, and is more likely to be done, then when therapeutic aims pertain to the vaguer, though sometimes more important, states of mind that other patients present as their problems.

The definition of therapeutic aim as a change in overt response rather than a change in psychological state, moreover, facilitates experimental research by giving relevance to experiments which would not otherwise have been thought pertinent to psychotherapy. When therapy is conceived as effecting change in states of mind that drive people to seek professional help, ethics and practical circumstances of professional practice generally prevent controlled experiments. A therapist cannot ordinarily divide his patients randomly into experimental and control groups. But when therapy is conceived as effecting change in response, controlled experiments become possible on relatively trivial changes. Research subjects may, as in other experiments, be assigned at random to differently treated groups, if one treatment promises at most a slight benefit and the other treatment guarantees that the subject will end up no worse off than if he had not participated in the experiment. The behavior therapist is more likely than other therapists to consider relevant to therapy controlled experiments that are done quite outside the context of professional help to pateients.

Attitudes toward behavior therapy are often strong and warmly held. People with a humanistic orientation are likely to view the whole movement as completely destructive of any proper understanding of the processes leading up to problem behavior, and the processes through which behavior may be changed. This attitude is readily generated by the theoretical pronouncements that often accompany accounts of behavior therapy, especially by the application of conditioning theory to the origins as well as to the treatment of problems. To disregard the research on behavior therapy for this reason, however, is to fall into a trap. Behavior therapy does involve remarkably favorable opportunities for testing the effects of therapeutic procedures, and if detached from the misleading theory (as I consider it), the findings are just as relevant to a humanistic theory as to a mechanical theory of man. They are, therefore, an important source for reasoned surmise about the probable effectiveness of humanistic therapies as well as the behavior therapies.

The heated attitude of many behavior therapists is quite opposite. It is likely to include a rejection of all other kinds of therapy because they are not accompanied—as in their nature they cannot be—by entirely adequate evidence as to their effectiveness. It includes also the typical experimenter's fallacy—the belief that because an experiment establishes with high confidence a relationship between a particular cause and a particular effect, it justifies equal confidence in the theory that the experimenter happens to have about what intervening processes account for this relationship. (Or, in the case of a nontheoretical experimenter, confidence in his belief that attention to the intervening process would not improve the understanding of the relationship between cause and effect.)

In my opinion, these contradictory extremes of opinion are not justified. Much of the general reasoning which underlies behavior therapy is less mechanical and antihumanistic than some of its advocates wish to consider it. The humanistic therapies already mentioned are not so discrepant with the behavior therapies as they appear on the surface. And the research done on behavior therapy has, in the absence of a comparable amount of research on the humanistic therapies, likely implication for the humanistic therapies. All these points are, I think, best illustrated with the type of behavior therapy sometimes distinguished by the label of operant therapy or operant training—the type especially derived from the experimental work of B. F. Skinner on learning in animals.

Operant Training

Operant training is patterned after B. F. Skinner's analysis of operant behavior. Skinner distinguishes respondent behavior, where the organism is responding to stimuli from the environment, and operant behavior, where the organism is operating on the environment. Respondent behavior is typified by the "classical conditioning" investigated by Pavlov. In his well-known experiments with dogs, a buzzer (for instance), which at first does not elicit salivation but is repeatedly sounded just before food is presented, will eventually elicit salivation even when not accompanied by food. Here, environmental control of behavior has been extended from one stimulus to another, and this change is referred to as conditioning; throughout, the organism is considered to be passively responding to specific external stimuli. Operant behavior is typified by equally well-known experiments with rats in a "Skinner box." A hungry rat is placed in a box where depression of a certain lever will cause a pellet of food to drop into a tray, readily available for eating. Any action of the rat that does not depress the lever will fail to result in delivery of food. A considerable time may pass before the rat first happens to press the lever. After he does so, and gets a bit of food, he repeats the act more quickly. The rate of responding is affected by such variables as amount and timing of food. The rat's behavior in the box, at first highly diffuse, has been modified in the direction of selecting that class of responses which successfully operates on the environment.

The model of operant training has been applied to a variety of human problems, and they include some for which the term *therapy* would very obviously be appropriate. By making candy, praise, or other special rewards contingent on speech (or, initially, on mouth movements akin to speech), mute and socially withdrawn patients have been led to talk; return of speech, in addition to its immediate value, facilitates further therapeutic interaction. The model of operant training has also been applied to educational procedures—for example, in devising programs of computer-assisted instruction. Of special interest are some of the applications in a border area between therapy and education.

A variety of these applications are illustrated, for example, in a series of studies reported in a recent book by Robert L. Hamblin and four colleagues, *The humanization processes.* Their work derives from Skinnerian thought, in the special form given to it by the sociologist George Homans, who has emphasized the mutual reinforcement that people provide each other in daily social interchange, and the role of this reinforcement in maintaining or altering the pattern of group interaction. Hamblin et al. apply this approach to inner-city children who are uninterested in school or seemingly incapable of the tasks that they are expected to master there. In their experimental procedures, the existing pattern of teacher-child interaction is broken up through the alert cooperation of the teacher, so that the positive reinforcements she provides to the problem child are more ample and are more specifically contingent than before on the child's emitting desired kinds of acts.

One experiment, for instance, was directed at reducing the violently disruptive behavior of certain boys in two classrooms. Systematic observation indicated that for these particular boys attention from the teacher was apparently a powerful reinforcer, and that it was being provided primarily when the boys threatened to disrupt the class. The teachers were told about these observations, were asked to try to ignore the disruptive behavior and instead to give attention, accompanied by tokens, specifically as a reward for the response of studying. The tokens could be exchanged later for movie viewing and other special privileges. These changes in the interaction between teacher and children led to a dramatic drop in the disruptive behavior, and a corresponding increase in studying. In a variety of experiments similar to this, improvement in attention, responsiveness, verbal and arithmetic skills, and constructive interaction with peers, were found in many—though not in all—children, and the changes were often very great. More generalized effects, such as increase in IQ, were also frequent and they, too, were sometimes very large.

The research of Hamblin et al. is not unique; studies by others strengthen the evidence for the conclusions I have just cited. Such studies do not, of course, tell us that operant training is the only effective way to deal with the problems confronted by inner-city children, nor that operant theory is the most productive way to formulate even that kind of training. But they do provide overwhelming evidence of the great practical value of operant training for many children. Equally strong evidence for a comparable value of other educational or therapeutic procedures can hardly be forthcoming except from the application of comparable research techniques to those procedures too.

The theoretical model provided by Skinner's account of operant learning has guided formulation of these programs of therapy and education; through its association with the research tradition, moreover, Skinner's account has facilitated and encouraged research directed at evaluating the outcome. All this is to the good, insofar as these programs are found to have the real value they seem to me to have. Their origin in Skinner's theoretical model does have a drawback, though, and it comes at the point where these programs are considered in relation to humanistic thought.

Skinner's writings seem to me to give his theory a context of aggressively mechanistic philosophy, and this atmosphere pervades much of others' work on operant therapy. Now this is very curious, for the model offered by Skinner is distinguished among theories of learning by its humanistic qualities. It is as though Skinner, only half aware of this fact, were struggling hard to maintain the semblance of fervent commitment to a mechanical conception that he is really abandoning.

There are several relevant points of distinction between Skinner's model of operant behavior and the earlier models of learning with which it was, several decades ago, competing.

1. The theories formerly predominant offered stimulus-response models, in which every act is thought of as a response elicited by a stimulus. Skinner rejects this conception, and takes as given the emission of a response by the organism.

2. Earlier theories each included an explicit general law about what

causes reinforcement, or learning. Different theories offered various laws. Some, for instance, asserted that reinforcement of a stimulus-response connection comes from the reduction of a drive—for example, reduction of hunger as a result of ingesting food. The effort here, in each theory, was to objectify the nature of reinforcement, to view it as basically uniform in all organisms. In Skinner's model of operant learning, what brings about reinforcement of an operant act is defined by the outcome in the particular organism; if any consequence of the act is found to increase the rate of performance of the act, that finding justifies its being considered a reinforcement. Some consequences (like ingestion of food while hungry) are so dependable as reinforcements that they are regularly used in experiments; but the basic definition of reinforcement includes any consequence that in a particular organism does lead to increased rate of performance of the act that precedes it.

3. As might be expected from his model's starting with the organism's emitting some response, and having the response reinforced by some consequence that may be distinctive to the particular organism, Skinner focuses on the behavior of an individual organism. Most other learning theorists had tried to establish laws directly applicable to a whole class of organisms, and their experimental results pertain to averages of a number of organisms tested. Skinner, while expecting the same laws to hold true for different individuals, applies them separately to one organism at a time—expecting regularity or lawfulness within the history of a real, individual organism, not within the mathematical abstraction of an unreal average organism.

4. Where Skinner shifts from a whole class of subjects to the single subject, he moves the other way in his definition of behavior. Many earlier learning theorists had tried to keep to an objective, even a physical, definition of their subject matter, viewing a response as a specific movement of a particular part of the body, for instance. Skinner, on the contrary, is very insistent that "operant" should always be taken to mean a class of responses. The criteria for what forms a class of responses are often complex and psychological, definitely not limited to physical qualities. In Skinnerian research on operant therapy, for instance, "abstractness in interpreting proverbs" or "commonness of associations" may be found as operants whose occurrence can be assessed and which can be subjected to reinforcement. The behaving organism is here very unratlike, decidedly and distinctively human. By defining an operant as any class of responses that can function as a class in the particular organism, Skinner opens the way for his general terminology to be applied in a humanistic model for human beings and in a rat model for rats, with the vast difference in the models effectively obscured.

I think anyone who looks at Skinner's account both sympathetically and critically, but with a humanistic point of view, is likely to sense in these four characteristics a definite departure from perfect mechanism. Suppose a psychologist wanted to apply a free-will, purposive model to human life, but to do so in a thoroughly objective manner, incorporating only the most externally definable of psychological events. He would have to disregard the thoughts that might precede emission of a response, the thoughts that lead up to a freely-chosen decision. He would begin, then, as Skinner does, with the organism's emission of some act as the basic given. He would also have to disregard any surmises about the purposes that the person had in mind, so he could not indicate in advance which possible consequences of the act would achieve the purpose to some degree; he would have to wait and find out by observing the effects. Reinforcement would have to be defined empirically as whatever consequences were found to increase the response rate (or to increase the probability that this response would be made when similar conditions recur), just as Skinner defines it. Acknowledging that purposes and hence reinforcements may differ from one person to another, as may the acts that happen to be followed by reinforcement, the humanistic thinker would with Skinner emphasize the need for studying each person individually. To allow for the complexity and individuality of thought processes leading up to response, finally, and yet not mention them, he would have to define the behavioral unit as any class of responses that have a unity in the particular instance.

A humanistic psychologist would be unlikely to want to reason in this very indirect way. He would feel that he is neglecting useful evidence obtainable directly from the person studied and is incurring unnecessarily the risk of frequent and gross error. He would find the terminology confusing, too. It is very difficult, for instance, to keep in mind that "reinforcement" is supposed to denote only some objective event if the criterion for identifying the event is a complex interaction between person and world with a clearly subjective element, that is, the person's obtaining and using some information about how his purposes may be attained. Someone proceeding from a humanistic position would be much less likely than Skinner to adopt such confusing terms, because he would see no need to try to conceal the subjective element intrinsic to his subject matter and unavoidable in its adequate consideration. But it is important that if a humanistic psychologist were to accept for some reason the restrictions of a purist objectivism, the model his humanistic orientation would lead him to would look very much like Skinner's.

It is important, in evaluating Skinner, to note that he began with studying the behavior of rats and pigeons, and has himself done little research on human beings. To have devised for the study of animal learning something so close to a humanistic model, and to have applied it so successfully, with rigorous objectivity, to animal learning, is in itself a monumental achievement. When Skinner turns his attention back to human beings, he tries to hold to the strict objectivity so useful in applying the model to animals and, since he is now speculating rather than doing research, he allows other humanistic aspects of his thinking—consideration of what a person wants and thinks—to slip in without much notice. Consistent recognition of them might well prompt an explicitly different model for human beings, one much more genuinely pertinent to their psychological structure. The changes to be expected are parallel to those I have already traced in recent social psychology, in the chapter on attitudes, opinions, and motives.

Many therapists influenced by Skinner obviously consider clear thinking about their clients more productive than philosophical purism; in their writings the hidden humanistic nature of the Skinnerian model begins to be explicit, and the simplified mechanical assumptions in which Skinner embeds it are sometimes abandoned. The special and valuable emphasis coming from behavior therapy is on the importance of real alteration of person-environment relationships. Manipulation of environmental response to a person's acts may have a profound and lasting internal effect on the person; here is the potentially great therapeutic value of behavior-therapy techniques themselves. An alteration of the person from within, moreover, induced by quite different techniques, may never have its full effect until it has altered external relations through an expression in behavior; that is the lesson that behavior therapy has for other therapeutic traditions. These important values could be trivial in comparison with the loss that might result from adopting a simple-minded behavioral model and applying it with rigid consistency. That would be like trying to operate the entire government of the United States by applying a few demogogic slogans. This sort of outcome in psychology seems improbable today. We can well afford to seek for an integrated humanistic psychology, I believe, all the positive advantages that can come from considering a behavioral emphasis, without any fear of being led to abandon a humanistic for a mechanical model of man.

Convergence of Humanistic and Behavioristic Points of View in Therapy

In most recent books that consider behavior therapy at length, a mechanistic model still predominates; but it is not so pervasive or exclusive as it once was. The practical experience accumulated both in therapeutic work and in research by those working in the tradition of behavior therapy seems to induce in many the more humanistic mode of thought that an outside critic like me is also likely to consider as required.

Of the recent books, the one by Yates might be expected to be most mechanistic, since he seeks in Hull's stimulus-response rather than Skinner's operant approach his general theoretical framework. Even here, there is a decidedly humanistic tone in Yates' repeated emphasis on the single case;

he considers the only unique feature of behavior therapy to be "the stress on the experimental investigation of the single case," a view that marks as irrelevant much of the least humanistic research other writers have thought relevant to behavior therapy. Yates sees as a future trend increased attention to the problem of how to move from external control to internal control—a perfectly clear though partial convergence with humanistic psychology.

Another behavior therapist whose thought shows a decidedly humanistic strain is Leonard Krasner. In castigating a hospital program that had been considered to exemplify bad features of behavior therapy, he argues that it was not behavior therapy at all, for the reason that it demonstrated "no respect for the integrity of the individual." A major technique of behavior therapy, Krasner feels, is training professional personnel to "react to the individual not as a sick patient but as a responsible individual who is acquiring new skills in learning to behave adequately in his environment." This, too, is not a full convergence with humanistic psychology, but a long move toward it; it places the behavioral emphasis in a context very different from that in which it originated.

The abandonment of a mechanistic model is most conspicuous in the recent book by Arnold Lazarus, *Behavior therapy and beyond.* Lazarus is one of the founders of behavior therapy, but even some of his earlier writings displayed a humanistic approach somewhat discordant with the partial espousal of a mechanistic model. His new book is entirely explicit about the predominance of a humanistic approach. It provides a brilliant demonstration of ways in which the techniques originating in experimental studies of learning can play an important role in humanistic therapy that is centered on the individual patient and directed at increasing his own control of his destiny. Lazarus discusses clinical practice rather than research, and he is concerned to show how a humanistic approach (or personalistic, as he more often calls it) can improve the value of behavioral techniques and can facilitate their being fruitfully blended with other techniques. Equally, though more by implication than by explicit argument, he shows how other forms of humanistic therapy can sometimes be improved by the introduction of techniques derived from behavior therapy. His chapter on group methods illustrates most directly the fusion of the two therapeutic traditions, humanistic and behavioral.

These various humanistic trends in behavior therapy, and the increasing research orientation of humanistic psychology, might lead us to expect an important convergence in the near future in research as well as in practice and in theoretical discussion. Indeed, this convergence has already begun on one important topic I have already considered—schizophrenia. In the previous chapter I described research based on a humanistic model of psychosis. The outcome of that research suggests that the humanistic model offers a great improvement over the disease-entity model of psychosis. That humanistic research is closely paralleled, as I will now indicate, in some recent work by behavior therapists. The two sets of research seem to have been done in complete independence from one another, so that their similarity is all the more noteworthy.

In the previous chapter I considered some humanistic research on the degree to which psychotic patients displayed bizarre symptoms or, in general, presented themselves as sick or healthy. This is paralleled by operant research in which "sick-talk" and "healthy-talk" are viewed as classes of behavior to be differentially reinforced. Leonard P. Ullmann and others did such an experiment with hospitalized schizophrenics. With some patients, an interviewer gave signs of approval after healthy-sounding statements such as reasonable planning for the future and realistic comments on hospital life; with others, the interviewer gave signs of approval after sick-sounding statements such as descriptions of symptoms and bizarre irrelevancies. Even the single 20-minute interview used in this experiment brought about a significant difference in the proportion of sick and healthy talk, in the direction expected from the theory of operant learning. This finding tends to confirm the humanistic research reported in the previous chapter, in adding to the evidence that psychotic behavior is not a stable product of a disease state but is instead highly alterable when pertinent changes occur in the social environment.

Also, the humanistic research suggests a different and, in my opinion, a more convincing interpretation of the operant research. Ullmann and his collaborators apparently regard the reinforcement of the healthy (or sick) class of responses as mechanically bringing about an increased rate of emitting that class of responses. The humanistic research shows that the same outcome may be obtained without any reinforcement—indeed, without any opportunity for the patient to make any responses that could be reinforced—by merely telling the patient something that alters the personal meaning of the situation he is in. My inference would be that in the operant research, the examiner's indications of approval were effective not by providing mechanical reinforcement, but by defining the social situation in relation to the patient's wants. These competing interpretations may sound like different ways of saying the same thing. I do not think that they are. The humanistic interpretation leads us directly, for example, to the expectation that the examiner's approval of healthy responses would have opposite effects in patients who want to be discharged and in patients who want to remain in the hospital, increasing their frequency in the former group and decreasing it in the latter. If future research should establish this point, the very loose definition of reinforcement in Skinner's theory could, of course, be adapted to the findings, by saying that the examiner's approval, considered to be positively reinforcing in the operant research thus far done, turns out to be positively reinforcing only for certain patients, and negatively reinforcing for others. To me, though, there seems to be more scientific virtue in a theory that can lead us to important facts than in a theory that can merely be adapted to fit them.

Recent operant research also has explored methods of overcoming the deficit commonly shown by schizophrenics in tests of intellectual performance. Studies on this issue are diverse. Sometimes the reinforcement for high-quality responses consists of the examiner's approval; sometimes it consists of coupons or tokens to be used like cash in the hospital canteen. The classes of test response reinforced have included attentiveness, abstractness, interpretation of proverbs, and commonness of word association. The reinforcement session is in some research preceded by explaining to the patient just what class of responses will be rewarded, though so far no one seems to have tested whether this procedure alone can be as effective as reinforcement alone.

Patients positively reinforced for correct or high-quality responses on early items in a test give good responses on later items more often than do patients who receive no special reinforcement. This general outcome strengthens the tentative conclusion that is justified by the few humanistic studies of this issue. The evidence from these two sources agrees in showing that intellectual test-performance of many schizophrenics can be easily and greatly modified. The operant research on intellectual performance has been prompted by viewing quality of performance as an operant that is mechanically modified by reinforcement. A humanistic point of view leads to a different interpretation of this operant research. Several of the operant researchers seem to be aware of these humanistic possibilities, and sometimes their conclusions closely resemble those of the humanistic research except that terms derived from Greek and Latin are substituted for more familiar words. One of them says, for example, "The present study indicates that the functional consequences of the schizophrenics' behavior play an important role in the emission of pathognomic verbalizations." The humanistic research argues that the pertinent factor is, more precisely, what the person *expects* to result from his behavior, and how the expected results fit with his wants. If he comes to expect that high-quality responses will increase his chances of discharge from the hospital, he is likely to perform better or worse than previously according to whether he wants to be discharged. The findings of the operant research are readily seen as a special case of this point in the humanistic understanding of schizophrenic behavior. The converse does not seem to be true; the operant theory of behavior seems applicable to the humanistic research only by an extremely loose use of words which renders that theory essentially a vague and disguised form of humanistic theory.

The whole line of humanistic thought about therapy, then, contributes to an enlargement and correction of the implications of the operant research. Yet theoretical considerations alone could hardly suffice for a persuasive presentation of this enlargement and correction; the research I reviewed in the chapter on schizophrenia, done under the guidance of that theory, provides the support essential to the argument. The psychological research tradition and humanistic thought, as I see it, need each other for mutual enrichment.

11
Conclusion

Modern psychology began as an effort to apply scientific method to studying the human mind. Many participating in this effort restricted their discipline within very narrow limits, fearful that a broader definition would hinder progress. Believing that mind could be studied—if at all—only through its behavioral manifestations, some redefined psychology as the study of behavior, excluding conscious experience altogether as a subject for study; some even banned all reference to internal conditions (such as motives or traits) that might be inferred from behavior. Recognizing that cause-effect sequences are most clearly identifiable through experimental manipulation of variables, some psychologists restricted their study to only those variables they could study experimentally. Seeing that measurement and precision have advantages especially exploited in the physical sciences but potentially useful in any discipline, some restricted psychology to the study only of variables that could be measured reliably and precisely. Some psychologists, moreover, finding that they could formulate quantitative laws about these variables with greater confidence and state them with a greater sense of importance if they paid no attention to the context, began to restrict their observations strictly to the measured variable under study, disregarding the context of ongoing individual life within which the measurements occurred. All these restrictions, moreover, could be imposed with less frustration or doubt if the observations were made only on lower animals, unable to describe their experience or comment on a misinterpretation of their actions, and apparently having anyway a less individual and less rich context of thought and action.

This narrowing of psychology reached its extreme many years ago; we have been gradually recovering from it. Today, few psychologists who are fundamentally interested in understanding people approach their aim indirectly by doing research on lower animals. Research is increasingly extended beyond the use of the experimental method. Measurement is less likely now than a few decades ago to be a goal of its own, divorced from scientific or practical use. More and more psychologists investigate the experience as well as the behavior of their subjects. The developments I have traced throughout this book are a part of this movement away from a narrowly defined and overly simple objectivity, toward more adequate ways of turning science to the study of man. Reliance on hyperobjectivity as the main guide has clearly failed. Yet the research tradition tends to retain the image of its past.

Some anomalies result. Consider, for instance, two books by psychologists which have recently been best sellers with the American public: Rollo May's *Love and will* and B. F. Skinner's *Beyond freedom and dignity*. People who have studied psychology, I suspect, place Skinner's book very decidedly in the scientific tradition in psychology, and May's hardly at all.

Yet Skinner's book seems to me to be connected with the scientific tradition only in a personal sense, having been written by a psychologist who is a most distinguished leader of the experimental analysis of animal behavior. What Skinner's book has to say about human beings—and they are the subject of the book—seems to me to be in the philosophical or religious tradition rather than the scientific. It appears to me an expression of the author's personal values and beliefs, stated with papal confidence and buttressed principally by wild extrapolations from rats and pigeons to man, making almost no contact whatever with the great body of psychological research on man, which might be drawn on to present a very different picture from that drawn by Skinner.

May's book, on the other hand, grows out of his years of clinical experience with patients, and that of many other psychologists and psychiatrists. It draws on the interaction of hypothesis and observation, displays humility about the author's wisdom, and looks toward future modification of knowledge. All this seems to me very much in keeping with the spirit of science, and with one reasonable opinion about what methods are at present most useful in scientific inquiry into human psychology. I am sorry May does not seem to find systematic, quantitative research on people any more important than Skinner does. But, at least, he seems to have an attitude conducive to other people's doing or learning about systematic research. That Skinner's book should be thought to represent the research tradition, and May's not, is an indication of the persistence even now of attitudes that formerly were a very serious threat to the development of an adequate psychological science.

One of those attitudes, as I indicated in Chapter 2, is the feeling that the psychological study of man should be confined to relating his observable acts directly to the external variables that influence them. Humanistic thought suggests that the psychological study of man should also include the study of internal system or structure, even though that is not directly observable. The need emerges clearly in some of the research that I have surveyed. A person's interest in being hypnotized, or his resistance to it, pertains to his feelings about broad changes in internal conditions, in general state of consciousness. Changes in a person's thinking about moral issues result partly from developmental changes in the general structure of his thought. In neither case can observable behavior be adequately understood without attention to the internal conditions from which it emerges.

How very narrowing this unfortunate extreme in the psychological research tradition is, can be made clear by comparison with another science. Let us consider that part of astronomy concerned with the solar system (and other such systems as they may become accessible to study). The solar system might be compared to the individual person in psychology. Each is a system or structure of internal parts and relationships. If astronomers were obsessed with the conception of science shared by many psychologists, they might well have taken the solar system as the unit whose behavior they were to study. As causal variables they would then be able to consider only the occasional intrusion of alien objects from outer space; events within the system itself would be banned from notice. The effects they could study would lie in the overall relation of the solar system to objects in outer space. For example, if objects from outer space are captured by the gravitational field of the solar system, what is the effect on the direction and velocity of the movement of the solar system in relation to the nearest other stars or systems? The capture of an alien object by the solar system might have a great many reverberating effects on the relationship of the elements already within the solar system, but these would be missed.

This seems to be essentially what is done by the behavioristic tradition in psychology in its approach to the person. The internal structure is disregarded. Only forces from the outside are considered—only, indeed, simple forces that can be specified as single quantified variables. Effects within the system are disregarded, and all that is considered is the gross effect on the observed relationship of the person to objects outside—a friendly approach, an aggressive lunge, a speeding up of movement. It seems hardly conceivable that astronomers could ever have dealt with the solar system in this way. Our position on one of the planets forming this system makes interrelationships within the system a first object of inquiry.

Had there been a number of other nearby solar systems available for study, perhaps the external approach would have been the characteristic one to be made initially. That is the situation in psychology. We each have an inside view of one person, but we see every other person from the outside. With the valuable emphasis on objectivity brought by the scientific tradition, we tend to emphasize the study of others, and readily fall into the trap of forgetting that each of these others is himself a person with just as much complexity as our own self. We may then forget for a while that the internal view—the person as a center of awareness, and the complex pattern underlying his conscious experience—not only *can* be an object of study but may *need* consideration to understand even the causes and the effects of the behavior directly observable from outside.

That the person can be studied, and with valuable consequences for scientific psychology, is well illustrated by Piaget's research on development. Piaget brings to his work a very strong sense of the value of science and an equally strong view of the necessity of studying the subject matter he intends rather than some other subject matter which can be more easily subjected to scientific study. The great bulk of us psychologists take one of two much easier routes. Many of us restrict our psychological study to questions very easily placed in a simple framework of an antecedent variable and a consequent variable. In doing so we gain some ability to predict certain limited phenomena, and to state precisely how well we can and cannot predict. But we lose much in understanding and, I believe, in ultimate capacity to improve prediction. Some of us take the other route, making our subject matter the whole structured human being, but skipping the difficult task of systematically testing ideas about the subject matter. By this choice we may gain in sense of understanding, feeling that we are genuinely studying the human mind. But we lose any capacity to discriminate between the accurate and the inaccurate things we say about it. More of us than at present should take the unifying path chosen by Piaget, studying the human person and constantly subjecting our ideas to the test of systematic observational inquiry.

It is time for psychologists to renounce the experimenter's fallacy—the implicit notion that the dependability of the specific facts established by a good experiment confers a special aura of validity on all the ideas that may be associated with the experiment. Development of scientific knowledge about man is a long process, with great uncertainty at all stages that we can as yet discern. Neither experimentation nor any other device is likely to eliminate all of the complexities and to supply a perfect and simple understanding. If we truly confined ourselves to knowledge having the clear certainty of experimental findings, avoiding all those extensions, inferences, and generalizations that contaminate their purity, psychology would be a collection of trivia. In claiming a broader significance for even the best experiment, uncertainty is introduced. It may far exceed the uncertainty intrinsic to studying historical records or to observing in the clinic and in everyday life. The uncertainty in these instances is more apparent, because it lies so close to the observations themselves. Where the uncertainty pertains to the remoter stages of inference from data that are themselves secure, it can go unnoticed. Then can arise the strange mixture of firm insistence on tight evidence for narrow statements, and complete abandon in zealous adherence to broad statements unrelated to evidence, which has recurrently plagued and demeaned the psychological research tradition.

On issues close to the factual level, it is reasonable to expect a high degree of certainty. The initial question about ESP—can a person obtain knowledge of the world outside him by presently unknown channels?—is close to the factual level. In the absence of dependably repeatable demonstrations, skepticism is reasonable here despite the many strong items of evidence to support a positive answer. (On the other hand, the position of parapsychologists, who choose to generalize the positive evidence despite its lack of perfect dependability, and to go beyond it in pursuit of the more interesting questions, is also reasonable; and if their judgment is correct, their course is the one infinitely more conducive to scientific progress.)

Rarely, however, is a major issue in psychology really close to a simple fact. No one, for instance, would doubt that people generally act in ways that bring them a dependable supply of food and water. The issue concerns the processes responsible: do they consist only of automatic strengthening of the previous response whenever food is eaten, for instance; or do they include the preparation and execution of plans? On such issues, as I hope I have shown, we need to avoid confusing certainty of evidence about particular facts with certainty of conclusion about broad theoretical problems. In reaching tentative conclusions about the broad problems, we may often infer with greater confidence from closely relevant information lacking in certainty than from information high in certainty but remote in relevance.

For example, early Freudian theory was modified in a humanistic direction by many separate dissident movements as well as by its founder. Many separate clinicians were making similar inferences from their study of patients. Each of them encountered difficulties in understanding patients adequately when he brought to the task only the simple mechanical model of drives which formed the main bulk of Freud's early theory. Each found the difficulties reduced when he modified this model in a humanistic direction or, perhaps, abandoned it in favor of a wholly humanistic one. None of these clinicians, naturally, could report his clinical observations and their relation to theory in the manner of an elegant experimental report requiring everyone's acceptance. Every clinician concluding in favor of a humanistic modification of theory was doing so on evidence less than completely adequate. Yet the fact that so many clinicians reached similar conclusions from their varied observations has more value as evidence, I believe, than any single experiment that might with some difficulty be planned to test the same issue.

Experimenters on social attitudes and opinions, as I have argued in an earlier chapter, have shown changes that likewise have a cumulative evidential value. The dialectic of their interaction with experimental data, like that of clinicians with their patients' problems, has moved them toward a more humanistic model of man. Again, the similarity of shift of many investigators may outweigh the specific substance of their experimental findings.

So, too, for other topics I have considered: The results of an experiment on behavior therapy may have their own immediate importance, but the fact that the experimenter found a personalistic rather than a mechanical approach necessary may be the major link connecting it with other experiments in contributing to general scientific progress. In research on schizophrenia, the repeatedly felt need to get at the patient's own view, and the clarification that results, may contribute more to cumulative knowledge than the particulars of separate studies. The fact that behaviorists studying hypnosis often violate their own methodological principles, in studying the conscious experience as well as the behavior of their subjects, joins with the outcome of humanistic research, in persuading us that modifications of consciousness may well be intrinsic to the phenomenon of hypnosis. Knowledge progresses, then, by an accumulation of uncertain judgments, as well as by an uncertain extrapolation of isolated certainties.

Though I share the humanistic view rather than the narrow mechanical or behavioral view associated with the extreme of the research tradition, I do not mean to criticize only the latter. Extremes in either direction may impede the progress of psychology. The issue of determinism versus free will provides an apt and important illustration.

Many psychologists in the research tradition have held that belief in determinism is an essential precondition for science, that without it the analysis and observation from which science grows would not occur. I know that as a general proposition this is false, for I can see in myself a negative case. I have taken part in scientific research with enthusiastic interest, and I have never been a believer in determinism.

Long ago it was widely held in Western society that without a firm belief, then presumably held by all decent people, in an afterlife of eternal reward or punishment no one would live a moral life. Now we know the falseness of this contention; anthropological studies show that whole societies lacking a creed of immortality are at least as moral as ours, and common observation in our varied society of today indicates that those rejecting a creed of immortality are not uniformly wanting in morality. Where the belief in immortality was universally present (or, at least, never openly denied), the claim for its essential role in morality could not be disproved.

The relation between determinism and science is closely akin, I think, to that between immortality and morality. When determinism is a creed shared by scientists (or, at least, never openly denied) its claim to be essential to science is hard to disprove. The relation, obviously, is not a logical one that could be established by a priori reasoning. The relation, if there is one, is psychological. A belief in perfect determinism is required (some people claim) to motivate the scientist in his search for regularities in nature. Perhaps that may have been true at one time, but I doubt it. Of other human activities—business, art, or making love, for instance—we do not say that the activity is justified only if absolute perfection is attainable. With the variety of incentives and gratifications associated with science today, I cannot believe that this one is really important for very many scientists.

Within the humanistic tradition, some psychologists have held that firm belief in the doctrine of free will—belief in the absolute reality of human freedom—is essential to the discipline. This absolute belief in freedom is not as often claimed to be necessary for scientific research as for clinical work. Many therapists conceive their aim as that of enlarging the patient's sphere of freedom, and of strengthening the patient's confidence in the reality of his freedom. How could therapists work effectively toward this end unless they genuinely believed in the absolute reality of human freedom? I think if I were a clinician I could offer myself again as a negative case. I know that I have a strong sense of my own freedom of choice. I believe this feeling is important to me, I would expect a corresponding feeling to be important to most people, and I believe I would gladly work to help them attain it. Yet I have never been a believer in the doctrine of free will.

I suspect, in short, that beliefs about unprovable propositions—metaphysical or religious beliefs—are not normally essential as motivators of psychological work. A chronic nonbeliever like me is not, I think, incapacitated either for research or for clinical practice. A true believer in free will could, moreover, be a successful researcher, and a true believer in determinism (like Sigmund Freud) could be a successful clinician—perhaps at the cost of some inner tension, but yet with great effectiveness.

Although I am sure metaphysical beliefs are less influential than often supposed, they may still be important. The role I see them most often playing is that of inhibiting, not motivating, the progress of psychology. Fervent belief in determinism leads some psychologists to be embarrassed about feelings of freedom, to avoid attention to them, or to speak of them as illusions. Since feelings of freedom are central to the processes under study and to the proper aims of therapy, this attitude imposes crippling restrictions. Fervent belief in free will leads some psychologists, perhaps—certainly many students or potential students of psychology—to disregard the scientific research tradition, and the rich outcome of its application to human behavior and experience; to disregard this tradition means to lose the many opportunities it provides for help in sustaining and extending human freedom.

The danger here is that holding to the doctrine of free will may lead one to find offensive any evidence that human behavior is greatly constrained, in any but the obvious ways, by external forces. The findings of much psychological research offer the threat of establishing previously unnoticed limitations on freedom. If a person's choice of a spouse is found to be influenced by nationality, religion, race, education, and nearness of residence, we may still be able to say that he is choosing freely among the possibilities his environment most readily provides. If a person's choice of a spouse is found to be influenced also by many traits in his own personality, and in that of the possible spouses, or by the series of events that established those traits, we may have more difficulty placing the facts in a framework of belief in personal freedom.

Disregard of some psychological research could be justified by its lack of relevance to the concerns of a humanistic approach. Much psychological research, on the other hand, is manifestly relevant, as I have shown in discussing art, moral development, schizophrenia, and several other topics. Too, much of the seemingly irrelevant research is in fact, I have tried to show, highly pertinent to humanistic interests—some through supporting indirectly a general humanistic position, as does the recent work of social psychologists on attitudes, opinions, and motives; some through providing a structure of knowledge that can fit a humanistic framework at least as well as the framework of origin, as I have argued is true of research on behavior therapy.

When the humanistic psychologist does undertake research, his viewpoint provides no guarantee of perfection. One virtue of the humanistic viewpoint is its encouraging attention to the context of experience and action, to their meaning for the whole person. Yet the humanistic psychologist may, like the extreme behaviorist, become so absorbed in his specific topic that he forgets the context. Social psychologists of humanistic bent, for instance, have sometimes assumed a basic human need for cognitive consistency. Humanistic estheticians have sometimes seemed to make, though less explicitly, the contrary assumption, that people have a basic human need for complexity or inconsistency. Two very different pictures of human nature emerge. They both, I think, have some validity. Social psychologists, by paying more attention to the context in which they observe a striving for consistency, have come to modify their initial sweeping generalization—considering it valid, for instance, only where inconsistency would threaten self-esteem. Estheticians may similarly gain by greater attention to the context in which the persons they study are acting. Eventually, then, the apparent contradiction between a rage for order and a rage for chaos may be resolved. Greater attention to context, from which a resolution of the contradiction is likely to emerge, is favored by a humanistic viewpoint, though clearly not guaranteed.

A humanistic psychologist may, like anyone else, exaggerate the importance of his own particular interest. A humanistic researcher on hypnosis might so emphasize the role of individual personality as a source of hypnotizability, that he would neglect the very real influence of environmental factors. A developmental psychologist, while holding the general view that a person advances through his own autonomous interaction with the environment, might so exaggerate the uniformity among people in stages of development that he would fail in practice to recognize the autonomy genuinely present in each individual.

If I am right in expecting that a humanistic viewpoint will increasingly dominate psychological research, we should not on that account relax vigilance against narrowness of conception, nor expect that psychology will lose the attractions of diversity and controversy. The present movement in psychology is toward eliminating only one source of difference, a source productive in the past of alienation rather than productive controversy. It is the vast separation between the extremes of the research tradition (requiring certainty to a point where broader significance is foresaken) and of humanistic thought (demanding human relevance so immediately that verification is not sought).

The research tradition has in recent years come to be applied with great efficacy under the guidance of humanistic thought, or in directions supporting humanistic thought. Humanistic psychology is thus gaining a place in the established body of detailed scientific research; it is becoming embedded in the research and transformed by it. We are moving toward a single general psychology adequate to modern conceptions, free of the inhibitions acquired in its infancy. In the future, then, a modified humanistic psychology may become one discipline, comprising the whole range of psychological activities ultimately useful to man. The outsider looking at that modern psychology, and comparing it with the diverse psychologies from which it arose, can be understanding and tolerant even if amused to hear a psychologist, immersed in his more intimate relations with his discipline, exclaiming with Fernando in *The Tempest,*

> *. . . but you, O you,*
> *So perfect and so peerless, are created*
> *Of every creature's best.*

Notes

General Note

In citing books, I have generally referred to the original publication, usually in hardback, because that is most useful for library purposes or for suggesting the time of writing or of translation. Many of these books however, are also available in paperback.

Notes to Chapter 2, The Research Tradition

Page 8 Skinner's statement appears in *B. F. Skinner: The man and his ideas* by Richard I. Evans (Dutton, 1968). In his 1971 book, *Beyond freedom and dignity* (Knopf; pp. 190–192, for example), Skinner seems to have taken a very small step toward the humanistic position on the role of awareness in psychology.

Page 11 For cognitive psychology and its models, see George A. Miller, Eugene Galanter, and Karl H. Pribram, *Plans and the structure of behavior* (Holt, 1960) and Ulric Neisser, *Cognitive psychology* (Appleton-Century-Crofts, 1967).

Page 11 An especially valuable critique of excesses in the psychological research tradition, in my opinion, is that offered by David Bakan in his book *On method: Toward a reconstruction of psychological investigation* (Jossey-Bass, 1969).

Notes to Chapter 3, Humanistic Psychology

Page 13 The Allport quotation is from page 309 of his article, "The open system in personality theory", *Journal of Abnormal and Social Psychology* for November 1960 (vol. 61, 301–310).

Page 14 James' humanistic viewpoint is represented both in his *Principles of psychology* (Holt, 1890) and in his *The varieties of religious experience: A study in human nature* (Longmans, Green, 1902). The humanistic aspect of James' psychology is discussed by several present-day psychologists in *William James: Unfinished business,* edited by Robert B. MacLeod (American Psychological Association, 1969).

Page 16 An introduction to these and other "growth techniques" is provided by William Schutz' *Here comes everybody* (Harper Row, 1971) and, in completely noncritical fashion and mixed with a great deal else, by Severin Peterson's *A catalog of the ways people grow* (Ballantine, 1971).

Page 20 For Maslow's work on peak experiences and on self-actualizing persons see, for example, his book, *Toward a psychology of being* (Van Nostrand, 1962). On sensitivity to artistic styles, see R. B. Morant and A. H. Maslow, "Art judgment and the judgment of others: A preliminary study," *Journal of Clinical Psychology* 1965 (vol. 21, pp. 389–391).

Notes to Chapter 4, Psychology and Moral Development

Page 23 Bogachevsky's developmental view of conscience is quoted from page 76 of Gurdjieff's *Meetings with remarkable men* (Dutton, 1969).

Page 25 Kohlberg's theory is presented in some of the specific references cited below. A general account readily available is his chapter, "Stage and sequence: The cognitive-developmental approach to socialization," pages 347 to 480 in the *Handbook of socialization theory and research* edited by David A. Goslin (Rand McNally, 1969). A shorter summary is given by Elliot Turiel in his chapter, "Developmental processes in the child's moral thinking," pages 92 to 133 in *Trends and issues in developmental psychology,* edited by Paul Mussen, Jonas Langer, and Martin Covington (Holt, Rinehart & Winston, 1969).

Pages 25–30 An authoritative, though difficult, account of Piaget's theory appears in his own article entitled "Piaget's theory," pages 703 to 732 in volume 1 of *Carmichael's manual of child psychology, third edition,* edited by Paul H. Mussen (Wiley, 1970). Introductions to his theory are provided by Piaget in *Six psychological studies* (Random House, 1967) and by Piaget and his co-worker Bärbel Inhelder in *The psychology of the child* (Basic Books, 1969). Piaget's writings require concentrated effort, but are worth it.

Page 28 The two quotations from Piaget are from page 725 of his 1970 article cited just above.

Page 31 Piaget's book on moral development is *The moral judgment of the child* (Free Press, 1932); the story I have quoted appears on pages 250 to 251.

Page 36 The research in other societies will be reported more fully in a chapter of the forthcoming book edited by Lawrence Kohlberg and Elliot Turiel, *Recent research in moral development* (Holt, Rinehart, & Winston).

Page 36 Research comparing the sexes will be reported by Turiel in his chapter, "Sex differences in the development of moral knowledge and judgment," in the book just cited.

Page 37 Effects of exposure to other reasoning are presented by Elliot Turiel, "An experimental test of the sequentiality of developmental stages in the child's moral judgments," in the *Journal of*

Personality and Social Psychology for June 1966 (vol. 3, pp. 611–618).

Page 37 For the experiment on understanding and evaluating others' reasoning, see James Rest, Elliot Turiel, and Lawrence Kohlberg, "Level of moral development as a determinant of preference and comprehension of moral judgments made by others," *Journal of Personality* for June 1969 (vol. 37, pp. 225–252).

Page 40 See especially the chapter by Elliott Turiel, "Stage transition in moral development," to appear in *Second handbook of research on teaching* edited by R. M. Travers (Rand McNally, 1972).

Page 40 The quotation is from page 109 of Lawrence Kohlberg and Richard B. Kramer, "Continuities and discontinuities in childhood and adult moral development," *Human Development* (1969, vol. 12, pp. 93–120).

Page 41 The examples of Stage 2 responses are quoted from the Kohlberg and Kramer article cited above, pages 109 to 111.

Pages 44–45 I have quoted by permission of the author from an unpublished paper, "Progressive and regressive aspects of moral development," by Elliot Turiel.

Notes to Chapter 5, Psychology of Art

Page 47 The lines by Stevens form part of "The poems of our climate," pages 193 to 194 of *The collected poems of Wallace Stevens* (copyright 1964 by Alfred A. Knopf, Inc.).

Page 48 Berlyne's book was published in 1971 by Appleton-Century-Crofts.

Pages 48–49 A summary of this Freudian theory of art is included in Robert Waelder's *Psychoanalytic avenues to art* (International Universities Press, 1965); Waelder's book has the great merit of reviewing also some of the many other ideas psychoanalysis has contributed to the study of art.

Pages 49–51 Rank's views on art are presented in several of his books, but most fully in *Art and artist* (Knopf, 1932). My quotations are from chapters in that book entitled "Life and creation" and "The artist's fight with art." Together with several other chapters from the same book, they are included in the paperback, *The myth of the birth of the hero and other writings by Otto Rank* (Vintage, 1959), where the quotations appear on pages 142, 191, and 192.

Page 51 The emphasis on personal growth recurs through all of Maslow's later writing. See, for example, *Toward a psychology of being* (Van Nostrand, 1962) or *The farther reaches of human nature* (Viking, 1971).

Page 51 A summary of Barron's study of soundness appears as Chapter 5 in his book, *Creativity and personal freedom,* (Van Nostrand, 1968) and the earlier version of it, *Creativity and psychological health* (1963).

Pages 51–55 MacKinnon has described his study of architects in several articles. The one stressing its relation to Rank's theory is "Personality and the realization of creative potential" in *American Psychologist* for April 1965 (vol. 20, pp. 273–281). The quotations are from pages 278 to 280 of that article.

Page 55 Taft discusses "Creativity: Hot and cold" in the *Journal of Personality* for September 1971 (vol. 39, pp. 345–361).

Page 55 Barron has written on creative personality in the book I have already cited and in *Creative person and creative process* (Holt, Rinehart & Winston, 1969).

Page 56 Allport's monograph, *The use of personal documents in psychological science,* was published in 1942 as Bulletin No. 49 of the Social Science Research Council, New York.

Page 56 Rothenberg's study of O'Neill, "The iceman changeth: Toward an empirical approach to creativity," was published in the April 1969 issue of the *Journal of the American Psychoanalytic Association* (vol. 17, pp. 549–607).

Pages 56–57 The quotation about O'Neill is from pages 197 to 198 of Rothenberg's article, "The process of Janusian thinking in creativity," in *Archives of General Psychiatry* for March 1971 (vol. 24, pp. 195–205, copyright 1971 by American Medical Association), which summarizes the several studies of his that I describe.

Page 58 These arguments of the new criticism are beautifully presented in Cleanth Brooks' *The well wrought urn* (Harcourt Brace, 1947).

Page 64 Judgments by Japanese potters have been reported by Sumiko Iwao and myself in "Comparison of esthetic judgments by American experts and Japanese potters" (*Journal of Social Psychology,* February 1966, vol. 68, pp. 27–33), those of Pakistani students by Mah Pervin Anwar and myself in "Personality and esthetic sensitivity in an Islamic culture" (*Journal of Social Psychology,* June 1972, vol. 87, pp. 21–28. Judgments by architects, other art experts, and students in Greece will be reported in an article by Mika Fatouros and myself.

Pages 65–67 The development of this measure of esthetic sensitivity, and its personality correlates among United States college students, are presented at greater length in an article of mine, "Personality correlates of esthetic judgment in college students," in the September 1965 issue of *Journal of Personality* (vol. 33, pp. 476–511), which has been reprinted in the 1969 Penguin paperback, *Psychology and the visual arts,* edited by James Hogg.

Page 65 This measure of independence of judgment, and its development, are described by Barron in "Some personality correlates of independence of judgment," *Journal of Personality,* March 1953 (vol. 21, pp. 287–297).

Page 66 Personality correlates of esthetic sensitivity among United States school students and Japanese college students were reported by I. L. Child and Sumiko Iwao, "Personality and esthetic sensitivity: Extension of findings to younger age and to different culture," *Journal of Personality and Social Psychology* for March 1968 (vol. 8, pp. 308–312). Corresponding results from Pakistan and Greece are considered in the articles already cited.

Page 67 Some of the personality measures found correlated with esthetic sensitivity seem likely to be correlated also with intelligence, and the question may be raised whether intelligence is the only link between them. The esthetic sensitivity measure is itself too little related to intelligence for this to be possible; in the college group I studied, esthetic sensitivity had a correlation of only +.17 with the verbal aptitude test, and −.01 with the mathematical aptitude test, of the College Entrance Examination Board.

Page 67 For the use of aniseikonic lenses, see *Cognitive control* by Riley Gardner, P. S. Holzman, G. S. Klein, Harriet Linton, and D. P. Spence (Monograph no. 4 in *Psychological Issues,* 1959). The effect of putting aniseikonic lenses on has been related to esthetic sensitivity in my 1965 article cited above and in a paper by Pavel Machotka and Richard R. Waite, "Form distortion and ego defense: A replication," presented at the 1968 Convention of the American Psychological Association. Machotka and Waite found an even closer relationship than had been reported in the original article. (With 49 subjects, they found a correlation coefficient of .51, compared with the earlier coefficient of .29 obtained with 138 subjects.)

Notes to Chapter 6, Hypnosis

Page 69 White presented this question in "A preface to a theory of hypnotism," an article in the *Journal of Abnormal and Social Psychology* for 1941 (vol. 36, pp. 477–506).

Page 70 Research on hypnosis by Hull and his students was summarized in his book, *Hypnosis and suggestibility: An experimental approach* (Appleton-Century, 1933).

Page 71 The two quotations about hallucination are from pages 270 to 271 of Hull's book.

Page 72 Hull's statement about anesthesia is on page 282 of his book.

Page 73 Hull's comparison with conditioning appears on page 280 of his book.

Page 73 For evidence about subjects' motives in human conditioning experiments, see the article by C. D. Noblin, E. O. Timmons, and H. C. Kael, "Differential effects of positive and negative verbal reinforcement on psychoanalytic character types" (*Journal of Personality and Social Psychology,* 1966, vol. 4, pp. 224–228).

Pages 73–81 The work of the Hilgards is presented in Ernest R. Hilgard's book, *Hypnotic susceptibility* (Harcourt, Brace & World, 1965) and Josephine Hilgard's book, *Personality and hypnosis* (University of Chicago Press, 1970). An abbreviated version of the former has been published as a paperback, *The experience of hypnosis* (Harcourt, Brace & World, 1968). Further valuable discussion, and a brief account of some later research, appear in E. R. Hilgard's article, "Hypnotic phenomena: The struggle for scientific acceptance" in *American Scientist* for September–October 1971 (vol. 59, pp. 567–577).

Page 80 The quotation is from page 342 of E. R. Hilgard's *Hypnotic susceptibility.*

Page 81 A summary of Sarbin's theory of hypnosis is included in the more general article by Theodore R. Sarbin and Vernon L. Allen, "Role theory" (pp. 488–567 in vol. 1 of *The handbook of social psychology,* second edition, edited by Gardner Lindzey and Elliot Aronson, Addison-Wesley, 1968). An instance of new discovery guided by role theory appears in an article by William C. Coe and T. R. Sarbin, "An alternative interpretation to the multiple composition of hypnotic scales" (*Journal of Personality and Social Psychology,* 1971, vol. 18, pp. 1–8).

Pages 81–83 Barber's research and his views on hypnosis are summarized in two recent books by him: *Hypnosis: A scientific approach* (Van Nostrand Reinhold, 1969) and *LSD, marihuana, yoga, and hypnosis* (Aldine, 1970).

Page 82 The quotations are from pages 236 and 244 of Barber's 1970 book.

Page 83 Paul L. Wachtel's paper, "Wanting nothing and getting nothing: On negative results in hypnosis research," is in the April

1969 issue of *The American Journal of Clinical Hypnosis* (vol. 11, pp. 209–220).

Page 84 Tart reports this greatly altered state of consciousness in "Transpersonal potentialities of deep hypnosis," pages 27 to 40 in the 1970 *Journal of Transpersonal Psychology* (vol. 2, no. 1).

Page 85 "Increases in hypnotizability resulting from a prolonged program for enhancing personal growth," by Charles T. Tart, appears in the June 1970 issue of *Journal of Abnormal Psychology* (vol. 75, pp. 260–266).

Page 85 Tart's findings have now been confirmed in a better controlled experiment by Jerrold L. Shapiro and Michael Jay Diamond, reported in their article, "Increases in hypnotizability as a function of encounter group training: Some confirming evidence" (pp. 112–115 in the February, 1972 issue of the *Journal of Abnormal Psychology,* vol. 9). Shapiro and Diamond found increased hypnotizability to result from encounter group participation of only 26 hours' total duration. They attribute the effect, however, to increased trust rather than to an increased readiness for novel experience.

Page 85 The personality correlates of hypnotizability are markedly similar to the personality correlates of creativity, considered in Chapter 5. This relation is explored directly by Kenneth S. Bowers and Sandra J. van der Meulen, "Effect of hypnotic susceptibility on creativity test performance," in the March 1970 issue of *Journal of Personality and Social Psychology* (vol. 14, pp. 247–256).

Notes to Chapter 7, Attitudes, Opinions, and Motives: Recent Social Psychology

Page 88 The quotation is from pages 50 to 51 of *Notes from underground, Poor people, The friend of the family: 3 short novels* by Fyodor Dostoyevsky, translated by Constance Garnett (Dell, 1960). *Notes from underground* first appeared in Constance Garnett's translation as part of *White nights and other stories,* and I am quoting from it by permission of The Macmillan Co. (American copyright owner) and William Heinemann, Ltd. (British copyright owner).

Page 89 I would not want, by describing the manipulative background of attitude research, to encourage too easy a dismissal of such research by humanistically oriented readers. So I want to add some cautions beyond those provided by this chapter itself. First, the same methods of research can be turned to antimanipulative ends in studying resistance to manipulation, and the resulting analyses may better serve humanistic purposes than does the undiscriminating resistance otherwise likely. See, on this point, William J. McGuire, "Inducing resistance to persuasion: Some contemporary approaches," pages 192 to 229 in *Advances in experimental social psychology,* 1964, vol. 1. Second, the outcome of the whole body of attitude research may include disproving facile assumptions likely to be made by practical manipulators of attitude, and to confirm that phenomena of attitude change have the degree of complexity humanistic theory would suggest. That is one conclusion that might reasonably be drawn from McGuire's thorough review, "The nature of attitudes and attitude change," pages 136 to 314 in vol. 3 of *The handbook of social psychology, second edition,* edited by Gardner Lindzey and Elliot Aronson (Addison-Wesley, 1969).

Page 89 An account of Lewin's role in the history of social psychology is included in Alfred J. Marrow's *The practical theorist: The life and work of Kurt Lewin* (Basic Books, 1969).

Pages 90–92 My account here is based on Festinger's book, *A theory of cognitive dissonance* (Row, Peterson, 1957). The quotation is from pages 261 and 264.

Page 92 L. Festinger and J. M. Carlsmith describe this experiment in "Cognitive consequences of forced compliance," *Journal of Abnormal and Social Psychology,* March 1959 (vol. 58, pp. 203–210).

Page 93 J. W. Brehm and A. R. Cohen's *Explorations in cognitive dissonance* was published by Wiley in 1962.

Page 94 The quotations are from page 24 of Aronson's article, "Dissonance theory: Progress and problems," pages 5 to 27 in *Theories of cognitive consistency: A sourcebook,* edited by Robert P. Abelson and others (Rand McNally, 1968).

Page 94 The experiment using the issue of legalizing marijuana was by Elizabeth Nel, Robert Helmreich, and Elliot Aronson: "Opinion change in the advocate as a function of the persuasibility of his audience: A clarification of the meaning of dissonance," *Journal of Personality and Social Psychology* for June 1969 (vol. 12, pp. 117–124).

Page 95 Abelson discusses "Psychological implication" in his article of that name, pages 112 to 139 in the source book cited in the second note back.

Page 95 The experiment by Mark R. Lepper, Mark P. Zanna, and Robert P. Abelson is described in "Cognitive irreversibility in a dissonance reduction situation," *Journal of Personality and Social Psychology* of October 1970 (vol. 16, pp. 191–198). I have quoted from page 192.

Page 96 On attribution theory, see Fritz Heider, *The psychology of interpersonal relations* (Wiley, 1958); Edward E. Jones and Keith E. Davis, "From acts to dispositions: The attribution process in person perception," *Advances in experimental social psychology* (1965, vol. 2, pp. 219–266); Harold H. Kelley, "Attribution theory in social psychology," *Nebraska symposium on motivation* (1967, pp. 192–240); Ivan D. Steiner, "Perceived freedom," *Advances in experimental social psychology* (1970, vol. 5, pp. 187–248).

Page 96 Bem first presented his behavioristic version of self-attribution in "An experimental analysis of self-persuasion," *Journal of Experimental Social Psychology,* 1965 (vol. 1, pp. 199–218). A similar account, drawing less on behavioristic terminology, is "Self-perception: An alternative interpretation of cognitive dissonance phenomena," *Psychological Review* 1967 (vol. 74, pp. 183–200).

Page 97 The textbook by Bem is *Beliefs, attitudes, and human affairs* (Brooks/Cole, 1970). The experimental report is "Testing the self-perception explanation of dissonance phenomena: On the salience of premanipulation attitudes," by Daryl J. Bem and H. Keith McConnell, *Journal of Personality and Social Psychology* for January 1970 (vol. 14, pp. 23–31).

Page 97 What I have already said about Daryl Bem's writing illustrates that progress often lies in some creative fusion of humanistic and nonhumanistic approaches, but more can be said in support of that conclusion. Charles Walters points out to me that Bem is more humanistic than the consistency theorists in rejecting their ultra-rational view that man is always striving for consistency; with the indirection of wit, Bem seems to make the same claim in *Beliefs, attitudes, and human affairs,* pages 38 to 39. On the other hand, Bem's arguments against the importance of internal awareness seem to imply in him an ultrarational view of man, granting importance only to those experiences that can be clearly verbalized (see pages 52 to 53 in his book, for instance). The work of Albert Rothenberg, which I have described in my chapter on psychology of art, would suggest that the presence of these warring elements in Bem's thinking may have had something to do with the great originality of what emerged.

Page 97 Laing uses this term in *The divided self* (Tavistock, 1960).

Pages 97–100 These experiments by Brehm and by Zimbardo and colleagues are all presented in Philip G. Zimbardo's book, *The cognitive control of motivation* (Scott, Foresman, 1969), except for the hypnosis experiment, which is reported in Christina Maslach, Gary Marshall, and Philip Zimbardo, "Hypnotic control of complex skin temperature," *Proceedings of the Annual Convention of the American Psychological Association,* 1971 (vol. 6, pp. 777–778).

Page 100 The experiment is described fully by Schachter and Singer in "Cognitive, social, and physiological determinants of emotional state," *Psychological Review* for September 1962 (vol. 69, pp. 379–399).

Page 101 "Insomnia and the attribution process" by Michael D. Storms and Richard E. Nisbett is in the October 1970 issue of *Journal of Personality and Social Psychology* (vol. 16, pp. 319–328).

Page 103 Brehm's book was published by Academic Press.

Page 104 "Effect of threats to attitudinal freedom as a function of agreement with the communicator" by Stephen Worchel and Jack W. Brehm, appeared in the January 1970 issue of the *Journal of Personality and Social Psychology* (vol. 14, pp. 18–22).

Page 105 Wicklund's paper, "Prechoice preference reversal as a result of threat to decision freedom," appeared in the January 1970 issue of the *Journal of Personality and Social Psychology* (vol. 14, pp. 8–17).

Page 105 The emergence of perceived freedom as an important concept in dissonance research is thoroughly reviewed by Ivan Steiner in the article cited earlier, and he also reviews there the evidence that perceived freedom plays an important part in attribution (that is, in making inferences about why a person acts as he does).

Page 105 The noise experiments I describe were reported in "Psychic cost of adaptation to an environmental stressor," *Journal of Personality and Social Psychology,* 1969 (vol. 12, pp. 200–210). The general outcome was confirmed in a somewhat different experiment by Glass, Bruce Reim, and Singer, "Behavioral consequences of adaptation to controllable and uncontrollable noise," *Journal of Experimental Social Psychology,* 1971 (vol. 7, pp. 244–257).

Page 106 For summaries of the obesity research, see Stanley Schachter, "Some extraordinary facts about obese humans and rats," *American Psychologist* for February 1971 (vol. 26, pp. 129–144), and Richard E. Nisbett, "Eating behavior and obesity in men and animals," *Advances in psychosomatic medicine,* in press.

Page 107 Rotter presented the questionnaire in "Generalized expectancies for internal versus external control of reinforcement," *Psychological Monographs* 1966 (vol. 80, no. 1). For recent research, see the following examples and other articles cited in them: Christine B. Williams and James B. Nickels, "Internal-external control dimension as related to accident and suicide proneness," *Journal of Consulting and Clinical Psychology* for August 1969 (vol. 33, pp. 485–494); John R. Forward and Jay R. Williams, "Internal-external control and black militancy," *Journal of Social Issues,* 1970 (vol. 26, pp. 75–92).

Page 107 Kiesler's discussion is on pages 159 to 164 of his book, *The psychology of commitment: Experiments linking behavior to belief* (Academic, 1971).

Page 108 The paper by J. T. Tedeschi, B. R. Schlenker, and T. V. Bonoma is "Cognitive dissonance: Private ratiocination or public spectacle?" *American Psychologist* for August 1971, (vol. 26, pp. 685–695).

Notes to Chapter 8, Extrasensory Perception

Page 109 The Blake quotation is from *The marriage of heaven and hell.*

Page 110 My grandfather's experience is quoted from pages 85 to 86 of James I. Long, *Pioneering in Mexico* (Long Co., 1942).

Page 112 Upton Sinclair's *Mental radio* was originally published in 1930. Recent editions, including the 1971 Collier paperback, contain a lengthy analysis by W. F. Prince in which statistical reasoning is applied.

Page 112 Jung's autobiography is *Memories, dreams, reflections* (Random House, 1961).

Page 112 *William James on psychical research* (Viking, 1960) is a compilation of his statements. Gardner Murphy has published, in addition to various papers, *Challenge of psychical research: A primer of parapsychology* (Harper & Row, 1961).

Page 114 Admission that other alternatives are exhausted, and resort to fraud as the only acceptable explanation, appear in "Science and the supernatural" by George R. Price (*Science,* August 26, 1955, vol. 122, pp. 359–367). Several discussions of his paper were published in the issue of January 6, 1956 (vol. 123, pp. 9–19). Readers of this material should be aware that in the issue of *Science* for January 28, 1972 (vol. 175, p. 359) under the title, "Apology to Rhine and Soal," Price published the following letter: "During the past year I have had some correspondence with J. B. Rhine which has convinced me that I was highly unfair to him in what I said in an article entitled 'Science and the Supernatural' published in *Science* in 1955 (26 Aug., p. 359). The article discussed possible fraud in extrasensory perception experiments. I suspect that I was similarly unfair in what I said about S. G. Soal in that paper."

Page 116 Recent consideration of distance effects and of their bearing on a theory of ESP appears in "ESP over distance: Research on the ESP channel" by Karlis Osis, Malcolm E. Turner, Jr., and Mary Lou Carlson, published in the *Journal of the American Society for Psychical Research* (1971, vol. 65, pp. 245–288).

Page 116 Rhine's 1934 book is *Extra-sensory perception* (Boston Society for Psychic Research; reprinted 1964 by Bruce Humphries).

Pages 117–120 Studies of individual differences are surveyed in the book by Gertrude R. Schmeidler and R. A. McConnell, *ESP and personality patterns* (Yale University Press, 1958).

Page 118 In some of the group experiments, subjects could by violating instructions have produced spurious results, but this problem does not pertain to the individual experiments. See Schmeidler's note, "ESP: Schmeidler to McNemar," *Contemporary Psychology* 1960 (vol. 5, pp. 59–60).

Page 118 Palmer's review, "Scoring in ESP tests as a function of belief in ESP", is in two parts. "Part I. The sheep-goat effect" is in the *Journal of the American Society for Psychical Research* for October 1971 (vol. 65, pp. 373–408). Part II is to appear in a later issue of the same journal.

Page 119 Honorton's study is reported in "Creativity and precognition scoring level", *Journal of Parapsychology* 1967 (vol. 31, pp. 29–42).

Page 119 Johnson and Kanthamani's article, "The Defense Mechanism Test as a predictor of ESP scoring direction," is in the *Journal of Parapsychology* (1967, vol. 31, pp. 99–110).

Page 119 Eysenck's "Personality and extra-sensory perception" appeared in the June 1967 issue of the *Journal of the Society for Psychical Research*, vol. 44, pp. 55–71. (This is the journal of the British society, not the American.)

Page 120 Moss and Gengerelli's first study was "Telepathy and emotional stimuli: A controlled experiment," *Journal of Abnormal Psychology* for August 1967 (vol. 72, pp. 341–348).

Page 122 The second study by Moss and Gengerelli was "ESP effects generated by affective states," *Journal of Parapsychology* 1968 (vol. 32, pp. 90–100).

Page 122 The third study in this series is Thelma Moss' "ESP effects in 'artists' contrasted with 'non-artists'", *Journal of Parapsychology* 1969 (vol. 33, pp. 57–69).

Page 122 The paper by Moss, Chang, and Levitt is "Long-distance ESP: A controlled study" in the October 1970 issue of the *Journal of Abnormal Psychology* (vol. 78, pp. 288–294).

Page 123 The critique by Baron and Stampfl appears as "A note on 'Long-distance ESP: A controlled study'" in the December 1971 issue of the same journal (vol. 78, pp. 280–283). Though neither they nor Moss, in a reply following immediately in the same journal issue, mention the fact, the criticism applies to none of the other papers thus far published in this series.

Page 123 As evidence for the presence of ESP, the qualitative data cannot, however, be given as much weight in the UCLA studies as in the dream experiments to be taken up later. The UCLA experiments leave open the possibility that qualitative findings (but not, except in the first study, the quantitative findings) could be influenced by a subject's possible advance communication with prior subjects.

Page 123 Previous experiments varying the type of target are reviewed and a new experiment of his own is presented by James C. Carpenter, in "The differential effect and hidden target differences consisting of erotic and neutral stimuli", *Journal of the American Society for Psychical Research* 1971 (vol. 65 pp. 204–214).

Page 123 Two studies of mood or group atmosphere are available: G. R. Schmeidler, "Mood and attitude on a pretest as predictors of retest ESP performance," *Journal of the American Society for Psychical Research* for July 1971 (vol. 65, pp. 324–335); G. R. Schmeidler and James G. Craig, "Groups' moods and ESP scores" to be published in the same journal, probably in the issue for July 1972.

Page 124 The psychotherapy study is "ESP scores following therapeutic sessions," in the *Journal of the American Society for Psychical Research* for April 1971 (vol. 65, pp. 215–222).

Page 124 Claims of evidence for telepathy in dreams are presented and discussed by several writers in a book edited by George Devereux, *Psychoanalysis and the occult* (International Universities Press, 1953) and by Jule Eisenbud in his book, *PSI and psychoanalysis* (Grune and Stratton, 1970).

Page 124 The quotation from Freud is from page 435 of *Collected papers, Volume IV* (authorized translation under the supervision of Joan Riviere; Hogarth Press, 1925).

Page 124 Charles Honorton and Stanley Krippner, in "Hypnosis and ESP performance: A review of the experimental literature," *Journal of the American Society for Psychical Research* for July 1969 (vol. 63, pp. 214–252), report this analysis of data compiled by L. E. Rhine, "Psychological processes in ESP experiences. I. Waking experiences", *Journal of Parapsychology* for 1962 (vol. 26, pp. 88–111).

Page 125 The initial report by Ullman, Krippner, and Feldstein was "Experimentally induced telepathic dreams: Two studies using EEG-REM monitoring technique," in *International Journal of Neuropsychiatry* 1966 (vol. 2, pp. 420–437). Like later studies, it is also described by Ullman and Krippner in "Dream studies and telepathy: An experimental approach," *Parapsychological Monographs,* number 12 (1970).

Page 125 This experiment with a single subject is described in the two publications just cited for the group experiment.

Page 126 The second individual experiment, with the same subject, is reported by Ullman and Krippner in *Biological Psychiatry* for 1969 (vol. 1, pp. 259–270), under the title, "A laboratory approach to the nocturnal dimension of paranormal experience: Report of a confirmatory study using the REM monitoring technique."

Page 126 The third individual experiment, with a new subject, is reported by Krippner and Ullman in "Telepathy and dreams: A controlled experiment with electroencephalogram-electro-oculogram monitoring," *Journal of Nervous and Mental Disease* for 1970 (vol. 151, pp. 394–403).

Page 127 The experiments reported to lack statistically significant results are summarized in the monograph already cited and in Krippner's paper, "The paranormal dream and man's pliable future," *Psychoanalytic Review* for 1969 (vol. 56, pp. 28–43).

Page 127 Ideas about the processes involved in ESP are presented in the final chapter of the monograph already cited, and in the paper by Krippner cited in the previous note.

Page 127 The experiment on precognition in dreams is reported by Krippner, Ullman, and Charles Honorton in "A precognitive dream study with a single subject," *Journal of the American Society for Psychical Research* for 1971 (vol. 65, pp. 192–203).

Page 128 Mary Craig Sinclair's account of the state of consciousness she found conducive to ESP appears in Chapter 21 of her husband's book, *Mental radio*, cited earlier.

Page 128 Baba Ram Dass describes pertinent experiences in *Be here now* (Lama Foundation, 1971).

Page 128 Van De Castle's summary, "The facilitation of ESP through hypnosis", appears in *The American Journal of Clinical Hypnosis* for July 1969 (vol. 12, pp. 37–56). The other summary, by Honorton and Krippner, has already been cited in a preceding note.

Page 128 "Hypnosis and ESP: A controlled experiment," by Thelma Moss, Morris J. Paulson, Alice F. Chang, and Marc Levitt, appears in *The American Journal of Clinical Hypnosis* for July 1970 (vol. 13, pp. 46–56).

Page 129 The article by William N. McBain, Wayne Fox, Susan Kimura, Miles Nakanishi, and John Tirado, "Quasi-sensory communication: An investigation using semantic matching and accentuated affect," is in the April 1970 issue of *Journal of Personality and Social Psychology* (vol. 14, pp. 281–291).

Page 129 The report by Osis and Bokert, "ESP and changed states of consciousness induced by meditation," appeared in the January 1971 issue of the *Journal of the American Society for Psychical Research* (vol. 65, pp. 17–65).

Page 129 Kamiya's discovery is reported in "Operant control of the EEG alpha rhythm and some of its reported effects on consciousness", pages 507 to 517 in *Altered states of consciousness,* edited by Charles T. Tart (Wiley, 1969). Kamiya's paper is also reprinted, along with later pertinent papers, in *Biofeedback and self-control,* edited by Joe Kamiya and others (Aldine-Atherton, 1971). *Biofeedback and self-control 1970,* edited by Theodore X. Barber and others (also published by Aldine-Atherton in 1971) is the first in a series of annuals on the same topic.

Page 129 The 1970 and 1971 volumes of the *Journal of the American Society for Psychical Research* include several studies of ESP in relation to brain waves, mostly by Charles Honorton and colleagues at the Maimonides Medical Center or by Rex Stanford and colleagues at the University of Virginia School of Medicine. I found especially interesting the discussion by Larry Lewis and Gertrude Schmeidler in their paper, "Alpha relations with non-intentional and purposeful ESP after feedback," pages 455–467 of the October 1971 issue (vol. 65).

Page 130 Schmeidler's suggestion about the personality of the researcher appears in her introduction to a book of readings she edited, *Extrasensory perception* (Atherton, 1969).

Page 130 Considering ESP a reality is alien to the general belief-systems of many psychologists, including myself. For this reason, the acceptance of ESP even as probable generally depends on personal observation; it seems rarely to be arrived at in the way that we arrive at most scientific beliefs, through fully crediting the testimony of others. While this book was in the process of publication, I for the first time made personal observations arguing for the reality of ESP, and this experience has greatly changed my own attitude on the issue. As a result, I slightly altered several passages in this chapter which had expressed doubts that for me seem no longer justified.

This experience centers on my recent acquaintance with Bill Delmore. A second-year student in the Yale Law School, he withdrew early in 1972 for at least one semester, to devote himself to exploring unusual talents he had long been aware of but had of late been developing further. Through my colleague Dr. Sidney J. Blatt, a psychologist in the Yale Department of Psychiatry, I had a chance to observe him at several sessions in which he displayed these talents. His specific skills having been developed and practiced in social situations, the materials he used were playing cards. He did a variety of remarkable things with cards. Some of these could have been done by sleight of hand. Others, I thought, could not; but I have had little experience with card tricks or their detection. What influenced me most toward crediting the genuineness of the apparent "psychic" element in his performance was, therefore, the circumstances: his relation to the friends who apparently accepted their genuineness, and the fact that he was leaving law school to explore his skills.

The presence of a "psychic" element was confirmed by Bill Delmore's performance in a variety of experimental procedures when he then spent several weeks at the Institute for Parapsychology in Durham, North Carolina—the Institute founded by Dr. J. B. Rhine on retiring from his professorship at Duke University. Dr. Edward F. Kelly and Dr. B. K. Kanthamani were in charge of the work he did there, and they have permitted me to adapt from their report ("A note on a gifted subject," *Journal of Parapsychology*, September 1972) a table summarizing what he did on a variety of tasks. The lines in the table refer to various procedures that test psychic abilities by departure from randomness. Some procedures are intended to test for clairvoyance or precognition, some for psychokinesis (that is, psychic influence on physical events). For each testing device are given the number of trials, the chance number of hits (the various devices have, as may be seen, from 2 to 6 equiprobable alternatives), the actual number of hits, and two columns pertaining to statistical evaluation. The CR, or critical ratio, is the ratio between the observed departure from chance and the standard error of the chance value,

Device	*Number of Trials*	*Chance Number of Hits*	*Actual Number of Hits*	*CR*	*p*
1. Fast PK machine	1000	500	541	2.6	<.01
2. 4-button machine	5377	1344	1542	6.2	<.000000001
3. Dart board	144	62	85	2.2	<.03
4. ESP cards	500	100	164	7.2	<.00000000001
5. Dice tumbler	144	24	44	4.5	<.000001
6. Sand timer	29	14.5	24	3.5	<.001

and p is the probability, derived from the normal probability curve, that so large a departure could occur by chance. Even if all mankind had been playing with these devices through many generations, such a combination of separate improbabilities in one person would remain improbable on a chance hypothesis. The diversity of devices prevents explanation by reference to special defects in any particular procedure. My knowledge of the experimenters—one of them a former student of mine—and my own observations of Bill Delmore's performance on the 4-button machine eliminate for me the "last-resort" explanation by postulating fraud. (The 4-button machine and its use are described by Helmut Schmidt briefly on pages 28 to 35 of *Progress in parapsychology,* edited by J. B. Rhine and published in 1971 by The Parapsychology Press; a fuller account is available in Schmidt's two articles in the 1969 *Journal of Parapsychology,* vol. 33: "Precognition of a quantum process," pp. 99–108, and "Clairvoyance tests with a machine," pp. 300–306.)

Here then, for me, is some of the dependably repeatable evidence needed for conviction that "ESP" points to real events—not repeatable at all times by all people, but repeatable by a single person in different situations with different observers, over some extended period. Being persuaded by this partly first-hand experience that there is a real, though mysterious, phenomenon here, I have become rather less interested in research directed only at testing the occurrence of ESP in one or another specific circumstance. I now share the conviction, common among parapsychologists, that energies are better devoted to research that attempts to unravel the mystery, seeking to identify the underlying processes by studying systematically the conditions that influence ESP. So long as this conviction remains rare, because of doubt about whether any real phenomenon is present, research merely testing the presence of ESP can continue to play a useful role. To both kinds of research, I believe, a humanistic approach contributes a great deal.

Notes to Chapter 9, Schizophrenia

Page 131 The interview passage is from *An anthology of human communication* by Paul Watzlawick (text and tape, published together by Science and Behavior Books, Inc., Palo Alto, 1964).

Page 132 Rosenbaum's *The meaning of madness* was published by Science House in 1970.

Page 132 *Schizophrenia* does approximately correspond, though, to the nineteenth-century concept, *dementia praecox,* which it came to replace. Temporal changes, and variation from one country to another, in the application of mental illness categories have helped bring into question the very concept of mental illness. Discussions of this issue, often with a cross-cultural perspective, are to be found in several of the chapters written by diverse contributors to *Changing perspectives in mental illness* (Holt, Rinehart and Winston, 1969), edited by Stanley C. Plog and Robert B. Edgerton.

Page 133 Biological factors in schizophrenia are also discussed in some of the chapters in the volume just cited, edited by Plog and Edgerton.

Page 133 Descriptions of the experience of mental illness have been collected by Bert Kaplan in his volume, *The inner world of mental illness: A series of first-person accounts of what it was like* (Harper & Row, 1964). A longer account of schizophrenic experience, presented in the form of a novel, is *I never promised you a rose garden,* by Hannah Green (Holt, Rinehart and Winston, 1964).

Page 134 A concise statement of the theory developed by this California group is available in the paper "Toward a theory of schizophrenia," in *Behavioral Science* for 1956 (vol. 1, pp. 251–264), by Gregory Bateson, Don D. Jackson, Jay Haley, and John Weakland.

Page 135 The description of Nancy is from *Schizophrenia and the family* (International Universities Press, 1965), by Theodore Lidz, Stephen Fleck, and Alice Cornelison.

Page 136 See, for example, Jay Haley's account of "The art of being schizophrenic," pages 145 to 176 in his book, *The power tactics of Jesus Christ* (Discus-Avon, 1971).

Page 136 The papers by Lidz, Fleck, Cornelison and other collaborators are collected in the book by them cited aove.

Page 137 Laing's major account of schizophrenia is in *The divided self* (Tavistock, 1960). *Self and others* (revised edition; Pantheon, 1969), though not primarily focused on schizophrenia, initiates a synthesis between the humanistic approach to social psychology and to schizophrenia. (Pertinent to this is the recent pamphlet by two social psychologists, Stuart Valins and Richard E. Nisbett, "Attribution processes in the development and treatment of emotional disorders," published in 1971 by General Learning Press, 79 Madison Avenue, New York 10016.) Continuing to view some of what is labeled schizophrenia as the outcome of unusual family relationships, Laing here draws on attribution theory to analyze how it develops. In a more general recent book, *The politics of experience* (Pantheon, 1967), the chapter on schizophrenia begins with a clear statement of the general humanistic approach. It ends, however, with a passage which to me is very discordant with the early part. Laing here seems to claim for schizophrenics a special wisdom which is doubtful in the light of the humanistically oriented research described later in my chapter, research suggesting that many schizophrenics abandon all prospect of a better future in yielding to the seductive appeal that a hospital offers as a place of refuge.

Page 137 *Sanity, madness, and the family*, by R. D. Laing and A. Esterson, was published by Tavistock in 1964.

Page 138 Frances E. Cheek's paper, "Family interaction patterns and convalescent adjustment of the schizophrenic" is in *Archives of General Psychiatry* for August 1965 (vol. 13, pp. 138–147). This research was done by a sociologist, but it is no less psychological for that. In all the interrelated disciplines of the social sciences a humanistic orientation should make for weakening the barriers between disciplines, through focusing attention on the common subject of inquiry rather than on one special tradition of how to pursue the inquiry.

Page 138 Bannister and Salmon reported this study in "Schizophrenic thought disorder: Specific or diffuse?", *British Journal of Medical Psychology* (1966, vol. 39, pp. 215–219).

Page 139 Anchor Books published Goffman's *Asylums: Essays on the social situation of mental patients and other inmates* in 1961.

Page 140 The article by Braginsky and others, "Patient style of adaptation to a mental hospital" appeared in *Journal of Personality*, June 1968 (vol. 36, pp. 283–298). Along with the other research I will describe by members of the same group, this is summarized in the book *Methods of madness* by Benjamin M. Braginsky, Dorothea D. Braginsky, and Kenneth Ring (Holt, Rinehart and Winston, 1969).

Page 141 The study of inconspicuous paients is described on pages 113 to 120 of the book that I have just cited.

Page 141 The study involving attitudes toward the hospital is presented on pages 54 to 59 of the same book.

Page 143 The questionnaire study of old-timers and newcomers was reported by B. Braginsky, M. Grosse, and K. Ring in "Controlling outcomes through impression-management: An experimental study of the manipulative tactics of mental patients," *Journal of Consulting Psychology* for August 1966, (vol. 30, pp. 295–300).

Page 143 The interview study was reported in the same journal in December 1967 (vol. 31, pp. 543–547) by Braginsky and Braginsky under the title, "Schizophrenic patients in the psychiatric interview: An experimental study of their effectiveness at manipulation."

Page 144 Zarlock's experiment appears in his article, "Social expectations, language, and schizophrenia" in *Journal of Humanistic Psychology* (vol. 6, pp. 68–74).

Page 145 See Fontana and Klein, "Self-presentation and the schizophrenic 'deficit' ", *Journal of Consulting and Clinical Psychology*, June 1968 (vol. 32, pp. 250–256).

Page 147 The two studies of contact with ex-patients are reported on pages 142 to 157 of *Methods of madness.*

Page 148 The West Haven ward is described by Towbin in "Self-care unit: Some lessons in institutional power," *Journal of Consulting and Clinical Psychology*, October 1969 (vol. 33, pp. 561–570).

Page 148 The quotation is from page 569 of Towbin's article.

Page 149 The distinction between process and reactive schizophrenia is elaborated and discussed in many recent books and articles—for example, on pages 18 to 21 of the book by Rosenbaum cited above.

Page 149 A humanistic approach, while making more likely the views on schizophrenia discussed in this chapter, is of course not their only possible source. For example, Theodore R. Sarbin argues strongly against the mental-illness paradigm on grounds that seem quite independent of a humanistic point of view. The concept he favors as a replacement for the illness metaphor, "transformation of social identity," does, however, seem more compatible with a humanistic view than does the illness metaphor. Sarbin's criticism is developed most fully in his paper, "On the futility of the proposition that some people be labeled 'mentally ill' " in the *Journal of Consulting Psychology* for October 1967 (vol. 31, pp. 447–453). His argument for "transformation of social identity" as a substitute concept is presented at greater length in "The scientific status of the mental illness metaphor," pp. 9 to 31 in the Plog and Edgerton book cited above.

Notes to Chapter 10, Psychotherapy

Page 152 For a history of psychoanalysis as therapy, see Hans H. Strupp, "Psychoanalytic therapy of the individual," pages 293 to 342 in *Modern psychoanalysis: New directions and perspectives*, edited by Judd Marmor (Basic Books, 1968).

Page 154 *Client-centered therapy* is presented by Rogers in his 1951 book under that name.

Page 156 Jung's papers on therapy are brought together as volume 16 of his collected works, with the title *The practice of psychotherapy* (Princeton University Press; second edition, 1966). He speaks of therapy, of course, in many of his other writings, and the statement about uniqueness is from paragraph 358 of volume 10, *Civilization in transition* (Princeton University Press; second edition, 1970).

Page 156 Jung's statement about influence is in paragraph 163 of volume 16, cited more fully in the previous note.

Page 156 Rank's view on psychotherapy are most accessible in the one-volume edition, *Will therapy and Truth and reality* (Knopf, 1945).

Page 158 Adler's views are well represented in *The individual psychology of Alfred Adler: A systematic presentation in selections from his writings,* edited by Heinz L. Ansbacher and Rowena R. Ansbacher (Basic Books, 1956).

Page 158 Horney published several pertinent books—for example, *The neurotic personality of our time* (Norton, 1937).

Page 158 Of Fromm's many books, perhaps the most pertinent to what I have said here is *Man for himself* (Holt, Rinehart and Winston, 1947).

Page 158 Sullivan's developmental theory is presented in his *The interpersonal theory of psychiatry* (Norton, 1953).

Page 159 For an introduction to the existentialist movement, see *Existence: A new dimension in psychiatry and psychology,* edited by Rollo May, Ernest Angel, and Henri F. Ellenberger (Basic Books, 1958), or *Existential psychology,* edited by Rollo May (Random House, 1961).

Page 159 Frankl describes both his existentialist psychology, and its personal origins, in *Man's search for meaning* (Beacon, 1962).

Page 159 For Bettelheim's experiences and what he made of them, see his book *The informed heart* (Free Press, 1960).

Page 160 Rogers' increased emphasis on emotion is seen in several of the papers collected in *On becoming a person* (Houghton Mifflin, 1961) and in his more recent book *Carl Rogers on encounter groups* (Harper & Row, 1970).

Page 161 Encounter groups have been the subject of many recent books. I like especially the Rogers book cited in the previous note.

Page 162 A brief introduction to meditative techniques is included in Severin Peterson's paperback, *A catalog of the ways people grow* (Ballantine, 1971). A longer introduction is *On the psychology of meditation* by Claudio Naranjo and Robert E. Ornstein (Viking, 1971). Beginnings of systematic research on meditation are included in several collections of readings: *Altered states of consciousness* (edited by Charles T. Tart; Wiley, 1969), *Biofeedback and self-control* (edited by Joe Kamiya and others; Aldine-Atherton, 1971) and *Biofeedback and self-control 1970* (edited by Theodore Barber and others; Aldine-Atherton, 1971).

Page 164 Bergin and Garfield's book is *Handbook of psychotherapy and behavior change: An empirical analysis* (Wiley, 1971).

Page 164 For examples of the views of these writers on behavior therapy, see Joseph Wolpe, *The practice of behavior therapy* (Pergamon, 1969); H. J. Eysenck and R. Beech, "Counterconditioning and related methods," pages 543 to 611 in the Bergin and Garfield handbook cited above; B. F. Skinner, "Part IV: The analysis of neurotic and psychotic behavior," pages 183 to 219 in his book *Cumulative record* (Appleton-Century-Crofts, 1959).

Page 166 Arguments akin to mine have recently been applied to the techniques of behavior therapy advocated by Wolpe, and to Wolpe's theory about them, in the following two articles in the November 1971 issue of *Psychological Bulletin* (vol. 76): Wallace Wilkins, "Social and cognitive factors underlying the effectiveness of Wolpe's procedure," pages 311 to 317, and Edwin A. Locke, "Is 'behavior therapy' behavioristic? (An analysis of Wolpe's psychotherapeutic methods)," pages 317 to 327.

Page 167 *The humanization processes: A social behavioral analysis of children's problems,* by Robert L. Hamblin, David Buckholdt, Daniel Ferritor, Martin Kozloff, and Lois Blackwell, was published by Wiley-Interscience in 1971.

Page 171 Aubrey J. Yates' book, *Behavior therapy,* was published by Wiley, 1970.

Page 172 The quotations are from page 644 of Leonard Krasner's article, "The operant approach in behavior therapy," pages 612 to 652 in the Bergin and Garfield handbook already cited.

Page 172 Lazarus' *Behavior therapy & beyond* was published by McGraw-Hill in 1971.

Page 173 "Selective reinforcement of schizophrenics' interview responses," by Leonard P. Ullmann, Roderick G. Forsman, John W. Kenny, Titus L. McInnis Jr., Irving P. Unikel, and Ray M. Zeisset, appeared in *Behavior Research and Therapy,* 1965 (vol. 2, pages 205 to 212).

Page 174 A summary of operant studies on schizophrenic deficit appears in pages 621 to 625 of the Krasner article already cited.

Notes to Chapter 11, Conclusion

Page 176 Exaggeration of objectivity as the prime value in psychological research may be viewed with greater understanding when it is related to more general social phenomena, such as technology's role in industrial society. A very valuable treatment of this, "The myth of objective consciousness," appears as Chapter VII of Theodore Roszak's *The making of a counter culture* (Doubleday, 1969), no less provocative for containing in itself, as it seems to me, a bit of exaggeration.

Page 176 May's book was published in 1969 by Norton, and Skinner's in 1971 by Knopf.

Page 176 By failing to mention relevant human research, Skinner grossly misleads readers who are not psychologists. The linguist Noam Chomsky, for instance, in his lengthy review of Skinner's *Beyond freedom and dignity,* assumes psychology to have produced no scientific knowledge relevant to the issues Skinner discusses. I believe the research I have summarized here in the chapters on moral development and on attitudes, opinions, and motives amply refutes Chomsky's assumption. (Chomsky's review appeared in *The New York Review of Books* for December 30, 1971.)

Page 181 The issue of free will and therapy is discussed by Rollo May in *Love and will*—for example, on pages 197 to 201.

Page 181 The doctrine of free will has also been argued for by one psychologist, and very persuasively, on purely empirical grounds, as "an inescapable item among the facts of human experience." See Carroll C. Pratt, "Free will," pages 181 to 190 in *Mind, matter, and method,* edited by Paul K. Feyerabend and Grover Maxwell (University of Minnesota Press, 1966).

Page 181 Experimental psychologists have of late begun to consider again phenomena long avoided because of concern about the determinism-freedom controversy. Gregory Kimble and Lawrence C. Perlmuter have published a penetrating analysis of "The problem of volition" in the *Psychological Review* for September 1970 (vol. 77, pp. 361–384). I want to mention, also, two books I have not yet read that I'm sure are relevant: Thomas A. Ryan, *Intentional behavior* (Ronald Press, 1970), and Francis W. Irwin, *Intentional behavior and motivation: A cognitive theory* (Lippincott, 1971).

Page 182 I have borrowed the expressions, *rage for order* and *rage for chaos,* from Morse Peckham's application of them (influenced by Wallace Stevens) to the corresponding controversy in historical and critical consideration of the arts, in his book *Man's rage for chaos* (Chilton, 1965).

Index